Doing Academic Planning

Effective Tools for Decision Making

edited by Brian P. Nedwek

Society for College and University Planning

Library of Congress Cataloging in Publication Data (in process)
Nedwek, Brian Philip

Copyright © 1996 by the Society for College and University
Planning
All rights reserved
Printed in the United States of America
2nd Printing
ISBN 0-901608-3-3

Society for College and University Planning
339 E. Liberty Street, Suite 300
Ann Arbor, Michigan 48104

Phone: 734.998.7832
Fax: 734.998.6532
Email: info@scup.org
Web: www.scup.org

ELECTRONIC REFERENCE CITATIONS

Citations to electronic references (at the end of each chapter) are primarily to websites, though there are a few references to listservs and gophers. Citation practices for the Web are in flux. Based on user requirements we start all citations with the URL (Universal Reference Locator). Where websites have titles, the title follows, followed in turn by information on the sponsoring organization and the author. All these URLs will be accessible in a single online location through "SCUP's Planning Pages" at http://www.scup.org.

Because the Web is an actively evolving collection of documents, no assurance can be given that any particular URL will still be active at any time after the citation is printed, although most will remain valid. If that is the case with a Web reference you are trying to locate, please use the other information provided to perform your search with the various online search engines, or consult "SCUP's Planning Pages."

You are invited to contribute citations to online works you find of value in your professional work. Send URLs to <scup@umich.edu>. Thank you.

Preface

Academic leaders have been caught flat-footed by the convergence of two powerful forces. Rapid and pervasive introduction of information technology is one front moving through the landscape of higher education. Emerging storms of discontent from numerous stakeholders over the process and product of higher education form another. Together these environmental factors are transforming the academy.

Historically, academic managers were focused on factors of production—number of books in libraries, proportion of faculty with terminal degrees and the like. They assumed a relatively stable and noncompetitive environment. Organizational structures and role relationships were neatly hierarchical and autonomous. Core functions were executed with an insensitivity, even immunity, to external environmental forces. Stakeholder involvement was limited and passive. Education was a public good and the policy agenda was preoccupied with issues of access.

Today, academic leaders are challenged by an expanding universe of information technology and its uses, and by a changed focus from a provider-centered culture to a learner-centered world. The new era is one of networks of learners wherein the student, not the library, is the center of the information universe. Libraries can no longer be viewed as mausoleums with an insatiable need for additional resources; rather they must be seen in competition with a host of organizations to serve as interdependent resources to the learner. The traditional "provider-centered" model argued for highly formalized systems of data and information broadcasting to a relatively passive client. Traditional systems promoted place-bound learning as a preferred technique to promote efficiency in production. The "learner-centered" focus suggests individualizing the pace of learning, (i.e., each learner progressing at a rate tailored to individual abilities and balanced against other forces in competition for their time) and thus has powerful implications for space planning and its use.

The learner-centered focus has implications beyond individualization. Historically, curriculum planning and assessment systems were designed to fit the production model. Thus, what courses to offer and when, were to be determined on the basis of provider wants and expectations rather than learner needs. The emerging individu-alization suggests a very different approach to curricular and assessment information system design. With a focus on the individual learner, curriculum decisions are more likely to be guided by skills to be demonstrated and content to be mastered within each skill domain. This approach provides individualization of a curriculum, based on the readiness of the learner. Instructional settings are structured along the lines of individual needs, thereby minimizing the need for gross homogenization of a group of learners (i.e., the use of general survey courses in the core curriculum as a way to gain efficiencies in the curriculum).

A learner-centered education has powerful implications for traditional planning tools currently available to higher education leaders. For example, to what extent are existing models of space utilization appropriate in an environment that seeks to maxi-mize individualization of learning opportunities? Does assignable square footage per FTE (full-time equivalent) student have as much utility in this new information age compared with its use in a producer-centered milieu? What then replaces classroom utilization planning tools? As implied by Dolence and Norris' *Transforming Higher Education*[1], the learner's relationship to the production function changes as well.

The principle organizational model becomes focused on the networks between resources, agents, and learners. A network approach introduces design issues here-tofore unexplored within the planning community. This new metaphor suggests core concepts different from the production-centered educational model of old. Network access replaces access to the "goods," just as growing resources within a network re-places passive reception of predetermined goods. Thus, students will seek out and contract with a variety of learning resources to develop skills. Self-paced learning modules, occasional live lectures, simulations, tape-delayed lectures, and the like suggest that planning tools need to focus more on the resources available to a client group during episodes far more frequent than a 16-week semester. Networking also suggests a reconsideration of traditional articulation agreements between educational sectors. The emerging pattern is one of collaborative arrangements among sectors of society from private industry and service organizations to integrated educational sectors. A seamless network of opportunities, service providers, and learners is on the educational horizon.

Faculty/student relational changes have altered the role expectations of faculty from dispensers of information to facilitators. Students, in turn, are expected to take responsibility for managing their learning. Faculty roles in this expanding information universe are unfolding. Facilitator, coach, and navigator are role definitions in the new order. Individualization of education is coupled with collaborative learning arrangements. Education in this new environment is seen as a strategic investment; in this setting stakeholders are involved more deeply than ever before.

Demonstrated accountability and resource allocation decisions linked to academic plans are transforming how we teach, research, serve, and govern. Simply put, the academy has been asked to improve efficiency, effectiveness, and economy in what

[1] Dolence, M. G. and Norris, D. M. 1995. *Transforming Higher Education—A Vision for Learning in the 21st Century*. Ann Arbor, MI: Society for College and University Planning.

we do; more important, we must change while living in a fish bowl. How will academic leaders as planners respond to these challenges in creative ways without losing sight of the institution's core identity?

The various dimensions of this sourcebook, (e.g., how to assess information/technology use capacity), can serve the evolution of higher education well. In assembling this reader, the selection of materials was guided by a sensitivity to provide academic planners with tools to perform core functions and activities that facilitate the transformation of higher education institutions from provider-centered cultures and organizations to learner-centered franchises. Readings examine partnerships and alliances needed for higher education institutions to survive, if not lead, the transformation of society into the information age.

In summary, facing storms of change within and outside the academy, higher education officials have realized that major realignments are underway creating demographic, economic, political, and cultural imperatives. Demographic and economic forces have become translated into the political language of "return on investment" public policy. Quality, accountability, and institutional effectiveness have become part of the culture for stakeholders in higher education.

Program directors, department chairpersons, academic deans and their associates, and academic vice presidents—at two and four-year institutions in public and independent school sectors—are anticipating continued change and are ready to respond in a timely fashion using new planning approaches and techniques.

This introductory book is organized around eight core topical areas: environmental scanning and related policy analysis tools; curriculum planning; enrollment management; human resources planning; planning for information technology; student services; integrating academic with facilities and budget planning; and accountability tools. Marie E. Zeglen, in Chapter 1, provides a systematic look at stakeholder and issue analysis techniques to make plans rational and actionable. In Chapter 2, Thomas V. Mecca describes the concepts and basic approaches of environmental scanning that higher education leaders can use to identify major discontinuities and related changes in their external environments. Gertrude M. Eaton and Helen F. Giles-Gee examine classic academic program review in Chapter 3, but from a learner-centered perspective and the new accountability. Chapter 4 introduces academic managers to the planning issues surrounding curriculum planning through alternative delivery strategies and partnerships. Kathleen A. Corak and James L. Croonquist bring a fresh look at the issues of delivering a curriculum in nontraditional ways.

Enrollment management is examined in two chapters. In Chapter 5, Michael F. Middaugh and Dale W. Trusheim describe recruitment and retention analysis tools that are used at the University of Delaware, but are easily adaptable to other institutions. They also discuss the relationship between financial aid and enrollment management in Chapter 6, providing a proactive approach to financial aid management and strategic planning.

A range of human resources planning issues are examined in Chapter 7 by Carol Everly Floyd; faculty recruitment and retention, their roles and responsibilities, and a series of recommendations are discussed in actionable form.

Chapters 8 and 9 contain a systematic look at information technology—from how to assess institutional capacity to planning for its expansion. Linda Fleit provides a way to examine information technology resources in ten key areas. Susy S. Chan then examines planning for information technology and calls for the application of process reengineering as a component of organizational transformation.

Diana L. Sharp and G. Gary Grace take an integrated approach, in Chapter 10, to understanding student development by applying a service perspective. Gretchen Warner Kearney and Stephen P. McLaughlin examine a co-curricular framework as an experiential learning opportunity to augment classroom learning. Co-curricular involvement has emerged as a key component of holistic education and has a positive impact on educational attainment. Chapter 11 provides a good introduction to current approaches and practices in co-curricular planning models.

Putting academic planning into a larger context is the focus of Chapters 12 and 13. Dilip M. Anketell examines how to integrate academic and facilities planning, followed by Thomas K. Anderes' recommendations on how academic plans and processes should be linked with budget development and funding allocation processes.

The use of performance indicators (PIs) as a method to couple quality assurance with accountability is becoming increasingly common among higher education systems, institutions, and programs. The closing chapter by Brian P. Nedwek introduces academic leaders to a range of PIs of process and outcomes in higher education.

Brian P. Nedwek
Associate Provost, Saint Louis University
President, Society for College and University Planning

Acknowledgments

Doing *Academic Planning* is the first in a three-volume series of publications by the Society for College and University Planning (SCUP) for academic leaders and planners. Many individuals gave countless hours to the task of building the first sourcebook. Members of the Academic Planning Academy of SCUP assisted in identifying the core components for the sourcebook and potential contributors. SCUP's Director of Education and Research, Mendi Spencer, provided numerous ways to improve the quality and usefulness of the book to a wide range of readers. Terry Calhoun, SCUP's Publications Director, has been supportive throughout the project, keeping us all focused on the deliverables, and sensitive to the needs of the reader in the knowledge age. Danny Steinmetz, temporary staff in SCUP Publications, helped in many ways, including preparation of the index. J. Thomas Bowen, Jr., Chair of the Professional Development Committee, shared his keen insights on how to integrate academic and facilities planning, and provided considerable assistance with Chapter 12. Meredith Whiteley, Chair of the Publications Advisory Committee, helped in so many ways to bring this academy goal to reality. I am grateful to the staff at Saint Louis University, especially Barbara Lind for her assistance in manuscript management and preparation, and to Ryan Comfort for his critical insights.

Contents

Expanded Table of Contents and List of Figures and Tables

Curriculum Planning **25**

Academic Planning within the Larger Context 115

Integrating Academic and Facilities Planning 117

Linking Quality and Accountability **135**

Environmental Scanning

Policy Analysis:
Scouting for the
Academic Wagon Train

Marie E. Zeglen

Approaches to
Environmental Scanning

Thomas V. Mecca

oday's academic leader needs to marshal the best available information to guide the planning process. But good information alone is not enough. Policy analysis is a systematic tool which academic leaders can use to ensure that their plans will result in effective action.

Policy Analysis: Scouting for the Academic Wagon Train

Marie E. Zeglen

CORE PLANNING QUESTIONS

Visions, plans, and policy analyses are all part of the same effort to build the future. The pioneers in this country who drove wagon trains westward had a vision of a new life in a new land. They had a general plan for how to make their journey from east of the Mississippi to the mountains and seashores of the west. They used policy analyses to decide which particular path or direction should be taken whenever they encountered obstacles such as rivers or hostile populations along the way. Policy analysis is a systematic process for reducing issues or problems to actionable solutions. Wildavsky refers to policy analysis as "an activity creating problems which can be solved" (1979, p. 17). The process is systematic, in that policy analysis proceeds through a set of predictable steps once an issue or problem has attracted the attention of an individual or group. In policy analysis, however, the problem is not taken for granted. It is analyzed, clarified, and crafted in such a way as to allow for solution. Policy objectives are set and solutions are then developed to meet those objectives. The solutions have to be actionable, or capable of being implemented in the specific environment where the problem exists. The analyst uses a variety of research and modeling techniques to predict the effects of each potential solution. Policy alternatives are then systematically compared to identify policy outcomes, trade-offs, and impacts. Criteria such as cost-benefit, goal achievement, or actionability are typically used

in sorting out alternatives. The end product is a set of recommendations for future action which is presented to policy makers.

Planners and policy analysts as partners.
Policy analysis is grounded in the kinds of real world issues an academic leader already understands. Like all planning processes, policy analysis is iterative, seeking continually to refine and rethink assumptions and conclusions throughout a study process. Policy analysis does not ignore political processes. On the contrary, a good analysis takes into account the way political factors influence an issue or its resolution. Like planning, policy analysis is collaborative and involves continual consultation with stakeholders and policy makers.

Planning and policy analysis are kindred disciplines. Both activities "deal with the future, use similar methodologies, operate in institutional settings, exercise influence, and participate in similar implementation processes" (Benveniste, 1989, p. 53). Partnership is productive between analysts and planners. Analysts contribute skill and sensitivity in designing change, while planners bring knowledge and experience to make change happen. While judgment and intuition are part of both policy analysis and planning, the policy analyst also brings a background in quantitative techniques to the planning process.

Marie E. Zeglen

is Associate Provost for Planning and Institutional Research for Northern Arizona University, Flagstaff, Arizona. Zeglen is a member of the Society for College and University Planning who has presented at SCUP's annual, international conference.

The role of the analyst. Policy analysts need extensive access to policy makers, stakeholders, and others in order to function effectively.

An analyst's judgment is sharpened when opportunities to test and exchange ideas with policy makers and stakeholders are afforded throughout the planning process.

The analyst must have a thorough understanding of the issue and its context, and be able to judge the actionability of policy options. An analyst's judgment is sharpened when opportunities to test and exchange ideas with policy makers and stakeholders are afforded throughout the planning process.

QUESTIONS

Policy analysis can be used to study many types of academic planning issues. It is an optimal approach for answering questions such as:

- What is the real issue needing the attention of decision makers?

- What policy or other options do decision-makers have for resolving the issue?

- Which of the possible options provide the best resolution to the issue?

- What are the likely effects and side effects of implementing the option?

- How can change best be managed to ensure success?

- How will decision makers know if the change really works?

BASIC CONCEPTS

There are several basic concepts for the academic planner to understand before using policy analysis:

- Issues;
- Stakeholders;
- Policy partners;
- The iterative nature of policy analysis;
- The role of judgment, intuition, and savvy in policy analysis;
- The use of grounded models; and
- The need for actionability of recommendations.

Issues. An issue is any disagreement among stakeholders for which a solution is sought by policy makers. Issues that present planners with significant social, economic, or ethical problems are most likely to benefit from a policy study. Consider an example from academic planning. In response to anticipated enrollment pressures, leaders decide to promote several initiatives to enable students to complete degree programs more quickly. Plans are proposed to extend academic program delivery in terms of the calendar, the locations where courses are taught, and the mode of delivery by which students can receive instruction. In addition, course and facility scheduling are reviewed to eliminate barriers to efficient student access to required courses and programs. A committee is formed to make recommendations, but numerous issues emerge during discussion of potential options. Department chairs are concerned that facilities commonly used by the department faculty will be less available under the new plan. Faculty are concerned with equity in compensation for teaching courses outside the current academic year calendar on which most contracts are based. Courses are not available in alternative delivery formats, and faculty have no time to develop new instructional approaches. Students are concerned with the proposed pricing for the different program alternatives. Local employers are concerned that student workers may not be available in the time frame needed to support seasonal work. The administration is concerned that the enrollment opportunities created through the new approach will not create student access fast enough to forestall legislative intervention. The institution's financial officer believes that the committee has not shown clearly that the new programs will be cost effective or allow adequate time for facility maintenance. The array of issues arising from the committee's work demands the brokering of a political decision from institutional leadership. That decision can be informed by systematic study of the issues and the policy alternatives.

Stakeholders. Stakeholders are individuals or groups who are invested in a policy outcome. The investment may be made for personal, emotional, rational, economic, philosophical, artistic, or other reasons. Investment in a policy outcome forces stakeholders into the political process as either recognized, legitimate players in the decision, or illegitimate challengers to the political order. Benveniste (1989) describes two kinds of stakeholders: "the real clients or beneficiaries" (p. 18) and the implementers or "individuals within or outside the organization who would carry out the policy or plan" (p. 19). A third group should not be overlooked—the plan or policy designers. It is natural for the planner or policy analyst to have a stake in the acceptance of policy recommendations and in the successful implementation of the resulting policy. This kind of stakeholding is healthy, motivating, and not of concern unless the analyst or planner loses objectivity.

Stakeholders for academic issues can include a wide variety of individuals, such as administrators, faculty, staff, state and federal government officials, students, parents, alumni, trustees, politicians, taxpayers, professional societies, and members of the business and industry community. Policy analysis must take into account the various stakeholders' views and concerns about an issue either through direct or indirect means. Many information sources can be used to gauge stakeholder interests, such as surveys, research reports, or focus groups. Generally, more effort is expended to track the views and positions of those stakeholders with greater ability to influence change.

The "invisible" stakeholders of the past are not silent about academic issues today. Students and their parents are now concerned about academic curricula and their content. The business community now invests substantial funds in the preparation of college graduates for employment. Bringing these silent stakeholders into the planning process is important. Ignoring such stakeholders only postpones dealing with their needs.

Stakeholders who are unsupportive or adversarial should be sought out since they provide a lens for predicting the reaction of some groups to new policies. Participation of those without commitment to the customary way of operating can stimulate creative approaches to problems or encourage support for changes that are later implemented. As an example, when business leaders were named to the Task Force on the Future of Engineering Education in the University of Wisconsin System, there was an initial period of critical, even adversarial, discussion about the goals of the engineering programs. Ultimately, the business leaders contributed many innovative ideas to the planning process and later helped to seek better funding for the plan.

Policy partners. The problems academic leaders face today can't be solved without involvement of other organizations or individuals. Policy partners are individuals or groups who can be co-opted or invited to share in developing a solution to a problem. These policy partners may or may not initially be stakeholders to an issue. In many cases, the partner may choose involvement in the planner's issue in order to solve another unrelated problems. For instance, businesses are often willing to fund classrooms in their facilities to increase educational opportunities for their staffs. Academics may trade expertise for use of the classrooms, which can help institutions meet goals for delivering other programs. Business professionals can become stakeholders after being invited to collaborate as partners in policy making.

Policy analysis as an iterative process. There are few policy problems with only one acceptable solution. The task of the policy analyst is to identify and study solutions, proceeding until one is found that is actionable in the environment. The "best fit" solution may not be identified immediately, so policy analysis is often an iterative process. Quade (1975) indicated that analyses may need to be reshaped and redone for several reasons. The alternatives identified may not achieve the goals established for solving the problem. The goals themselves may be unrealistic and need redefinition or lowering. The recommendations may not be actionable because of political or other external constraints. Gill and Saunders (1992) explain that issues themselves can change as a study unfolds. The analyst needs to adapt to such changes and refocus the study.

The "messy" troika of judgment, intuition, and political savvy. The role of the policy analyst is like that of an organizational anthropologist. The policy analyst needs to use disciplined, rational approaches in assessing how an issue works in the environment. But the process changes when the analyst must identify the best solution to resolve an issue. Determining what solution will work

The "invisible" stakeholders of the past are not silent about academic issues today. Students and their parents are now concerned about academic curricula and their content. The business community now invests substantial funds in the preparation of college graduates for employment.

best in the environment is more craft than science. A cost-benefit analysis, for instance, can identify which solution delivers the greatest benefit at least cost, but cannot answer the question of whether any particular solution will be actionable. Judgment, intuition, and political savvy are at least as important as facts or analyses in selecting among policy alternatives. These skills are gained from immersing oneself in the environment of the problem and its solutions.

*J*udgment, intuition, and political savvy are at least as important as facts or analyses in selecting among policy alternatives. These skills are gained from immersing oneself in the environment of the problem and its solutions.

Models grounded in the environment. Policy analysts have a unique task compared to academic researchers. A physicist might build a model that describes how a phenomenon works. The goal of the model is to identify the underlying universal laws governing how the phenomenon behaves—water molecules exposed to heat, for instance. The physicist assumes that if the model is correct, it will work for any water molecules exposed to heat, in any location meeting the specified conditions. In contrast, the policy analyst does not look for universal laws in the systems studied. Instead, the analyst attempts to describe and model the uniqueness of an issue being studied. The representational world which is created by the analyst is unique to the issue and its particular set of stakeholders and environmental constraints. The analyst looks for the solution that best fits the particular issue, as expressed in its specific environment. In so doing, the analyst usually considers how the issue has been resolved in similar settings.

Actionability. A successful policy analysis creates more than an improved understanding of the issue or its stakeholders. It contains actionable recommendations. The solutions must work, and must be acceptable to stakeholders and policy makers.

APPROACHES AND PRACTICES

Policies are the vehicles of both organizational stability and change. They specify the rules and practices by which individuals inside organizations behave and how organizations manage their relationship to external individuals or groups. They may be formal or informal. Policies change in a cyclical manner, as illustrated in Figure 1. The three parts of the cycle are the processes of policy development, implementation, and evaluation. Policies are conceptualized, developed, and then implemented. At some point, stakeholders or policy makers agree that the policies either work acceptably or need change. Out of this evaluation come pressures and ideas for improvements or new policies. Then the cycle starts anew. Varying methods are used to progress through the cycle, ranging from decision making according to the simple preferences of a leader to structured techniques, such as cost-benefit analysis or risk assessment.

As a formal method, policy analysis is used in policy development, policy evaluation, and policy optimization. In policy development, policy analysis serves to identify viable policy options in response to issues. Policy evaluations focus on means of assessing whether or not a policy achieves its intended goals. Policy optimization is the use of formal methods, such as operations research or total quality management approaches, to analyze and strengthen goal achievement under a given policy.

Academic leaders most often come into contact with the use of policy analysis as a tool for policy development. There are four main steps in using policy analysis to develop new policy ideas: (1) issue crafting, (2) policy crafting, (3) policy selection, and (4) policy presentation.

Issue crafting. Policy analysis is similar to the activities of a wagon train scout. The scout's job is to go ahead of the wagon train to survey the territory, to determine what people and animals live along the way, to look for both obvious and subtle dangers, to define safe routes to the destination, and to make general recommendations to the wagon train master on how to proceed. When a mountain or river or desert lies in the path of the wagon train, the scout needs to alert the wagon master to the problem, to provide good information about the obstacle, and to offer an initial assessment of alternatives to explore. In policy analysis, the first step is to craft an issue scouting report. Issue crafting has six basic goals: (1) clarifying the issue, (2) establishing the context for the issue, (3) stating the policy objectives for solving the issue, (4) giving a broad overview of the range of feasible policy alternatives to explore, (5) suggesting criteria for determining whether a policy has successfully met policy objectives, and (6) recommending whether or not to proceed with a full analysis of the issue. A well done scouting report may be just as valuable to policy makers as a full fledged policy analysis. It helps sort out which issues are productive to address, and which issues are not. Some problems require policy study, while others can be solved by other actions, such as funding allocations or personnel changes.

Clarifying the issue. Policy issues are not always clear in reviewing controversy or problems. Conflicts may really represent symptoms of a problem rather than the real issue. The heat of the desert sun may be the first apparent problem, but lack of water is more serious. Student complaints, for instance, about small aid awards could be the result of changes in external financial aid programs or could result from finan-

cial constraints due to lowered enrollments. The policy analyst or planner must clarify the issue sufficiently to define meaningful approaches to its solution. Quade (1975, p. 71) recommends that an issue be defined with respect to "where it came from, what its symptoms are, why it is a problem, and what will be done with the analysis if it is carried out."

Establishing the context for the issue. It is important to put the issue into context in order to understand it. The context includes the issue culture, issue history, and potential constraints or opportunities related to the issue. The issue culture is the context in which the issue is viewed, discussed, and managed by potential stakeholders and policy partners. The history of the issue, and any policy actions addressing the issue, are a preview of how future policy actions might be received. Finally, the existence of any constraints on how stakeholders view what constitutes resolution of the issue is important in crafting the issue. For instance, policy makers may only be interested

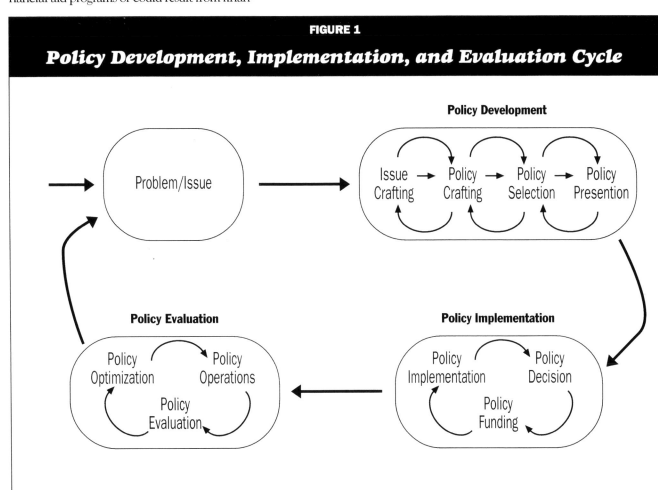

FIGURE 1

Policy Development, Implementation, and Evaluation Cycle

in reducing the current level of conflict or newspaper coverage over an issue, while other stakeholders may want full resolution. In such a case, the policy analyst may recommend a public relations effort rather than a full policy study to deal with the issue. Issues also create opportunities for policy makers or stakeholders to create pressure or enable change in related areas. Dan Quayle, for instance, used the stimulus provided by an episode on the television show, *Murphy Brown,* to raise a host of concerns about unwed parenting during the 1992 American presidential campaign.

Stating policy objectives. Once an issue is defined clearly and placed in context, policy objectives or goals can be identified. According to Quade (1975), the issue analysis should "suggest the objectives toward which programs for meeting the problem should be directed… [and] call attention to the ultimate goal toward which the solution is directed" (p. 73). Gill and Saunders (1992, p. 19) distinguish between the assigned objectives of the study and the objectives of the policy maker. If these different objectives are in conflict, the results of the analysis may not be actionable. The purposes of narrowing policy objectives are to create a manageable study focus and to communicate realistic expectations for outcomes to the policy maker.

> *The purposes of narrowing policy objectives are to create a manageable study focus and to communicate realistic expectations for outcomes to the policy maker.*

Stating broad range of policy alternatives. Issue crafting surveys the landscape of potential policy alternatives, striving for completeness and culminating in some judgment about potential alternatives. Here the analyst advises the policy maker about the likely policy paths to be recommended in a full study. Information about potential policy alternatives comes from review of the policy literature, networking with policy makers or stakeholders, or from other sources—such as historical works, client feedback, or focus groups. The information is synthesized, and used to decide whether or not a given policy alternative should be considered. Majchrak (1984) points out that policy changes may range from the incremental to the fundamental. By including this information in the issue crafting paper, the analyst gives the policy makers or other stakeholders an opportunity to shift the direction or scope of analysis, should the project go forward.

Quade (p. 75) suggests that the following information be included about each policy alternative in the presentation of issues: description, judgment of potential effectiveness, rough costs or cost areas, possible spillovers or unintended consequences, initial comparison of alternatives, and any other important considerations.

Suggesting success criteria. Criteria for assessing the success or failure of future policy changes are suggested in the issue report. If possible, quantifiable measures should be identified which can later be used in policy evaluation.

Recommendation on proceeding. The issue report is a thorough but preliminary study of the issue being faced. Its most important component is the judgment of the analyst whether the policy maker should pursue a more intensive policy study. Some potential reasons why further analysis may not be fruitful are: (1) the organization does not control the policy levers necessary to effect change, and so should pursue political action rather than policy action, (2) the issue can be resolved by a more direct action, (3) not enough information is available to sustain a reasonable policy analysis, or (4) the policy issue is already well studied and understood, so an educational rather than analytic effort might be useful. If the analyst recommends proceeding, the issue crafting report can set expectations for the scope, cost, and time frame of the study to follow.

Policy crafting. Policy crafting is the effort to identify, specify, and assess the viability of policy choices for resolving an issue. Continuing the wagon train scout analogy, the scout analyzes which routes are likely to bring the wagon train to its destination in a safe and timely manner. As part of this effort, the scout considers the characteristics and culture of the wagon train, specific information about each possible route, and other environmental factors (projected weather, food, and water along the route, and the possibility of dangerous encounters). The scout explores portions of each possible route to gather more information. In academic planning, the routes considered range from changes in existing policies or practices to entirely new approaches. Policy crafting proceeds iteratively through three steps: (1) refining the policy alternatives, (2) specifying and creating a model for each policy alternative, and (3) assessing the viability of each policy alternative.

Refining policy alternatives. In the issue scouting report, a number of potential policy alternatives are presented. The alternatives are described in broad-brush terms, and an informed guess is made concerning their viability. In policy crafting, each alternative must be fully defined and set in its environmental context.

All policies are embedded in a cultural environment with rules and norms by which individuals and organizations operate to achieve goals, choosing behaviors consistent with values and operating practices to maximize gains. Further, the extent to which individuals and organizations can achieve goals will be limited by their influence, authority, and power. In order to plan for a policy change, the analyst has to understand the values and modus operandi of stakeholders who direct or influence outcomes to achieve specific goals. Different stakeholders see policies as more or less beneficial or adoptable in light of their goals, so the analyst should examine how such factors will operate for each policy alternative being studied.

Gill and Saunders (1992) point out that it is useful to analyze history or trends in policy development concerning an issue. Any given policy alternative has probably been tried in other organizations or even in the same organization in the past. Review of successful and unsuccessful implementations of policies in similar settings can aid in identifying specific challenges or benefits of one policy approach over another.

There may be legal, judicial, economic, ethical, cultural, or political constraints on the kinds of policies that can be considered. For instance, the existence of a contract may eliminate some policy options. Some policy goals or initiatives may also create opportunity for change in other policies. Emphasis on research partnerships with business, for instance, may enable change in academic program delivery or academic support services.

Specifying and creating a model for each policy alternative. The analyst often creates a model for how a new policy would operate in the environment. The model is a representation of re-

ality accurate enough to give the researcher confidence in predicting the effects of a change in policy (Quade, 1975). Models range from thought experiments to complex mathematical representations of systems. In building a model, the analyst uses the best available tools and information and seeks first to represent the most important features of the environment for which a policy change is being planned. For example, in building a model to use in simulating policies for enrollment planning, the first step is to replicate the overall environment of the institution. Factors like demographics, high school enrollments, the economy, and institutional policies concerning admissions, financial aid, and academic standards, would be represented. Once the overall environment—the microworld—is modeled, ideas about the effects of policy changes can be tested. Models can help show the lag between policy implementation and actual change, or highlight unanticipated effects of policy. Quade points out that models can be very good as communication devices and as a way to focus the judgment and intuition of researchers and stakeholders on finding a policy solution (p. 49). The policy analyst or planner can use the model to verify understandings about the environment by sharing the model widely and using it to discuss potential changes with stakeholders. Since simulating policy changes in a model is less threatening than pilot testing such changes in the real world, open discussion of policy alternatives is facilitated. Participation of stakeholders in development and review of the model also promotes confidence in its later use in simulating policy impacts.

Assessing the viability of each policy alternative. Deciding whether or not a change is viable is one of the most difficult tasks in planning. Benveniste (1984) distinguishes between technical and feasibility methodologies associated with planning activities. Technical methodologies, such as systems analysis, forecasting, or trend analysis are helpful in analyzing among alternatives and in describing the environment for which change is being planned. Feasibility methodologies are more active than technical meth-

> *Since simulating policy changes in a model is less threatening than pilot testing such changes in the real world, open discussion of policy alternatives is facilitated.*

ods and help develop greater intuition about how policies might behave in the environment. They involve "providing technical assistance, networking ideas in the bureaucracy, creating incipient alliances of supporters, facilitating understanding of the issues, explaining the consequences of actions, negotiating with opponents, keeping tabs on implementation, and so on" (Benveniste, 1989, p. 32). Feasibility methodologies are used proactively to explore acceptability and workability of an idea for change in the environment. Their use involves active discussion with the stakeholders of how different changes might work or might not work in the environment. Floating ideas through discussions and focus groups can be helpful. In exploring the feasibility of policies, the analyst's role is more similar to that of a participant observer than to a scientist conducting an experiment. There is no substitute for active engagement with policy makers, stakeholders, and future implementers for gaining the intuition and insight needed to judge the viability of potential changes.

Active collaboration with stakeholders and policy makers throughout the study is important because ownership of the change process facilitates later acceptance of change (Fullan, 1991). Sharing the policy ideas helps to transfer ownership of the ideas from the planner or policy analyst to stakeholders and policy makers. Change may fail if this transfer of ownership is not successfully made.

Sharing the policy ideas helps to transfer ownership of the ideas from the planner or policy analyst to stakeholders and policy makers.

What are some of the common reasons a potential policy might be dismissed as unworkable? A policy proposed may not achieve the desired policy outcomes. Other hurdles a policy must leap are those of acceptability to stakeholders, economic affordability, and political feasibility. Proposed changes should not result in unwanted impacts unrelated to the change at hand. Solutions should not create new problems worse than those being solved.

Policy selection. Policy selection is the task of assessing the policy alternatives and identifying the best option or options for the policy maker to pursue. The wagon train scout elimi-nates some alternatives through exploring, mapping, and examining sections of each potential path. The scout's next step is to explain the narrowed choices to the wagon master and provide some judgment on the optimal route for the train to follow. In academic planning, policy selection relies in part on the use of formal methodologies or techniques to compare alternative courses of action, and in part on the more intuitive assessment of how actionable a policy choice would be. For that reason, every policy alternative must be studied and assessed within the context of the environment in which it will be implemented. The steps to follow in assessing the value of any policy alternative include: (1) setting the environmental context for each alternative, (2) identifying relevant policy attributes for each alternative, (3) comparing the policy alternatives with respect to the attributes, (4) ranking the alternatives on the basis of the comparison, and (5) making recommendations for change or stability.

Setting the context for each policy alternative. The environmental context for each policy alternative includes the influence of cultural, historical, and any other constraining or promoting factors on how a policy will operate in the particular environment under study.

Each policy alternative is seen as more or less consistent with the views, practices and philosophies of the different stakeholders for the decision. Once a new policy is adopted, there will be a shift in the relative power or influence of stakeholders in the policy area. The analyst must understand and assess both the willingness of different stakeholders to accept or support a decision, and the relative influence or power of those stakeholders. Is a decision likely to be blocked, regardless of the merits of the policy being suggested?

Given what is known about the way in which different policy alternatives have been treated in the past, what kind of reception will the policy idea receive? Are there particular stakeholder groups that need to be advocates for a given policy shift? How does the policy change compare to prevailing policy trends in the area?

A new policy direction may be seen as either a vehicle for enhancing change in a specific direction or a throwback to policy now seen as antiquated. The policy may also have implementation characteristics that make it less acceptable for other reasons, such as timing, level of change required, cost, or the time required for producing results.

Identifying policy attributes. Stokey and Zeckhauser (1978) point out that it is a fairly easy task to choose among alternatives if there is only one outcome of a policy and it can only be measured one way. For instance, if the only goal a policy needs to satisfy is to increase the number of students enrolling in an academic program, then ranking alternatives such as lowering admissions standards or awarding program-specific financial aid is straightforward. Preference is given to the alternative that results in the highest number of students in the program. But, "the trouble is that most policy proposals (intentionally or otherwise) serve a variety of objectives, and their outcomes are described in terms of more than one characteristic, some of which may be unfavorable" (p. 117). This "multi-attribute problem" (p. 117) means that analysts first need to define all of the attributes, or valued consequences, associated with each policy alternative before comparisons can be made. In the example on increasing enrollment in a program, there are probably some associated goals, such as maintaining quality standards or expanding in accord with curricular concerns, that need to be considered for any policy change. The analyst needs to know which attributes are most important to satisfy. No one policy is likely to have the same performance characteristics with respect to each attribute, so a decision is usually made favoring one attribute over another.

Comparing the policy alternatives. The analyst compares the anticipated performance of each policy alternative with respect to each attribute. There are three attributes traditionally considered in the comparison: goal achievement, cost-benefit, and actionability. Other impacts of policy change need review, such as unanticipated consequences or impacts resulting from how the new policy interacts with existing policies (Majchrak, 1984). Sometimes, doing nothing at all is the best alternative.

Goal achievement. To what extent does the policy alternative satisfy the desired policy attributes or goals? Projecting a policy's effectiveness in meeting goals can be difficult. Sources of information to help with this assessment include data from prior use of the policy in similar environments, views of stakeholders on how well a proposed policy might meet their interests or goals, willingness of key stakeholders or implementers to expend effort to make the policy change successful, and, if available, simulations or pilots of the potential effects of the policy.

Cost-benefit. Stokey and Zeckhauser (1978) indicate that "benefit-cost analysis is the principal analytical framework used to evaluate public expenditure decisions" (p. 134). This kind of analysis is related to the assessment of goal achievement, but focuses on linking the relative amount of success in meeting goals to the cost of the effort involved. There are at least two major limitations to cost-benefit analysis used in policy comparison. First, many of the desired policy attributes in higher education are not easily quantifiable. For instance what level of "benefit" can be assigned to delivering a higher quality versus a lower quality course in business economics? The cost of quality will usually be higher, given traditional methods of course delivery, and the benefits (better decision making by future executives?) may be very high but not easy to identify or demonstrate. The second major limitation is that cost-benefit analysis focuses only on costs and benefits that can be identified at the time of study. Stokey and Zeckhauser (1978) point out that such benefits or costs need to be discounted in some fashion to account for consequences experienced in the future (p. 136). Another difficulty to keep in mind is that costs and benefits of a future action are unknown and must be projected. The analysis must rely on either a model that can be used to simulate the policy effects, or on data from a pilot project or a project in another setting. Cost-benefit analysis is also insensitive to political issues. The question of who gets the benefits or who pays the costs may be more important than the ratio resulting from analysis (Quade, 1975; Majchrak, 1984).

Actionability. There are two components to the decision of whether or not a policy change is

*C*ost-benefit analysis is also insensitive to political issues. The question of who gets the benefits or who pays the costs may be more important than the ratio resulting from analysis.

"actionable" or able to be implemented. The first is stakeholder support of, or opposition to, the potential policy. The best ways to assess opposition are to study similar implementations of policy and to use structured interviews with key stakeholders. Organizational requirements for the success of the new policy are the second component. Majchrak (1984), for instance, lists three critical aspects of the organization that should be reviewed in assessing how actionable a policy might be: (1) the structure needed in the organization to implement a policy, (2) organizational resources needed for implementation, and (3) related policy mechanisms needed for implementation. For example, a policy change initiating on-line registration for students may require structural changes in terms of staffing or work processes. Implementing the new registration system would require technology, staff, time, and other resources in order to be successful. Related policy changes in the area of student course approval processes and faculty involvement in scheduling decisions may also be necessary.

Ranking the policy alternatives. The analyst usually stops short of recommending one final alternative and, instead, presents information on all actionable alternatives. Preferences for selection among policy alternatives do not always match the results of whatever quanti-

TABLE 1
Contents of the Policy Presentation

1. **Issue**	Clarify the issue addressed by the policy study.
2. **Policy objectives**	State what specific policy objectives are to be addressed.
3. **Context for change**	Review the key environmental factors that affect the issue and any policy solutions. Mention major stakeholders and potential partners with the ability to influence whether or not a policy change will occur or will work if implemented.
4. **New policy model(s)**	Describe the new policy model(s) recommended in the study. Attempt to "encapsulate the vision in a short metaphor, slogan, or memorable statement that conveys its essence and captures attention" (Nanus, 1992, p. 127).
5. **Policy rationale**	Give the underlying rationale for selecting the policy model(s), including results of the policy comparison process, and the judgments of stakeholders, policy makers, and/or the analyst concerning the viability of the models reviewed.
6. **Policy outcomes, tradeoffs, impacts**	Give informed estimates of policy outcomes, tradeoffs with other organizational outcomes, and impacts that can be expected on other areas of the organization.
7. **Critical success factors**	List any factors needed to ensure the success of the policy change, such as required investments, related policy changes, provision of staff training, or involvement of particular stakeholders or partners in the change.
8. **Implementation concerns**	Alert stakeholders and policy makers to any challenges that can be expected in implementing the change(s), and include suggestions about the handling of any implementation issues.
9. **Recommendations**	Recommend one or more new policy models be adopted, or that no alternative model is better than the current approach. Suggest other actions to help resolve the issue under dispute if recommending the status quo.
10. **Future evaluation strategy**	Recommend an approach to evaluation of the policy change, including method of study, monitoring measures, or periodic review to assess goal achievement or cost-benefit. If relevant, point out the need for baseline data on current policy or practices to enable evaluation after implementation of policy change.

tative approaches are used in the comparison of policies. In the end, policy preferences are based both on quantitative assessments and a judgment about what policies will be most effective and actionable in the environment at hand. The perfect policy would be one that achieves the organization's policy goal in the least costly manner, with positive benefits to all stakeholders, and can be implemented without creating any new problems. Needless to say, such a policy usually does not exist! The challenge for the analyst is to synthesize all the information available on context, potential performance, and implementation for each policy alternative, and to arrive at a slate of acceptable policy choices.

Policy presentation. How the scout presents the choices to the wagon master is important. The wagon master wants good information on which to base a decision, but does not necessarily want to be told what to do! Recommendations for the content of a policy presentation are given in Table 1 (page 12). The presentation may be written or oral, or both. If written, the presentation should always begin with a brief executive summary communicating the main points and recommendations in the proposal. Any detailed material should be included as an appendix, or referenced as a separate report. The analyst should assume that many of those interested in the study will review *only* the executive summary.

MANIPULATION AND DELIVERY

The packaging and delivery of the proposal is part of the political process for building support for the policy decision about to be made. Policy makers may want to use the analyst's report as an independent expert document, a statement of a new policy direction for the organization, or a vehicle for floating some new ideas on a topic under discussion. Since the analyst does not "own" the delivery process (policy makers do), it is important to tailor the structure of the policy proposal report to its intended use. Generally, the analyst or planner will need to deliver the report to many different kinds of audiences in a variety of oral and written forms. As an alternative, other staff within the organization may adopt the project, officially or unofficially, to carry the process forward. At a minimum, the report delivered by the analyst should be sufficiently complete and well constructed to allow for further repack-

TABLE 2	
General Guidelines for Policy Analysis Reports	
Directness	• Provide a brief executive summary.
	• State conclusions first.
	• State the problem addressed by the study.
	• State study limitations.
	• Clearly state factors needed for success.
	• Use the active voice.
	• Forego jargon.
Focus	• State the issue.
	• State and discuss all actionable alternatives.
	• State tradeoffs and impacts of each alternative.
	• Use concrete examples.
Format	• Limit data tables or move to appendix.
	• Use graphics to convey information.
	• Create oral and written versions of the report.
	• Be brief.

aging to meet the communication needs of decision makers.

Packaging of the proposal. Stokey and Zeckhauser point out that "many policy analyses are gathering dust because they are too long or too hard to understand" (1978, p. 329). Policy researchers are often academicians and may package a policy proposal using the same style as in academic research. Academic papers typically follow a format: state a problem, summarize all relevant literature and information about the problem, state an hypothesis about the problem, describe the research design for studying the problem, present results of the study, interpret the results, and then make recommendations for further research or improvement of the study. The audience for a policy report is much less patient than the audience for an academic paper! A good discussion of the style and format of a policy report is found in Majchrak (1984). Table 2 contains general guidelines for preparing a useful report for policy makers or stakeholders.

The challenge for the analyst is to be concise as well as credible. Only a limited amount of the thought and work behind the analysis can be presented in the policy report, but supplemental materials can give detail on the contextual or comparative information used to support conclusions. Different readers have different needs and desires for information. "Some will desire more detailed information, some will only want the major findings, and some will only want information that directly helps them" (Majchrak, 1984, p. 94). Ultimately, the success and credibility of the analysis will depend on the quality and workability of the ideas within it. Packaging needs to be effective, without getting in the way of the ideas in the report.

ACTIONABILITY ISSUE

Actionability is enhanced when the analyst is positioned to understand thoroughly both the technical and political aspects of the problem being studied. Four factors are extremely important in helping assure actionable results: (1) access to stakeholders and policy makers, (2) regular feedback among the analyst, stakeholders, and policy makers, (3) effective study design, and (4) effective study delivery.

Access. The analyst needs to understand the views of stakeholders and policy makers if a successful policy path is to be plotted. Such understanding is impossible if the analyst does not have access to individuals and organizations influential in the policy process. Majchrak (1984) points out that both the policy analyst and the policy maker learn from the interaction. The policy analyst learns about the political process while the policy maker learns about the study process. Without access, the analyst has to resort to second- and third-hand information and must make guesses about political positions, values, and impacts. Lack of access can result in incorrect assumptions about issues and policies, or policy effects going unchallenged during the study. The consequence may be that unreasonable or unacceptable solutions will be posed to stakeholders and policy makers.

> *Ultimately, the success and credibility of the analysis will depend on the quality and workability of the ideas within it. Packaging needs to be effective, without getting in the way of the ideas in the report.*

Feedback. Effective policy analysis cannot be done in isolation; the analyst needs to seek and obtain reasonable feedback **during** the study process in order to maximize the workability of resulting recommendations. Feedback at the end of the process of study is too late. Intraprocess feedback from stakeholders and policy makers is critical at almost every step during the study. Examples include the restatement of the issue, the statement of policy objectives, the initial cut at policy alternatives, the reasonableness of policy models, the policy comparison, and the assessment of actionability. Even the packaging of the final policy report is dependent upon feedback concerning the specific audience, and goals for presentations or written reports.

Design. Good study design maximizes the chance for workable results. However, there is a pragmatic aspect to policy research as compared to academic research. Thoroughness in analysis trades off to some extent against the timetable for policy action. As Stokey and Zeckhauser (1978) stress, "a less ambitious study that is in hand when policy is debated will be far more valuable" (p. 329) than one which is thorough but late. Policy studies have to be as thorough as possible—given the timetable for discussion and change, and the resources available for the study. Recommendations may not be actionable if the study design is flawed or if insufficient information is available to support the conclusions. But the study effort will be wasted if policy decisions are made before its completion.

Delivery. If policy makers, stakeholders, or policy partners do not understand the results or recommendations of the study, there is little likelihood of action. Good delivery is sensitive to the culture, background, and priorities of the audience for policy change.

RECOMMENDATIONS

Policy analysis is a powerful tool for improving the academic planning process. Properly launched, it helps elevate the conversation beyond politics and results in more effective plans. Policy analysis is also an imperfect art. There are seven essential admonitions for the academic leader using policy analysis in planning: (1) define issues so that solutions are achievable, (2) find and include the views of all stakeholders on issues, (3) know the environment of the problem and of the solutions, (4) recognize the quasi-political role of the analyst, (5) balance quantitative and qualitative approaches, (6) share responsibility for policy outcomes, and (7) recognize when reengineering is needed instead of incrementalism.

Defining the issue. One principle of total quality management is to invest more time in designing good processes than in checking for errors later. Similarly, policy analysis benefits from investing time in the definition and clarification of the issues to be studied rather than relying on later evaluation techniques to discover if a new policy is working effectively. Good policy crafting depends on good issue crafting. Issues that are unclear or misidentified or misfocused will lead to policies with similar characteristics.

Including the stakeholders. Understanding the views, environment, and goals of stakeholders is critical to success in an academic planning effort. Not including the views of relevant stakeholders leads to stale analyses which do not address the needs for change of different groups or individuals. Policy recommendations that are not embraced and owned by both stakeholders and policy makers eventually fail.

Knowing the environment. Issues cannot be understood without knowing the environment in which the problem developed. Policy crafting cannot be done effectively without understanding the environment in which solutions to the problem must operate. Implementing a policy designed for another time, another place, or another culture is usually fruitless.

Recognizing the quasi-political role of the analyst. A good policy analysis incorporates information about the biases and points of view of stakeholders in selecting and comparing potential policies. To understand the political side of the environment, the analyst, like the participant-observer, has to become involved, even immersed, in the thinking patterns and culture of the organization. The challenge is to maintain objectivity in the way the analyst uses and assesses the information gained from this participation. If the policy analyst or planner becomes a stakeholder, analysis may be distorted. This can happen if the analyst becomes committed to a particular course of action, either because of employment with the academic organization or due to attachment to a particular idea or position. The process itself may influence the judgment of

PRINT REFERENCES

Benveniste, G. 1989. *Mastering the Politics of Planning: Crafting Credible Plans and Policies That Make a Difference*. San Francisco: Jossey-Bass Publishers.

Dolence, M. and Norris, D. 1995. *Transforming Higher Education: A Vision for Learning in the 21st Century*. Ann Arbor: Society for College and University Planning.

Fullan, M. 1991. *The Meaning of Educational Change*. New York: Teachers College Press.

Gill, J. and Saunders, L., eds. 1992. *Developing Effective Policy Analysis in Higher Education. New Directions for Institutional Research* No. 76. San Francisco: Jossey-Bass Publishers.

Majchrak, A. 1984. *Methods for Policy Research. Applied Social Research Methods Series. Volume 3*. Newbury Park: Sage Publications, Inc.

Nanus, B. 1992. *Visionary Leadership: Creating a Compelling Sense of Direction for Your Organization*. San Francisco: Jossey-Bass Publishers.

Norris, D. and Poulton, N. 1991. *A Guide for New Planners*. Ann Arbor: Society for College and University Planning.

Quade, E. S. 1975. *Analysis for Public Decisions*. New York: American Elsevier.

Skulley, J. 1995. "Building Blocks of a New Society". *Educom Review* 30(5): 28–31.

Stokey, E. and Zeckhauser, R. 1978. *A Primer for Policy Analysis*. New York: W. W. Norton & Company Inc.

Wildavsky, A. 1979. *Speaking Truth to Power: The Art and Craft of Policy Analysis*. Boston: Little, Brown and Company.

ELECTRONIC SAMPLER

http://cause-www.colorado.edu/
CAUSE (the association for managing and using information resources in higher education).
This is a good source for reams of on-line information about higher education policy pertinent to information technology.

http://epn.org/
EPN (Electronic Policy Network: Idea Central).
This website contains links to a number of policy centers and think tanks on a wide variety of issues and topics, some of which are related to higher education.

http://seamonkey.ed.asu.edu/epaa/
Education Policy Analysis Archives: A Peer Reviewed Journal. College of Education, Arizona State University. Gene V. Glass, ed.
In addition to the website, there is a listserv for related discussions. Instructions on how to join are located on the Web pages. A related listserv, EDPOLYAN, is for discussion of education policy. You may subscribe from http://info.asu.edu/asu-cwis/epaa/discuss.html.

http://www.ed.uiuc.edu/coe/eps/prof/Prof.html
Professional Information. College of Education, University of Illinois at Urbana-Champaign. Nick Burbules.
A set of links to colleges of education and related departments, education resources, philosophy of education resources, and more.

http://www.fsu.edu/~air/home.htm
Internet Resources for Institutional Research. AIR (Association for Institutional Research).

the analyst, as the pressure to produce satisfactory results comes to bear.

Overemphasizing quantitative approaches.
There is a great danger in giving too much emphasis to quantitative measures and results in policy analysis. Quantitative information is important in providing a rational basis for the policy selection or comparison process but may mislead if not coupled with expert judgments and the intuitions of those closely associated with the policy area. The pressure to maximize the cost-benefit or other performance ratios estimated for policy alternatives should not automatically outweigh intuitive judgments on the viability of policies. Ultimately, the policy analyst needs to make recommendations balancing both qualitative and quantitative assessments.

Sharing responsibility for policy outcomes.
The policy analyst becomes part of the arena for decision making, sometimes even assuming the role of assistant or partner to the policy maker. The price of access and participation in the planning process is shared responsibility with the policy makers and policy implementers for the outcomes achieved. The policy analyst who embraces this responsibility as a team member is more likely to be invited into the policy process again. Changing overnight from a policy developer to a policy evaluator, while maintaining political innocence, is generally not well received!

Going beyond incrementalism. Policy analysis often leads to incremental change. Incremental changes are easiest to make, since they manipulate practices that already exist in the culture of the organization. The focus on actionable change creates a dilemma for the analyst when only incremental change seems acceptable, but only real reengineering can solve a problem or meet a planning goal. The policy analyst may have to choose between playing it safe with incremental recommendations or taking the risk of a bolder recommendation. Incremental change is usually doable, but not always meaningful!

SUMMARY

Policy analysis is a critical tool for higher education leaders and planners who are trying to reinvent the academy. Strategic vision is needed to see a new future, and careful planning is needed to move an institution toward that future. But the vision and plan are not enough to ensure successful change. Good information is needed, but it is not enough. Many obstacles and issues arise during a process of cultural, political, or institutional change. Policy analysis is the tool for articulating solutions to those issues that would otherwise impede progress. The methods and techniques used in policy analysis combine sophisticated use of information with the judgment, intuition, and political savvy needed to find actionable solutions to problems. A partnership among leaders, planners, and policy analysts is needed to craft the new academy successfully. ◆

his chapter describes the concept of environmental scanning, outlines basic approaches higher education administrators can take to identify change in the external environment, and suggests ways to project the consequences of change into strategic and long-term planning.

Approaches To Environmental Scanning

Thomas V. Mecca

CORE PLANNING QUESTIONS

College and university administrators who can identify major changes in the external environment—changes affecting the future of their institutions—are equipped for more effective strategic planning. By expanding their knowledge of external changes disrupting the relationship between their institutions and the environment, administrators can develop more effective long-term strategies. Typically, however, academic leaders gather strategic information passively, on an informal and irregular basis, selecting strategic information without the benefit of specific criteria to apply in identifying change across all sectors of the environment.

Moreover, unanticipated changes in the environment render conventional approaches to strategic planning inadequate, unable to address the uncertainty created by change. Such approaches lead administrators to base long-term strategies upon expectations of a "surprise-free" future, ignoring unanticipated change by relying on extrapolations of historical data.

But the future of colleges and universities is not predetermined. A complex interaction of **trends, chance events,** and **human interventions** creates the future environment. **Trends** are changes in environmental factors that are measurable over time (fluctuations in funding of public higher education nationwide). An **event** is a discrete, confirmable occurrence that makes the future different than the past. (Congress mandates two years of military service for all eighteen-year-olds.) **Human interventions** are

policies, strategies, or tactics adopted by groups or organizations to effect a desirable change.

The core planning questions include:

- To deal with the uncertainty of the external world, how can higher education administrators process information about emerging trends and potential events that forecast future conditions?

- How can academic managers and planners collect external data systematically and lessen the randomness of information flowing into their institutions?

- To what extent can sufficient lead time be built into the planning processes for managers to understand external changes and develop appropriate strategic responses to resulting issues?

BASIC CONCEPTS

Simply put, the external environment comprises everything beyond the direct control of the college or university that administrators and staff see as affecting its future, directly or indirectly. Researchers categorize such factors into four sectors: social, technological, economic, and political (STEP).

Levels of the environment. Environmental factors also exist at several levels (Morrison, 1992). The **task environment level** includes external factors specific to a particular institution (e.g., students/

Thomas V. Mecca

is Senior Vice President of Piedmont Technical College, Greenwood, South Carolina. Mecca is also a member of SCUP's Academic Planning Academy and has presented a workshop on environmental scanning at SCUP's annual, international conference.

potential students, their parents, their future employers, donors, other revenue sources). The **industry environment level** contains external factors directly affecting all institutions of higher education (e.g., federal student aid, public attitudes toward higher education, federal legislation). The **macroenvironment**, the broadest level, embraces factors that affect all organizations, including colleges and universities. For example, the advent of computers affected not only the workplace, but all segments of higher education (e.g., two- and four-year, public and private, research and comprehensive).

Approaches to environmental analyses. Administrators employ two basic approaches when analyzing the external environment. With the **inside-out-approach**, common in most strategic planning processes, decision makers examine a limited number of specific trends or external factors and their effect on a set of strategic goals and objectives already seen as important to the institution's future. With the **outside-in-approach**, decision makers first identify major trends and factors emerging across the environment and then determine which of them may be critical to the institution's future. With this information, they develop strategies that capitalize on predictable environmental opportunities and/or cope with possible environmental threats.

Components of environmental scanning process. Comprehensive environmental scanning includes: scanning, monitoring, forecasting, and assessment. **Scanning** identifies the signs of social, technological, economic, and political change. Aguilar (1967) distinguishes among four modes of scanning. In the first two, **undirected viewing** and **conditioned viewing**, decision makers exposed to environmental information are either unaware of its significance or inactive in assessing it. In the **informal search** and **formal search** modes, however, decision makers actively collect information either through unstructured efforts (obtaining environmental information limited to a specific purpose) or preestablished procedures (securing information related to broad changes in the environment).

Monitoring complements scanning by tracking, systematically and over time, trends and developments identified previously. Monitoring identifies changes in environmental trends and developments critically important to the institution.

Forecasting determines the direction and magnitude of change in key external factors. When decision makers lack sufficient knowledge of causal relationships among environmental factors, they are unable to identify, with certainty, developments that may disrupt the future. Forecasts allow administrators to base their strategic decisions on estimates regarding the probable occurrence of environmental change.

Assessment allows administrators to analyze forecasts of environmental trends and developments relevant to the institution. Assessment focuses the attention of decision makers particularly on the nature and degree of impact each trend or development will have. Administrators use the information from such assessments to formulate appropriate strategies.

APPROACHES AND PRACTICES

Models of environmental scanning. In formulating strategy, administrators use four distinct models of environmental scanning, representing different levels of sophistication (Jain, 1984). They use a **primitive model** when scanning passively and informally, with no attempt to distinguish between strategic and nonstrategic information. Administrators employ an **ad hoc model** when they obtain information sporadically about particular environmental sectors seen as important to the institution. They adopt a **reactive model** when they continuously monitor, store, and analyze information about specific environmental sectors but do not use a formal scanning system. When using the **proactive model**, administrators establish a formal system of environmental scanning to conduct ongoing, systematic scanning, monitoring, forecasting, and analysis across a broad range of environmental sectors.

Environmental scanning systems. Those who research academic planning encourage college and university administrators to establish formal systems of environmental scanning (Hearn and Heydinger, 1985; Morrison and Mecca, 1989). In a formal system, decision makers systematically review an assortment of print materials (magazines, newspapers, reports) electronic media (TV, radio, electronic databases) and human sources (conferences, meetings, personal conversations) for information.

*C*omprehensive environmental scanning includes: scanning, monitoring, forecasting, and assessment.

In the simplest system, one or more persons abstract information from a variety of publications (national and regional newspapers, leading magazines, specialty publications, other relevant literature) and circulate the abstracts, in their original form or in an internal newsletter, among administrative offices and staff. A modern variant of this is forwarding email newsletters and web pages electronically. Clearly, however, the idiosyncratic nature of the scanner's perceptions of the environment greatly affects the objectivity of the resulting information.

A more comprehensive system utilizes a cadre of staff volunteers who systematically scan material from a broad range of information sources representative of external change. Recruited from personnel within the institution, these volunteers can include faculty members, key administrators and staff members, planning committee members, and senior administrators. Morrison (1992) recommends that scanners be trained in a full-day workshop how to scan assigned sources and prepare abstracts.

The sources scanned include material from the social and behavioral sciences, natural sciences and technologies, business and economics, politics and government, and education. Because information sources should represent all STEP sectors and all levels (task, industry, macro) of the environment, diversity is the important criterion in selecting scanning materials (Morrison, 1992).

The publications shown in Figure 1 represent print information resources generally scanned. Developments in the macroenvironment are recorded in national newspapers, popular magazines, professional magazines, special interest publications, popular intellectual publications, and non-establishment periodicals. Futurist literature is an excellent source of information about emerging trends and new developments in the macroenvironment.

FIGURE 1

Typical Scanning Information Resources

Macroenvironment	National newspapers	e.g.,	*New York Times, USA Today, The Wall Street Journal, Christian Science Monitor*
	Popular magazines	e.g.,	*Time, U.S. News and World Report, Newsweek*
	Professional magazines	e.g.,	*Training, IEEE Spectrum, Datamation, Foundation News, Nation's Business*
	Special interest publications	e.g.,	*BYTE, Psychology Today, American Demographics, Technology Review*
	Popular intellectual publications	e.g.,	*Atlantic Monthly, Harper's*
	Non-establishment periodicals	e.g.,	*Utne Reader, Mother Jones, New Age, The Noetic Review*
	Futurists literature	e.g.,	*The Futurists, Futurics, Futures Research Quarterly*
Industry Environment	General publications	e.g.,	*The Chronicle of Higher Education, Planning for Higher Education, Change, Education Week, Community College Week*
	Specialized publications	e.g.,	*Journal of Medical Education, Graduate, Women, CASE Currents, Academe*
Task Environment		e.g.,	institutional research reports; local and state government reports; regional, state and local newspapers (many now available online)

A number of general and specialized publications serve as basic sources of information about the industry environment. Information resources for scanning the task environment generally include institutional reports; state boards of higher education reports; local, state and regional newspapers; and local and state government reports. Any published material, however, can be a source of information.

The trends and developments monitored in the scanning process are generally those identified as critical to the future of the institution by participants in the initial workshop and by major decision makers.

Scanners are asked to review publications they regularly read. Materials not regularly reviewed may have to be assigned so that the group covers all relevant information sources. If the number of scanners is sufficient, two or more should review the same source to prevent items of potential interest being missed. Volunteers scan their assigned materials for articles containing signals of departures from expected futures or discontinuity in current trends. The trends and developments monitored in the scanning process are generally those identified as critical to the future of the institution by participants in the initial workshop and by major decision makers. Specifically, scanners identify items that contradict assumptions about what is happening, represent trends or ideas never before encountered, contain forecasts, represent new twists to old arguments, present opinion polls showing shifts in attitudes or values, or discuss technological breakthroughs.

The scanners prepare one-page abstracts of each article, explaining the idea or development that indicates change, its implications for their institution, and for higher education in general. Implications may appear as emerging strategic issues, identification of stakeholders affected, or future trends resulting from social change. Scanners also prepare abstracts of conferences, books, TV and radio programs, movies—publications in all forms of media.

Scanners forward completed abstracts to the staff member coordinating the program, who then catalogues and files them according to a previously developed taxonomy. The collected information can then be quickly and conveniently classified and retrieved.

Periodically, an analysis committee—representing a cross-section of the institution's administration, faculty, and staff—reviews the abstracts. The committee evaluates new abstracts to identify emerging trends, events, and strategic issues they consider to have the most significant implications for the future of the institution.

A summary of the committee members' evaluations is prepared and forwarded to the institution's strategic planning committee, the scanners, and other key decision makers. The summary contains a brief description of ten to fifteen trends, possible events, and emerging issues. It should also include a brief analysis of the environmental forces influencing the rate and direction of each trend, the likelihood of each event occurring, and the emergence of each issue.

The analysis committee distributes the information developed from its analysis of the abstracts in several ways. A scanning newsletter focuses the attention of all members of the institution on critical trends and developments emerging in the environment. Distributing selected abstracts can draw attention to a particularly significant trend or issue. Information can also be available institution-wide through campus email, and electronic bulletin boards.

Planning staff members incorporate the summaries of the analysis committee's meetings into alternative scenarios. Members of the strategic planning team analyze the scenarios and develop institutional strategies.

Summaries direct the scanners by identifying emerging changes in the environment that warrant continued monitoring. Faculty and curriculum planners use the summaries to revise existing academic programs and to create new ones.

The office responsible for administering the system described here will vary by institution (Morrison, 1992). Depending upon the institution's planning capability and resources, the planning office may be responsible. Institutions with neither a planning nor a research office may assign a faculty or staff member to oversee the scanning system as part of their regular duties.

Senior administrators should recognize that a scanning system requires time and resources. According to Morrison (1992) a continuous scanning system requires, at a minimum, one professional who can devote half-time to the activity.

MANIPULATION AND DELIVERY

Three methods commonly used for environmental scanning are: Delphi, cross-impact analysis, and scenarios. Each helps decision makers clarify the future by studying unanticipated discontinuities and environmental changes.

The Delphi technique obtains forecasts from a group of "experts," on the assumption that many heads are better than one. In conventional Delphi, a panel of experts forecasts the likelihood, rate, and impact of emerging developments—through a series of questionnaires. Anonymity of panel members is maintained while determining the degree of consensus among them.

The typical panel of experts includes planning team members, key decision makers, and other individuals, in and beyond the institution, judged to have knowledge critical for the institution's future. Information gained from the Delphi procedure is used to formulate scenarios defining alternatives.

Before formulating alternative scenarios, planners create a cross-impact model to assess relationships among critical trends and developments predicted through Delphi. Such a model traces enhancing and inhibiting interrelationships among a set of events or developments, allowing decision makers and planners to identify, in particular, those that play a major role in affecting the future (Morrison and Mecca, 1989). A cross-impact analysis process defines explicitly and completely the pairwise causal relationships within a set of events or developments. The process asks how the prior occurrence of a particular event might affect the occurrence of other events or developments. Once these relationships are specified, analysts can "let events happen" and trace a new set of forecasts representing an alternative to the "most likely" future.

Scenarios describe possible futures, illustrating alternative outcomes of a set of forecasts, and illuminate critical uncertainties created by the major forces affecting the institution (Wack, 1985). Each scenario defines a unique mix of future environmental forces. By providing a range of possible futures, alternative scenarios facilitate identification of common features likely to have an impact on the organization—no matter which future materializes.

In most colleges and universities, a single individual within the scanning team or planning staff writes a series of alternative descriptions of the institution's future environment. With this approach, however, the quality of the scenarios depends upon the writer's analytical abilities, creativity, and experiences. The scenarios may be so idiosyncratic that decision makers find it difficult to develop institutional strategies sufficiently objective and robust.

More sophisticated techniques use interactive computer models to generate scenarios. PASS (policy analysis simulation system), for example, is designed specifically for application in higher education planning. It incorporates trend-impact analysis techniques to generate outlines of alternative futures that display a chain of events occurring over time as well as resultant variations in the level of trends affected (Mecca, 1993, p. 266).

Decision makers conduct policy analysis by reviewing each scenario. Within the particular future described by a scenario, they identify opportunities and threats (explicit or implied) posed by environmental forces, the causal relationships among these forces, and key points for policy interventions. Interventions seriously considered as possible strategies seize the opportunities and avoid the threats.

ACTIONABILITY

Administrators use various approaches to incorporate scanning information into their strategic decision making activities.

Vulnerability audit. Colleges and universities that lack sufficient resources to support a comprehensive system of environmental scanning can conduct a vulnerability audit. A vulnerability audit focuses the institution's scanning efforts on assessing only those environmental factors that pose direct threats to the control feature of the institution (Ashley and Morrison, 1995).

The process consists of five sequential steps. First, members of the analysis team identify factors critical to the institution's stability. These can either be tangible (a large pool of entering students) or intangible (the public's view of the economic worth of a college degree).

During the second step, members of the team identify external developments that could

> *Colleges and universities that lack sufficient resources to support a comprehensive system of environmental scanning can conduct a vulnerability audit.*

undermine the factors identified in step one-environmental threats requiring a strategic response from decision makers and administrators.

In step three, the team members first restate the particular development as a forecast of an event or condition that could happen within a specific time period (e.g., within three years the federal government will require a SAT score of 850 for a student to qualify for financial aid). Members then assess the probability of each forecast and its impact on the institution. Individual assessment of each forecast (threat) is then mapped on a master chart according to the dimensions of impact and probability of occurrence. Members complete this step by discussing individual assessments that deviate from the general consensus.

In step four, the team reviews the overall pattern of threats to the institution, identifying those to which the institution is most vulnerable, and determining the degree of its vulnerability.

In the fifth and final step, the team designs strategies to address each area of vulnerability, assigns persons to implement each strategy, and allocates resources to carry out the priorities.

ED QUEST process. The ED QUEST strategic planning model links environmental scanning information directly to strategy formulation. Adapted from the QUEST model (quick environmental scanning technique), ED QUEST integrates future research techniques and divergent thinking methods into a participatory group process that produces visions of alternative futures and institutional strategy (Mecca, 1993).

Because it comprises the generic elements of strategic planning, ED QUEST allows administrators of institutions implementing strategic planning to design a more elaborate planning process and apply more advanced planning techniques incrementally. Thus, it allows college and university administrators to manage the evolution of their strategic planning capability, increasing the likelihood that the institution's planning system will mature appropriately.

Because it comprises the generic elements of strategic planning, ED QUEST allows administrators of institutions implementing strategic planning to design a more elaborate planning process and apply more advanced planning techniques incrementally.

The ED QUEST model includes six procedural components, each incorporating various methodologies and procedures used in environmental scanning, including Delphi forecasting, cross-impact analysis, and scenario analysis.

The institution's strategic planning committee initially determines the current status of the institution by identifying the elements of its mission and key indicators of its performance. Using published materials (magazine and newspaper articles, graphs, trend extrapolations, book excerpts) collected in a "future prospects notebook," team members identify critical trends and future events by using a Delphi procedure. They then forecast the direction/institutional impact of each critical trend and the likelihood/impact of each event.

The team next conducts a cross-impact analysis to determine the interrelationship within a set of critical trends and events. From the information obtained, they create alternative scenarios of the future. Each scenario consists of a particular configuration of critical trends and events describing a potential future environment. Team members assess each scenario to determine its institutional consequences should it materialize. After they formulate strategies addressing the anticipated consequence of each alternative future, they evaluate the impact of each strategy on previously identified strengths and weaknesses and incorporate it into the strategic management of the institution.

The issue management model. Unless anticipated and managed, emerging issues can compromise institutional performance. The issue management model suggested by Morrison (1992) allows administrators to integrate raw information obtained through environmental scanning into a process for identifying and managing complex issues. By identifying issues in the early stages of development, administrators gain sufficient time to develop an orderly and rational response.

Once issues are identified through scanning, the nature of each is framed in a succinctly written issue brief. A set of issues is assigned to one of three categories:

Category I—Issues requiring the implementation of the issue management model.

Category II—Issues that do not require immediate action because of their maturity, their inability to be managed, or their relative unimportance.

Category III—Issues that require no action.

The issue management model comes into play with issues in Category I. Once an issue's significance justifies spending further resources on its management, the following 10-step process is initiated:

1. Designate an individual as issue owner whose institutional responsibility is most closely aligned with the issue.

2. Form an action team of individuals from areas in the institution most sensitive to the issue.

3. Conduct a situational assessment by defining the issue, gathering information, and studying the results.

4. Define the impact of the issue on the institution's future.

5. Identify and assess the ramifications of the issue from the perspective of stakeholders.

6. Formalize a position on the issue directing the institution to achieve the desired outcome.

7. Help stakeholders develop objectives that contribute to the institution's position.

8. Develop technical objectives that change the way the institution "does business."

9. Implement an action plan containing specific changes the institution will make to implement its strategies.

10. Measure progress on the issue and fine tune accordingly.

RECOMMENDATIONS

The literature on environmental scanning reveals a discrepancy between the "ideal" and the "real" model of environmental scanning. Jain (1984) finds that only one-third of corporations engaging in environmental scanning activities actually develop formal systems of scanning.

Developing a comprehensive, systematic approach to environmental scanning requires a commitment of time and resources. Managers of environmental scanning units typically encounter difficulty in identifying relevant information and scanning material because they have an inadequate concept of the general environment (Jain, 1984). Limiting the scope of the environmental scan information collected addresses this problem.

PRINT REFERENCES

Aguilar, F. J. 1967. *Scanning the Business Environment.* New York: Macmillan.

Ashley, W. C. and Morrison, J. L. 1995. *Anticipatory Management: Ten Power Tools for Achieving Excellence Into the 21st Century.* Leesburg: Issue Action Publications, Inc.

Hearn, J. C. and Heydinger, R. G. 1985. "Scanning the University's External Environment—Objectives, Constraints, Possibilities." *Journal of Higher Education* 56(4): 419–445.

Jain, S. C. 1984. "Environmental Scanning in U. S. Corporations." *Long Range Planning* 17: 117–128.

Mecca, T. V. 1993. "A Case Study of the ED QUEST Strategic Planning Model in a Public Two-year College." Doctoral dissertation, College of Education, University of South Carolina.

Morrison, J. L. 1992. "Environmental Scanning." In *The Primer for Institutional Research*, edited by M. A. Whiteley, J. D. Porter and R. H. Fenske. Tallahassee: Association for Institutional Research.

Morrison, J. L. and Mecca, T. V. 1989. "Managing Uncertainty: Environmental Analysis/Forecasting in Academic Planning." In *Higher Education: Handbook of Theory and Research*, edited by J. C. Smart. New York: Ag athon.

Wack, P. 1985. "Scenarios; Uncharted Waters Ahead." *Harvard Business Review* 63: 72–89.

ELECTRONIC SAMPLER

http://apollo.gmu.edu/~jmilam/air95.html
Internet Resources for Institutional Research.

http://sunsite.unc.edu/horizon/
On the Horizon. School of Education, Program in Educational Leadership, University of North Carolina. James L. Morrison.

Encourages discussion about emerging issues, trends, events in the social, technological, economic, environmental, and political sectors of the macro environment (national/global levels) that will affect education—elementary and secondary schools as well as colleges and universities. You will also find instructions on how to subscribe to a related listserv.

http://www.cua.edu/www/eric_ae/search.html
Search ERIC. Educational Resources Information Directory.

http://www.gactr.uga.edu/Scanning/scan0796.html
Lookouts: The Newsletter of Environmental Scanning. Georgia Center for Continuing Education. Donna L. McGinty (ed.).

http://www.newwork.com/Ed_watch.html
BraveNewWorkWorld & NewWork News. Gary Johnson.

As the masthead of this electronic journal says, "All about work. All the time. For business, education, and careers." Sample article on September 7, 1996 was "What if They Gave an Education and Nobody Came" by Mark Champion (Grand Rapids Community College).

http://www.rrpubs.com/heproc/
HEPROC (Higher Education Processes). R&R Publishers.

HEPROC is a collaborative, participatory discussion and research environment for higher education interests.

Also, finding sufficient readers to scan a variety of information sources regularly can prove problematic. Institutions without the human resources to implement a continuous scanning process can subscribe to environmental scanning newsletters. Examples of such publications include *Future Survey* published by the World Future Society, *What's Next* from the Congressional Institute for the Future, *John Naisbitt's Trend Letter*, and *Technotrends* from Burrus Research Associates, Inc, in Milwaukee, Wisconsin.

Some valuable websites include *On the Horizon, Academe this Week, EDUCOM,* and *Internet Resources for Institutional Research*. See references to these and other sites in this chapter's "Electronic Sampler."

According to Ashley and Morrison (1995), databases such as those available through Edu-

cational Resources Information Center (ERIC), Public Affairs Information Service (PAIS), Dialog, and Bibliographic Retrieval Service (BRS) are also valuable sources to monitor.

Filing and storing scanning information requires a good deal of time and effort. Managers of scanning systems, however, can easily create and maintain a taxonomy with a database program.

The complexity of environmental scanning systems has evolved over time in a patterned fashion, from simple processes of information gathering to complex systems of information analysis. Administrators and planners interested in committing their institutions to a comprehensive environmental scanning system should do so incrementally, and over an extended period of time. ◆

Curriculum Planning

Planning an Academic Program Review

Gertrude M. Eaton and
Helen F. Giles-Gee

Alternative Delivery Strategies, Partnerships and Articulation Agreements: New Recipes for Favorite Dishes

Kathleen A. Corak and
James L. Croonquist

This chapter provides a model of the content and process of program review: administrative structures employed, definition/selection of key indicators and a format for their display, critical steps in the review process, faculty and student expectations, and alternative links to institutional planning.

Planning An Academic Program Review

Gertrude M. Eaton and Helen F. Giles-Gee

CORE PLANNING QUESTIONS

Increased demands for accountability have affected traditional program review practices. In earlier decades, institutions simply added the cost of inflation and new initiatives to their annual budget appropriations (Solomon, 1990). As legislatures and consumers began to question pricing and costing decisions about products and services, program review became a central element in planning, especially since program inventories failed to adjust to declining financial resources. This chapter provides a model of both the content and process of program review: administrative structures employed, definition/ selection of key indicators and a format for their display, critical steps in the review process, faculty and student expectations, and alternative links to institutional planning.

The higher education community has typically regarded program review as an assessment of quality and/or an opportunity to request more resources. Consideration of a program's contribution to the long-range goals of an institution, system, or state were often overlooked. Increasingly, however, institutions expect that program reviews will inform decisions about where to reallocate resources effectively. Barak (1986) observes that an integrated approach among program review, planning, and budgeting is advantageous because goals and objectives are clarified, units are evaluated consistently, and expectations are specified before the process begins. Institution-wide planning is leading program review from a faculty-oriented approach to a

student-centered approach. Inputs as yardsticks of quality are being replaced by outcomes as measures of performance/accountability. More and more, the following core planning questions guide decisions about what can be done to improve program quality:

- Are faculty involved in developing performance indicators and benchmarks to demonstrate whether the program is responding to institutional demands for accountability?

- Are assessments of student learning outcomes in place? Have any changes in curricula and/or teaching resulted?

- How productive is the program? What does it cost? How do expenses compare to similar programs at the institution and elsewhere?

- Does the program fit the institution's mission and plans for the future? Are redeployments necessary?

BASIC CONCEPTS

Program review is simply the evaluation of a program's contribution to students, faculty, the institution, and the larger community. Implemented on a five-to-seven

Gertrude M. Eaton
is Associate Vice Chancellor for Academic Affairs for the University of Maryland System, Adelphi, Maryland. Eaton was both a presenter at SCUP–31 and the Plenary Sessions Chair for the SCUP–31 Conference Committee.

Helen F. Giles-Gee
is Associate Vice Chancellor for Academic Affairs and Director of Articulation for the University of Maryland System Administration, Adelphi, Maryland. Giles-Gee was SCUP's 1992 Mid-Atlantic Regional Representative, served on the Executive Committee of SCUP's Board of Directors, and was SCUP's President in 1993–94.

year cycle, a common core of quality indicators usually includes, but is not limited to, information on students' preparation and performance, faculty qualifications and productivity, currency of the curriculum, level of instructional support, adequacy of facilities, and alumni/ae satisfaction.

Postsecondary institutions use the results of program reviews to make decisions about enhancement, continuation, merger/consolidation, and reduction or elimination of academic programs. Increasingly, motivations for program review include the need for an institution to become more efficient and thereby contain costs. In 1992, for example, the Maryland Higher Education Commission conducted a statewide review of programs, using such indicators as enrollments and degrees awarded, to target several hundred programs as nonproductive and/or duplicative. The University of Maryland System (UMS) Board of Regents responded by requiring institutions to justify retention of such programs. Through an arduous process that determined cost, productivity, and centrality to mission of all targeted programs, the board of regents mandated over 166 program actions and reallocated $10 million among UMS institutions.

*T*he overarching goal of the review process is to demonstrate how the program fits with the mission and future plans of the institution.

The experience in Maryland forced resident postsecondary institutions to recognize that "quality" as it is usually defined by faculty was, in and of itself, insufficient to retain a program. To the regents, clearly reflecting the opinions of external groups, comparative program cost, and productivity were essential—not alternative—components of quality. Thus, institutions had to demonstrate the particular value of targeted programs in sharpening their institution's role within the system. To the UMS community, the downside of the regents' approach to program review was the real threat to institutional autonomy.

APPROACHES AND PRACTICES

The basic concepts of program review build both upon indicators of accountability (often fiscal and external) and upon traditional measures of quality. Since the 1980s, national and regional accrediting bodies have developed stringent procedures for outcomes measure-

ment, forcing higher education institutions to search for better ways to conduct formative reviews (ongoing and continued program evaluation) and summative reviews (periodic analyses of the final product). A few examples follow in which institutions took varied steps to address predetermined objectives. Each engaged the faculty in the process. Each dealt effectively with reviews outside the department. Each validated institutional priorities through reallocation.

Thompson (1983) describes how the University of Washington, through its committee structure, identified priorities and allocated resources to maintain the enrollment level, to improve academic support for instruction, and to provide funds for equipment, computing, library, and physical plant. Some programs were eliminated, resulting in a surplus of tenured faculty who were either reassigned or provided with early retirement options. Bloomfield (1984) describes a mathematical and computerized program review model used at Oregon State University. Student credit hour trends were plotted on a logarithmic scale to enable the simultaneous review of programs regardless of size. Average expenditures were compared to those of peer institutions. Several programs were reduced by limiting enrollment and/or major areas of concentration.

In another case, the University of Montreal faced a $45 million budget deficit from 1982 to 1985. The university decided that service to non-majors, freshmen, and graduate programs were high priorities. Belanger and Tremblay (1982) developed an equation that compared course credits from different disciplines. The results of the analysis were used to reduce teaching resources by decreasing course offerings and sections, eliminating courses with low enrollment, promoting cyclical course offerings, and increasing section sizes and efficiency.

These historical examples demonstrate that within the canon of program review there are key steps in the process.

The program review process. The overarching goal of the review process is to demonstrate how the program fits with the mission and future plans of the institution. Therefore, the institution must orient chairpersons and faculty to new or unusual demands for accountability. For example, in the fall of 1995 the University of Maryland System Office of Academic Affairs held a systemwide workshop for new departmental chairs. One of the most widely attended sessions dealt with the effect of external accountability and fiscal need on program review. The chairs focused upon a single question, "what do the regents and the state want from us?" In brief, the answer was "accountability": 1) serve students better through more cooperation among the system's institutions, 2) use distance education technologies to maintain a solid market share of the state's students, and 3) increase access and maintain quality while simultaneously streamlining administrative services and downsizing programs. As they shared experiences in these areas, the chairs acknowledged the legitimate interests of governing boards and state agencies in redefining the focus of higher education. However, the imposition of the regents' tenets in institutional planning has proved to be a fundamentally new experience for departments.

Initially, program review is an effort undertaken by an entire department, facilitated by the chairperson; units and individuals outside the department are also key to the process. It is critical that the selection of program data and performance indicators be agreed upon by the academic leadership before a review begins. If the review is to be useful for planning, faculty must see the synergism among a program's quality, productivity, cost, and institutional priorities. The chairperson should work with faculty to develop preliminary recommendations, and with the planning officer to incorporate an institutional perspective into the department's thinking.

Following the departmental review, programs are usually evaluated by larger units within the institution (college/school or institution-wide planning committees, senior cabinet), with the levels of review determined by the size of the institution. The University of Maryland at College Park (UMCP), for example, requires several levels of review beyond the department in which programs are slated for downsizing, modification, merger, or elimination: the Campus Senate; the General Committee on Programs, Curricula, and Courses; and the campus Academic Planning and Advisory Committee (APAC). Comments are sought from UMCP alumni/ae and external constituents. Program duplication and comparative costs are examined, and final recommendations are forwarded

to the provost. An effective review process requires clarity of responsibilities among key individuals and groups.

Some institutions prefer to supplement the information developed during internal review processes by adding an external panel. The use of an external team can help to validate the findings of earlier reviews and to minimize the conflicts that might result from unpopular recommendations.

Role of the chief academic officer.

The chief academic officer must view each program review in three contexts: the institution and/or system mission and goals, the curriculum, with its prerequisites or co-requisites for other academic programs, and the services provided to the general education program. Additional considerations may include a program's reputation, gauged by regional or national rankings. The value of each program under review is measured against all other programs at the institution. Formerly, the chief academic officer might have made the first recommendations alone, but now it may be necessary to work more closely with the chief

---

FIGURE 1

Four Key Steps in Program Review Process

STEP 1

Prepare the Institution
- Determine common indicators[1]
- Establish cycles for reviews[2]
- Provide orientation to departments
- Clarify expectations

STEP 2

Gather and Analyze Data
- Academic unit/department gathers data
- Institutional research office gathers data
- Chairpersons assist departments with preliminary analysis of data and recommendations

STEP 3

Provide Institutional Context for the Program Review
- Determine strategic fit within the campus mission
- Obtain comments from campus and external constituents
- Determine impact on fiscal and other resources utilized across the institution
- Determine priority of program, in comparison to other programs, within the mission of the institution

STEP 4

Decision Making/Contribution to Institutional Planning
- President/senior cabinet decides on program outcomes
- Board of regents/trustees affirms program review outcomes
- Inform campus of decisions and next steps

---

[1] For public institutions, some indicators may be determined by external agencies such as a state higher education coordinating board. For institutions within systems, the indicators may be prescribed by the board of regents in consultation with the state higher education coordinating board.

[2] A board of regents for a system may establish a review cycle to ensure the simultaneous review of similar programs system wide.

financial officer and institutional planner to address issues of cost and strategic value.

Role of the department chair. The responsibilities of a department chair are very different from those of a faculty member. Increasing responsibilities in the areas of personnel management, cost containment, and accountability, are transforming the chair into a manager/administrator and report writer. Metz (1995) notes that decisions to strengthen the role of the department chair encounter strong resistance among faculty. Further, the task of implementing the results of program review my be hindered by frequent turnover in the departmental leadership, emphasizing again how critical it is that institutions have in place a staff development plan for new chairs. During the review process, the department chair must be prepared to assume the following responsibilities:

In today's accountability climate, program reviews are driven by fiscal need and pose a threat to faculty and staff, since one possible outcome is retrenchment.

- To interface with the institutional research officer, institutional planner, and academic administrators;
- To maintain a schedule ensuring completion of the review in timely fashion;
- To organize faculty and staff, and perhaps students, to assemble and interpret data; and
- To facilitate development of recommendations for improving the review process and strengthening the program; and
- To write the program report.

Role of the faculty. Historically, faculty members have had few expectations of program review, regarding the process either as an opportunity to identify improvements, or simply a bureaucratic necessity. However, in today's accountability climate, program reviews are driven by fiscal need and pose a threat to faculty and staff, since one possible outcome is retrenchment. Reviews driven by new fiscal implications may decrease the openness of faculty and require new strategies to keep the process objective and collegial (Harpel, 1986).

Program review identifies faculty utilization patterns, enabling the department to increase productivity in the following ways:

changing the student/faculty ratio, assessing the ratio of tenure/tenure-track faculty to core undergraduate course instruction, determining effects of that ratio on program cost, reducing the number of electives in the major, and increasing the instructional load of faculty–all within the constraints of the institution's mission and the department's definition of quality. Moreover, efforts to link the results of program review to financial planning will influence how faculty are assigned and evaluated. Personnel costs provide the most fungible resource for reallocation, tenure notwithstanding. It is critical, therefore, that program review engage faculty in analyses that will inform the outcomes of their programs.

External pressures may require new faculty workload models to justify distribution of effort in teaching, research, and service according to the institution's mission. Consequently, institutions must develop a reliable way to determine whether the productivity of the department is within an acceptable range. One measure of instructional productivity is the number of student credit hours generated by tenured/tenure-track faculty. Productivity levels of faculty at similar institutions with similar programs can provide a framework for comparison. Reporting productivity has become a key issue in state legislative appropriations processes. Two years ago, for example, external demands for accountability forced the UMS to develop a new way to report faculty workload or risk having $20 million withheld from their operating budget by the Maryland General Assembly.

Role of students. More and more outside institutions and agencies are demanding validation of the relevance and quality of student learning. What better way to justify spending? Students, too, have strong expectations regarding the curriculum's relevance to work or postgraduate study, the quality of the faculty, and the adequacy of resources to supplement instruction. Clearly, students enrolled in programs under review must be assured that their needs will be met, regardless of the outcomes of the review. If an institution decides to reconfigure or close a program, declared majors must be able to complete their work in equivalent or substitute courses.

Institutions may collect student input in three ways: 1) include them on institution-wide planning committees, 2) solicit their comments about program review recommendations, and 3) survey graduates about the adequacy of their preparation for employment or advanced study.

Role of the institutional research or planning office. Chairs and faculty are not often experienced in the development and presentation of accountability data, particularly in assigning program costs. The institution's research office can assist by providing data for indicators required for all program reviews and for those applicable only to a particular program. Most important, the office can assist the department in identifying how the program meets the strategic needs of the institution, the region, the state, or the nation. Generally, the institution's research office reports to the president or provost to enhance the objectivity of data collection and to ensure consistency with data reported to external agencies. Alternately, the office may report through a planning officer. In all cases, the institution should have assurance that the data used are accurate.

Role of the president/board of trustees. The president, relying upon the advice of the senior cabinet, will make final decisions about the status of programs and be held ultimately accountable for the outcomes of decisions about programs and reallocation of funds. Typically, the president will share decisions with the board of trustees for their understanding and affirmation. It is unusual for a board to micro-manage a president's decisions about an academic program, especially when a shared governance process has provided the various internal and external constituencies opportunity for input.

Finally, an action plan accompanied by a timeline for implementing changes is usually required. Actions taken to implement change will usually be done in stages that are consistent with decision cycles of the institution. Thus, a program scheduled for elimination will be carried on the operating budget for one or more additional fiscal years after the decision to shut it down. Faculty development or buy-out expenses will add expenses to one or more fiscal years.

MANIPULATION AND DELIVERY

Prior to the 1980s, colleges focused on resources and inputs rather than outcomes; therefore, quality as an outcome was assumed but not measured. In addition, most program reviews provided data on the status and direction of programs, but did not enable colleges to change or improve programs (Conrad, 1983). This approach is no longer viable.

Today, programs are evaluated according to a set of predetermined indicators. Judgments about programs are formed by identifying benchmarks—values of the data comparable to values gathered from similar programs on campus or at institutions with similar missions. Alternatively, institutions may simply decide to improve the value of the indicators by a certain percentage over a specified time period (e.g., a ten percent increase in sponsored research or minority enrollment). Benchmarks are important because they demonstrate the program's improvement in specific areas even after the goals have been reached.

The previous section, "Basic concepts," mentioned a number of traditional areas—faculty, students, curriculum—associated with evaluating the quality of an academic program. This section examines program cost and productivity, indicators that have assumed greater prominence in institutional planning, goal setting, departmental analyses, and recommendations.

Cost and productivity indicators. The process for ascertaining productivity and cost of offering should be simple, with judgments informed by data. The data elements in Table 1 were developed by University of Maryland System committees comprising faculty, campus academic administrators, budget and financial planners, and directors of institutional research. The elements were used by the institutions, the system administration, and the board of regents to recommend the extensive program actions mentioned above. One caveat: to many faculty the indicators in Table 1 appeared to value cost and productivity above quality. In fact, they were designed not to expedite budget cutting, but to provide a basis for redeploying resources. In addition, questions were raised about the paucity of indicators on research and service. The UMS decided that its systemwide review of programs would rely upon easily verified data. However, Table 1 includes faculty contributed indicators particularly useful to research institutions within the UMS.

Judgments about programs are formed by identifying benchmarks—values of the data comparable to values gathered from similar programs on campus or at institutions with similar missions.

TABLE 1

Academic Program Cost and Productivity Indicators[1]

Fall semester undergraduate enrollment (most recent)
Four-year change in undergraduate enrollment
Fall semester graduate enrollment (most recent)
Four-year change in graduate enrollment
Bachelors degrees awarded (most recent)
Four-year change in masters degrees awarded
Doctorate degrees awarded (most recent)
Total student credit hours (most recent)
    Number of lower division of total SCH
    Number of upper division of total SCH
    Number of graduate of total SCH
Full-time equivalent students (FTES)
Full-time equivalent faculty (FTEF)
FTES/FTEF
Number of tenured and tenure-track faculty
State supported expenditures (general funds and tuition)
State supported expenditures/FTES
State supported expenditures—total salaries
Research expenditures
Research expenditures/state supported expenditures
Research expenditures/number of tenured and tenure-track faculty

ADDITIONAL INDICATORS

Number of books published/number of
    core faculty (tenured and tenure-track)
Number of referred works/number of
    core faculty
Number of creative activities/number of
    core faculty
Number of presentations/number of
    core faculty
Number of research grants/number of
    core faculty
Number of days spent in public service/
    number of core faculty

[1] The indicators, when displayed by institution, constitute the Program Review Matrix

should be prorated according to the number of full-time equivalent students (FTES) produced by each program, since it is students who drive the administrative costs of a program. To supplement cost information, departments might add data on faculty non-instructional productivity or provide other indicators to demonstrate appropriate use of resources. For further discussion of the uses of program review indicators by the University of Maryland System, see Eaton and Miyares (1995).

Departmental analysis and recommendations. In ten case studies of state level performance indicators, Neal (1995) concluded that to contribute to the formation of institutional planning, indicators must be carefully integrated with other planning and funding strategies. The key to conducting a program review that will inform planning at any level is to select indicators and benchmarks that allow assessment of the current and future **impact** of the program. The UMS has found the following framework informative and useful.

- **Demonstrate contribution** of the program to the mission and planning priorities of the institution;

- **Identify duplication** of work done in the academic program with work done in other programs or departments and suggest modifications to reduce duplication;

- **Verify student demand** and projected enrollment in the subject matter taught in the program;

- **Indicate complementary nature** of the academic program with other essential programs or functions performed in the institution;

- **Correlate the assessment** of student learning outcomes to program objectives and **indicate changes** made as a result of strategies employed by faculty; and

- **Demonstrate consistency** of the faculty characteristics with the educational and service objectives of the program.

Some institutions have begun to connect program reviews directly with strategic plan development. In response to calls by regional accrediting bodies to demonstrate a capacity to continue planning and to invest in quality assessment after reaccreditation, colleges and universities have expressed program reviews as strategic planning objectives.

The data in Table 1 are available at most institutions. In order to facilitate examination of program costs at research institutions, those costs are not allocated among degree levels. State supported expenditures include both tuition and state funds. Private institutions should also work with the total departmental budget, whatever the sources of income. Data include only direct costs, since no savings accrue to the department when indirect costs are cut. One difficulty arose when some departments claimed that disaggregation of the data was difficult among programs housed in the same department. It was agreed that in departments where multiple programs are offered, costs

Saint Louis University's strategic plan, for example, contains an objective that the "University will support and maintain only those programs that meet standards of excellence, promote the University mission, and for which internal, external or emerging markets exist" (Saint Louis University, 1996, p. 11). Specific strategies are identified to realize the objective including the regular assessment of all programs against several criteria (e.g., proportion of faculty holding a terminal degree, number of graduates, faculty scholarship and external support levels, credit hour production, competitive viability, minimal duplication and redundancy, cost-effectiveness, capacity for external recognition of excellence, strategic advantage, and mission complementarity).

ACTIONABILITY ISSUES

Program review itself is not an exact science. Barak and Sweeney (1995, p. 15) stress the importance of simplicity in using the results of program review: "The more complex the decision-making process, the less likely that it will be successful. This seems counter-intuitive because the act of integration and use of program review results make the decision-making process more complex. It appears that the act of use itself is quite simple: someone just insists on using the results of program review " (p. 15). In the case of Maryland, it was the regents who made the first decision.

Program review is, however, informed by data. Consistently applied cost/productivity indicators allow institutions to identify the outliers, those programs that differ significantly from similar programs on the same campus or at peer institutions. Departments that single-mindedly show the best investment of institutional resources (e.g., reallocations, program modifications, increased productivity, entrepreneurship, strong student learning outcomes, and greater administrative efficiency) are most able to justify resources for their programs. In short, a final program review report proposes to the leadership anticipated changes over the next five to ten years, and indicates how faculty and students will incorporate these changes for the benefit of both program and institution.

RECOMMENDATIONS

Accountability is documentation of an institution's effectiveness in meeting its mission and goals. The use of resources to maximize effectiveness is the crux of serious

PRINT REFERENCES

Barak, R. and Sweeney, J. 1995. "Academic Program Review in Planning, Budgeting, and Assessment." In *Using Academic Program Review*, edited by R. Barak and L. Metz. *New Directions for Institutional Research* No. 86. San Francisco: Jossey-Bass Publishers.

Barak, R. J. 1986. "The Role of Program Review in Strategic Planning." *Association for Institutional Research, Professional File* 26.

Belanger, C. and Tremblay, L. 1982. "A Methodological Approach to Selective Cutbacks." *Canadian Journal of Higher Education* 12(3): 25–35.

Bloomfield, S. 1984. "Analytical Tools for Budget Reductions: A Case Study." Association for Institutional Research, 1984 Annual Forum Paper, EDRS 246 790.

Conrad, C. 1983. "Enhancing Institutional and Program Quality." In *Survival in the 1980s: Quality, Mission and Financing Outcome*, edited by R. Wilson. Center for the Study of Higher Education, Arizona University, Tucson, AZ.

Eaton, G. and Miyares, J. 1995. "Integrating Program Review in Planning and Budgeting: A Systemwide Perspective." In *Using Academic Program Review*, edited by R. Barak. *New Directions for Institutional Research* No. 86. San Francisco: Jossey-Bass Publishers.

Harpel, R. L. 1986. "The Anatomy of an Academic Program Review." *Association for Institutional Research, Professional File* 25.

Metz, L. 1995. "Program Review in Academic Departments." In *Using Academic Program Review. New Directions for Institutional Research* No. 86. San Francisco: Jossey-Bass Publishers.

Neal, J. 1995. "Overview of Policy and Practice: Differences and Similarities in Developing Higher Education Accountability." In *Assessing Performance in an Age of Accountability: Case Studies*, edited by G. Gaither. *New Directions for Higher Education* No. 91. San Francisco: Jossey-Bass Publishers.

Saint Louis University. 1996. *Strategic Plan: A Shared Vision and Commitment to Excellence*. St. Louis: Saint Louis University.

Solomon, L. 1990. "Rhetoric: Revising the Cost Spiral in Higher Education." Paper presented at the Seventh Annual Professional Development Seminar, State Higher Education Financial Offices, SHEEO, Chicago, August 17, 1990.

Thompson, R. 1983. "Maintaining Quality Programs During Periods of Fiscal Stress." In *Survival in the 1980s: Quality, Mission and Financing Options*, edited by R. Wilson. Center for the Study of Higher Education, University of Arizona.

ELECTRONIC SAMPLER

http://bridge.anglia.ac.uk/www/flexi.html
Flexible Learning and Higher Education. Faculty of Educational Services, Anglia Polytechnic University.

http://chronicle.merit.edu
The Chronicle of Higher Education.

http://rhythm.mecn.mass.edu/bhe/zassess.htm
Assessment in Higher Education. Massachusetts Board of Higher Education.

http://sshe7.sshechan.edu/mayplan.html
Imperatives for the Future: A Plan for Pennsylvania's State System of Higher Education. Office of the Chancellor, Pennsylvania State System of Higher Education.

An interesting look at how academic program review fits into this state's strategic plan.

ELECTRONIC SAMPLER

http://www.educom.edu/program/nlii/keydocs/massy.html

Using Information Technology to Enhance Academic Productivity. NLII (National Learning Infrastructure Initiative). William F. Massy and Robert Zemsky.

A white paper from the Wingspread Enhancing Academic Productivity Conference in June 1995.

http://www.schev.edu/paper.html

Paper Trail: Reports, studies, news releases, regulations, and other documents. SCHEV (State Council of Higher Education for Virginia).

Includes papers on state policy on transfer, transfer connection, and more.

planning at every level within an institution. The process that follows program review links tactical planning efforts on the program level with the institution's overall plan.

The integration of several planning activities into a single set of clearly defined goals ensures that the collective outcomes of program review reflect the institution's mission and vision. The ability of a department actually to link its review of academic programs with the planning and budgeting of the institution depends largely upon whether the institution itself has projected expenses, enrollments, and income over the next five to ten years. If so, the review should reveal how the program fits with the priorities. The University of Maryland System, for example, requires an institutional financial/accountability plan that includes reallocations, particularly those deriving from program reviews.

Even if an institution has not yet developed a financial plan, it will be wise for the department to select performance indicators and establish benchmarks to measure how well it is meeting its own objectives. Planning at the departmental level is critical because it is certain that, as resources diminish, institutions will turn to academic programs for significant redeployments, if not savings.

The goal of this chapter has been to provide the basic elements of a program review in the face of ever increasing demands for accountability. Departments and their faculties should be fundamentally influenced by the outcomes of program review. Program review will affect plans at every level: staffing, reallocation, enrollment, facilities, budget, and so on. The departmental plan must, therefore, demonstrate centrality to the mission and goals of the institution, accountability through data, and a willingness to redesign its use of resources. ◆

This chapter proposes a five-step model for constructing cooperative curricular agreements. First, clarify purposes for the agreement and determine whether it fits the institutional mission. Second, assess the collaborative environment to guarantee involvement by key decision makers. Third, structure a process to address matters of governance, curriculum, facilities, resources, revenues, and policy conflicts. Fourth, assess the product of the agreement and improve it. Finally, use assessment results to reappraise the agreement, revising or retiring it as necessary.

Alternative Delivery Strategies, Partnerships, and Articulation Agreements: New Recipes for Favorite Dishes

Kathleen A. Corak and James L. Croonquist

CORE PLANNING QUESTIONS

Preparing a generic recipe for success in cooperative agreement-making is a little like making spaghetti. Every chef knows what ingredients should be included in the sauce and how long the pasta should be cooked. But very seldom do two chefs agree upon the precise formula for the sauce or even how hot the stove should be. Nonetheless, they all assume that people who make spaghetti know how to fire up the stove and select the proper utensils. For the purposes of the following discussion on cooperative agreement-making, it is assumed that readers are at various stages of culinary expertise and will create their own recipes from the ingredients offered here.

Successful institutions are marked by innovation and creativity in marshaling resources to respond to new markets in a timely manner. No longer able to rely upon predictable and steady revenue streams, decision makers and planners seek to leverage their scarce resources through partnerships. The basic questions confronting academic leaders include:

- Why go off campus?
- How are off-campus articulation agreements and partnerships formed in a way that ensures the integrity of the process?

For many, the experience today is one of all-out warfare among institutions for operational dollars. Traditional curriculum delivery–the student travels to the campus for face-to-face faculty interaction–is no longer universally suitable or appealing to the learner. The search for alternative modes of delivery that will reach new markets and result in new revenues has intensified.

Kathleen A. Corak

is Executive Dean of Minot State University, Bottineau, North Dakota. Corak is a former Convener of SCUP's Academic Planning Academy, a current member of that academy, a member of SCUP's Planning Institute Subcommittee, and a former member of SCUP's Publications Advisory Committee.

James L. Croonquist

is Vice President for Academic Affairs at Minot State University, Minot, North Dakota. Croonquist is a member of the Society for College and University Planning.

BASIC CONCEPTS

Cooperative agreements. The most viable alternatives seem to be a collection of understandings loosely referred to as "cooperative," "collaborative," "joint," or "articulation" agreements between two or more institutions. These agreements are somewhat like contracts, although may not be as legally binding. They are likely to result eventually in written documents. But such physical evidence may be drafted well after the handshake of understanding has taken place–and even then, perhaps, only as problems with the agreement begin to surface.

Agreements of this sort are like treaties, the result of negotiations that transpire between one campus and another institution. Although subsequent agreements may be modeled after earlier versions, there are frequently no precedents to follow, for each venture is new territory explored. Developing procedures to make the agreement work can be most challenging and often requires some very creative thinking. But, whether defined as a partnership or couched as an alliance, it is important to remember that cooperation is the theme and revenue enhancement the goal.

> M*otivated by the prospect of "more bang for the institutional buck," cooperative agreements are often entered into prematurely.*

Key to the development of these agreements is the ability to deliver curriculum in nontraditional ways. Such alternative delivery strategies include courses taught through email or surface mail, interactive television seminars conducted simultaneously in multiple sites, satellite uplinks and downlinks, and audio and video conferencing. Added to those are the flexibly-formatted courses and workshops that range in length from overnight and weekend seminars to those that stretch over the full term. Alternative delivery strategies are central to some agreements because of the market enhancement potential. Because of their characteristic flexibility with regard to timing and place of delivery, they attract students who might otherwise be unable to participate in the higher education milieu.

To the uninitiated, cooperative agreements suggest an immediacy to revenue problem solving that is compelling. They have the desirable appearance of simplicity and efficacy.

Expectations of financial gain grow exponentially as administrators anticipate increased student credit hour production and/or tuition from a new clientele for only a minor investment in an already proven product: an existing academic program.

Regrettably, it is not as simple as that. When one enters the world of cooperative agreement-making with an uninformed perspective, the outcome is one of frustration. Motivated by the prospect of "more bang for the institutional buck," cooperative agreements are often entered into prematurely. That is, they are formed without structure, without clarity of intentions, and without a comprehensive appraisal of the environment in which they exist. This inevitably leads to misunderstandings and misconceptions about the purpose and direction of the agreement and can result in one or more of the parties withdrawing from it.

Planning model elements. Five elements are integral in building a foundation of trust upon which solid agreements can stand. These elements, listed below, are expressed as a series of steps toward forming a successful planning model:

- Establishing clear intentions;
- Analyzing the environment;
- Agreeing to the process;
- Assessing the product of the agreement; and
- Revisiting the plan.

Further, it is certain that no meaningful planning will occur unless each of the parties is thoroughly involved in the process and has a stake in the outcomes. This means that the process of constructing agreements must first address the benefits to be derived by each participant in the process. If value is not self-evident to all parties, and if there is no "buy-in," the agreement is doomed even before it is formalized.

Thus, although written agreements may look very different from each other, there must certainly be a structure to partnerships. There are also consistent rules to follow in assembling such partnerships. The key, then, lies in the planning. And, as always, the key in planning is to ask the right questions. Figure One provides a checklist of issues to be addressed in building cooperative agreements. The issues are grouped into four categories: general

FIGURE 1

Issues to be Addressed in Cooperative/ Articulation Agreements

GENERAL ISSUES

1. Yes ☐ No ☐ Is there a governing body such as a state or regional entity that controls who should cooperate with whom? If so, what are the procedures necessary to gain approval for the proposed alliance?

2. Yes ☐ No ☐ Has the regional accrediting agency been contacted? What are the procedures for gaining approval for an institutional change such as a new cooperative program?

3. Yes ☐ No ☐ Is the proposed articulation/cooperative agreement within the mission parameters of the partners?

4. Yes ☐ No ☐ Has the question, "Whose degree is it?", been answered. Is the degree "owned" by one of the partners?

5. Yes ☐ No ☐ Has the ownership of credits and student credit hour production been clarified?

6. Yes ☐ No ☐ Are credits compatible between/amongst the partners (e.g. is Math 101 offered at three hours on all the cooperating campuses)? If not, what is the process for determining commonalty of course values?

7. Yes ☐ No ☐ Are the credits assigned as either all semester or all quarter hours? If not, what provisions for accommodation will be provided for students?

8. Yes ☐ No ☐ Are there issues of transfer that need clarification? For example, do courses apply to the major area or are they only accepted as electives?

9. Yes ☐ No ☐ Do any of the partners have residency requirements that affect the delivery of course work to an extended campus? If so, how does residency impact the agreement?

10. Yes ☐ No ☐ Are there other campus policies that might affect the agreement? What are they?

ISSUES OF QUALITY—GENERAL

1. Yes ☐ No ☐ Has the faculty on each of the campuses been actively involved in the decision-making processes to cooperate with other institutions?

2. Yes ☐ No ☐ Have the proper campus governance structures been brought to bear on the proposed articulation(s)?

3. Yes ☐ No ☐ Are the cooperating institutions viewing the cooperative process in the same light?

4. Yes ☐ No ☐ Have the institutional agendas been deciphered to the satisfaction of all parties?

5. Yes ☐ No ☐ Have the needs of the students been considered in the planning process?

6. Yes ☐ No ☐ Are the human (faculty & support staff) and fiscal (budgetary) resources adequate to ensure that standards in the program are maintained when offered as a cooperative venture?

7. Yes ☐ No ☐ Are goals and outcomes for the cooperative agreement clearly established before it goes into effect?

8. Yes ☐ No ☐ Is there a realistic assessment plan to evaluate the articulation agreement in a timely fashion and on a regular schedule? If so, how does the assessment plan initiate changes to the agreement? If not, how will the agreement be evaluated?

continued on p. 38

FIGURE 1

Issues to be Addressed in Cooperative/ Articulation Agreements (continued)

9. Yes ☐ No ☐ Are there clearly stated timelines on the articulation agreement? Does it expire over time or is it continuous?

10. Yes ☐ No ☐ Is there a designated contact person (program coordinator) with line-authority to clarify areas of concern for students and faculty on all campuses? If not, to whom are questions directed?

ISSUES OF QUALITY—SPECIFIC

1. Yes ☐ No ☐ If the cooperative agreement includes a remote or extended site, are there adequate student services available at that site?
   Yes ☐ No ☐ library adequate?
   Yes ☐ No ☐ advising?
   Yes ☐ No ☐ materials? (books, computers, etc.)
   Yes ☐ No ☐ physical environment? (classrooms, housing?)
   Yes ☐ No ☐ other?

2. Yes ☐ No ☐ Does the agreement address issues of who teaches which courses?

3. Yes ☐ No ☐ Are faculty at an extended site to be used in the program? How are they approved to teach?

4. Yes ☐ No ☐ Will faculty from one site be asked to commute to another site? If so, how does that affect loads?

5. Yes ☐ No ☐ If faculty committees are involved (e.g. in a graduate program), have provisions been made to accommodate students at the remote site?

PROCEDURAL/MECHANICAL ISSUES

1. Yes ☐ No ☐ Have the kinds of delivery vehicles to be used been identified?

2. Yes ☐ No ☐ Are there technology applications such as interactive television, email, or satellite being considered. If so, what are they and how are issues of quality being handled?

3. Yes ☐ No ☐ Is there a process for securing priority scheduling on technology delivered programs? If so, how is priority scheduling arranged? By whom?

4. Yes ☐ No ☐ Have issues of financial aid been addressed?

5. Yes ☐ No ☐ Is there a mechanism for collecting fees?

6. Yes ☐ No ☐ Is there agreement on providing informational brochures for students? Who prepares and pays for them? Who distributes them? How do students obtain them?

7. Yes ☐ No ☐ Are promotional materials on the cooperative program available? If so, who prepares them? How are they distributed?

8. Yes ☐ No ☐ Is there an 800 line available? If so, what is it?

9. Yes ☐ No ☐ Are there issues of sharing equipment between partners? If so, how is that articulated? Who pays for what?

10. Yes ☐ No ☐ Is there a way to end the agreement if it proves to be unsatisfactory to any of the parties involved? If so, what is it and how does it affect students?

concerns, issues of quality, specific concerns about quality, and procedural matters.

The particular planning model promoted in this chapter converts the five key elements–establishing clear intentions, analyzing the environment, agreeing to the process, assessing the product of the agreement, and revisiting the plan–into the five pivotal questions that follow.

*1. What are the intended outcomes of
   this agreement?*

As elementary as this question seems, it is daunting to see how frequently it goes unanswered. Articulation agreements are formed without sufficient thought given to outcomes. A sort of "common understanding" of intentions is assumed. There is an implicit trust that all parties want to work toward the same ends. But it may be premature to discuss outcomes without a full questioning of motives.

One reason is that those elements thought to be part of a "common understanding" between the involved parties, turn out to be not so common. Misinterpretations are the norm. It will help to remember that agreements made between two different organizations are interpreted in light of the corporate language and the cultural context peculiar to each. (We may all speak the same language, but we don't speak the same organizational dialect.) Differences between two colleges or universities are significant. They are only magnified when negotiating with a different kind of organization. It can be very worthwhile to spend sufficient time in the early stages of negotiation just defining your terms. It may require great diplomacy and patience to understand and accept the oddities inherent to the other organization. But the importance of articulating individual expectations in truly mutual terms cannot be overstated. It lays the groundwork for discussing the outcomes issues.

Some specific questions posed and answered will greatly help the participants achieve a common understanding while also illuminating motives. First, think through carefully and discuss openly the many reasons for taking on the project. For example, are there financial antecedents? Do you need to increase revenues? Do they have to cut costs? Then, are there access issues? Do they need additional training that cannot be had elsewhere? Do you have students who cannot

attend your campus? Further, is there a mandate involved? Are there pressures from the state or federal government, or even from accrediting associations, that require one of the partners to take action?

Another important consideration is knowing which of the parties has initiated the collaboration. Ask, "Why now?" Is there more than one agenda being played out in the discussions? As these intentions are clarified, you must also ask yourself whether, in light of what you are learning, the project is in keeping with your institutional mission. If the answer is "yes," a fruitful discussion of outcomes can begin.

There are three main components to be addressed in regard to outcomes: revenues, curriculum and faculty. These components can be likened to ingredients in the spaghetti analogy. As varying quantities of ingredients result in very different tasting sauces, so will different emphases on revenue, curriculum, or faculty directly affect collaborative outcomes. Consider how each partner to the collaboration intends to measure each of these three critical ingredients as they are added to the agreement. If you cannot reach consensus (who should put in how much of each), then you have no collaborative recipe for success. The point is that consensus on intended outcomes must drive the combination of ingredients central to the goals of the collaboration. Well-articulated outcomes should drive the rest of the process.

Well-articulated outcomes are expressed in measurable terms that make the program evaluation phase much cleaner. To be specific: as outcomes are agreed upon, urge the group to decide what kind of evidence will convince others that a particular goal has been met. For example, if an intended outcome is to prepare, in two years, a sufficient number of licensed practical nurses to fill the local hospital needs, ask what evidence would convince the collaborators of success? A graduation rate of ten students per year? A decrease in LPN turnover rates at the hospital within three years? Employer satisfaction index increases? Measurable outcomes are second to none; arriving at them should be a goal of the negotiating team.

*B*ut the importance of articulating individual expectations in truly mutual terms cannot be overstated. It lays the groundwork for discussing the outcomes issues.

2. What is the environment for the agreement? Assuming the first question has been answered to everyone's satisfaction, the next phase is to analyze the environment within which the agreement will be struck. This is a four-step process: identify key players, establish a time frame, determine facilities needs, and conduct a SWOT (Strengths, Weaknesses, Opportunities, Threats) analysis.

*I*t is most important in the articulation process to identify the players promptly. Do this by listing all personnel—administrative, faculty, support—who must be involved to make the agreement work.

It is most important in the articulation process to identify the "players" promptly. Do this by listing all personnel–administrative, faculty, support–who must be involved to make the agreement work. Determine whether the right assortment of decision makers has been invited to the negotiating table. It is frustrating to work on a project with good intentions only to find that the ultimate decision makers have been left out of the loop. It can be useful for the negotiating team to construct a flow chart clarifying who does what in their respective organizations and with what level of authority.

Another essential step is the establishment of timelines. One timeline, of course, is the date by which you want to have the agreement completely articulated. Another is the duration of the agreement once it is in place. An agreement with an expiration date is always more desirable than one of indefinite duration, because it allows for review, revision, or even termination of the agreement as necessary. Once the initial agreement has been signed, participants can shift focus to other matters and quickly lose sight of the day-to-day administration of the project, especially those who administer collaborations from a distance. Include benchmark dates in the document. They gauge the extent to which the partners are achieving their desired outcomes.

A third crucial step is to determine the facilities requirements for the agreement, including the buildings, classrooms, and technologies. Computers, chairs, and desks obviously fall into this category, but so do postage, paper clips, copying costs, and telephone charges. All instructional support must be considered to project expenses accurately.

Having considered matters of key personnel, time frame, and facilities, conduct a SWOT analysis, a particularly effective tool for analyzing the environment. Project negotiators, individually or collectively, list items that fall into each of the four SWOT categories and then weigh the positives against the negatives.

An example: suppose the local high school wants to teach college-level courses to its seniors on its own campus and wants your blessing on the project. In the "Strengths" column you might note that you are the only postsecondary organization in the area that is in a position to work with them toward their goal. They need you. Also, you have the right faculty on board whose help could be enlisted. In the "Weakness" column you might note that the timing is bad. It is late April, and the faculty will soon be away for the summer. In the "Opportunities" column, though, you recognize that this partnership has the potential of increasing freshman enrollment. When those high school seniors graduate, they will be more committed to attending your campus. Conversely, in the "Threats" column, might this project actually result in a decrease in student credit hour production? If those students are earning college credit at no cost during high school, they will not need/pay for them at your college.

As these lists are shared among the collaborators, it often happens that others have put a very different spin on the concerns you yourself have raised. Consider the matter of classrooms, for example. In many agreements, one of the parties must assume responsibility for providing the space in which to teach. The organization that controls the space, usually one classroom or a group of them, determines which rooms are available, and when and which facilities are to remain unavailable to other partners. To the campus in charge of the classrooms, that "control" can be seen as an opportunity; space rental may be on the horizon. But to the partners, lack of influence over space usage may be a legitimate threat, especially if the articulation agreement does not reference charges normally levied for use of facilities. The surprise of an unforeseen cost after the agreement is in effect will undermine the partnership. Discussion of the SWOT analysis broadens everyone's thinking and increases understanding about what is at stake for the participants.

Sometimes an identified weak area can be transformed into a strength. Consider the matter of faculty "load" (the number of credits to be taught each term). Some proposals suggest or imply the use of faculty "above load" (greater than full-time; essentially, overtime) in order to offer extended programs. This is awkward for the home campus and particularly disadvantageous when the extended program is distant. To the home campus of the faculty member, then, this aspect of the collaboration constitutes a weakness. Campuses are forever having to justify overworking faculty for the "Greater Good" of service to students. But consider the possibility of involving other faculty already in the extended area. If qualified faculty are already on site and carry the credentials necessary to achieve mutually desired outcomes, by all means use them. Doing so converts the "weakness" (overworked faculty) into a "strength" (expanded faculty base in a new service region). It enriches the cooperative spirit of the collaboration by including new colleagues who share a common goal—a significant step toward cementing good relations between and among collaborators.

3. What are the processes for approval of the agreement?

The next step is to immerse the team in "process" issues. There are six issues that need to be carefully processed: governance; curricular; facilities; resources; revenues; and interinstitutional policy conflict resolution.

Before discussions, the team should establish some ground rules for itself, planning to meet regularly and often to handle the myriad of details that will emerge. No "wildcatting" should be allowed—that is, no one individual should be permitted to determine policy or initiate procedures unfamiliar to the others. Problems should be solved as a team. Remember that it will be common—and necessary—to hark back to the outcomes statements in order to clarify intentions and define each participant's role in bringing about the intended ends.

To ensure their success, agreements must consider issues of governance at all levels. The primary level is faculty governance. A common failing of articulation agreements is their lack of faculty involvement from the very inception of the project. By their nature, collaborative agreements address curriculum either directly, as in the sharing of programs, or indirectly, through concerns about accredita-

tion or transfer credit. Faculty have deeply vested interests in matters of curriculum. Most campuses rely on bodies like curriculum committees and faculty senates to oversee the curriculum. To form agreements that affect the delivery of curriculum, yet do not get plugged into faculty governance procedures, is akin to trying to make spaghetti without turning on the stove. Faculty left in the dark about "new academic agreements" have been known to stonewall mercilessly on principle alone.

Next, the team should look off campus. Colleges, universities, and other organizations usually have governing boards. There may be a local board of regents or a state board of higher education that needs to be consulted. If there is a state-coordinated system, consider how the agreement might affect other campuses. Will a commissioner or a chancellor ultimately have to authorize this agreement? What questions will they want answered before giving you their stamp of approval?

Next, the team should think in terms of accrediting bodies. Would the new agreement be in line with regional, national, or professional accreditation standards? Do you need to make a formal request for institutional change of affiliation status with an accrediting body? If a specific discipline is singled out for articulation, does it have accreditation standards that limit or prohibit clauses in the agreement? If so, how are those circumstances to be mediated? Accreditation issues can be tricky. It is best to look at them carefully at the outset.

Curricular issues constitute another important part of the articulation process. They are of two kinds: ownership and quality control. In forging an agreement, partners quickly have to come to terms with matters of ownership. Whose degree (or program or course) is this? You may all be contributing instruction, but only one awards the degree. (There are exceptions: the Joint Doctoral Program at San Diego State University and The Claremont Graduate School, for example). Who is responsible for determining the curriculum? Whose syllabi will be used? These questions are directly related to concerns of ownership.

Remember that it will be common—and necessary—to hark back to the outcomes statements in order to clarify intentions and define each participant's role in bringing about the intended ends.

Questions regarding quality control must also be answered. Some concern themselves with the learners. Who sets the admission standards? Who sets the retention standards? How are the learners to be evaluated? Other questions address quality of instruction. For example, who determines which faculty will be qualified to teach? What criteria are important in this selection? Who is responsible for evaluating faculty credentials and approving or disapproving them? Who hires the faculty? Who evaluates their performance and under whose governance structure? Still other questions should be raised about the quality of the program emerging from the agreement. How will the team know whether the program is successful? The intended outcomes already agreed upon will point toward an answer, but the team should specify responsibility for future gathering and analysis of data required to answer the question thoroughly.

It is important to keep in mind that determining curriculum and assigning faculty have great bearing on intended outcomes. The shape of the curriculum and the credentials of the faculty are main ingredients in "the sauce," if you will. The team will have to consider the proper mix of faculty when determining the design of the curriculum–and always while attending to the intended outcomes.

Facilities issues need articulation. They are of three kinds: availability, access, and cost. First, it must be determined whether the needed space is available during hours that meet the needs of the agreement. Premium space may not be available. Will the team consider different facilities? Or different times of delivery? Second, are the available facilities accessible to both students and faculty? If great distance is involved, what bearing will that have on access? Third, and not to be overlooked, are there costs for facilities usage? Will there be rental fees? Is there a charge for use of special equipment? What about hidden costs such as travel to and from the facility or meals on the road? Facilities issues need to be resolved as the agreement is taking shape.

Next are resource issues. Resources include the people and the services it takes to run our campus-based programs. For example, extended-campus agreements, largely academic in nature, will include some expectation that the learners have access to library materials. Which libraries can meet these needs for the learners? Are online library services available to students who study at a distance? Are available services sufficient given the nature of the agreement? If not, what can be done to address the deficit?

Another resource, often overlooked, is access to what we generally consider to be standard student services. Although we may tend to take their availability for granted on our own campuses, how will we provide the extended campus student with, say, academic advising? What about tutoring services or study skills assistance? Depending upon the nature of the agreement, your campus may be obligated, by virtue of accreditation requirements, to provide standard services to all students, even those who are not based at your site.

Revenues issues are undoubtedly the "sticky wickets" of articulation agreements. There are generally at least two revenue issues central to most agreements: student credit hour production; and collection of tuition and assorted fees. It is difficult to talk about one without the other. In some agreements they are resolved separately, but not easily. Apparently simple things, like collecting tuition, can become terribly complex. For example, in a three-way agreement among institutions with varying fee structures, will students be expected to pay three separate, partial fees, or one mutually acceptable amount? If the latter, who will collect it (and how, and when), and will it be split? If revenues are to be shared, what precisely does that mean? Who gets how much for doing what? What is meant by sharing? Is there a constant percentage involved or is it to be an enrollment-driven model, flexible with each offering?

What if the agreement brings together two fee structures that are really quite different? Suppose one institution charges by the credit regardless of credits amassed, while the other charges a flat rate to anyone exceeding twelve credits per term. What is to be done for the student taking three credits from the first campus and twelve credits from the second? How can you address the fiscal needs of both partners to the agreement without doing a disservice to the learner? Another scenario is

There are generally at least two revenue issues central to most agreements: student credit hour production; and collection of tuition and assorted fees.

one in which institutions Alpha and Beta share a program. Students at Alpha pay $90 a credit. Students at Beta pay $70. To complete this new program of study, students will soon be taking Beta courses on the Alpha campus. Because the degree is to be granted by Beta, students will take discipline-specific courses from Beta faculty. But, Alpha faculty will teach the general education component of the degree. Students will probably be taking Alpha and Beta courses simultaneously. Will they pay $70 or $90 per credit to earn the degree?

The bottom line: Who will pay? What is the learner's share and what are the partners' shares? Who will manage accounts receivable (tuition, fees, rents) and accounts payable (technological support, library materials, faculty salaries)? Resolving matters of revenue is frequently the most challenging and frustrating aspect of agreement-making. As with matters of curriculum and faculty, you cannot attain intended outcomes without a clear understanding of how revenues will influence the agreement. The document should clearly specify who controls revenues and how they are to be shared. Revenue sharing details, including a complete budget projecting expenses and income, should be presented to all participants before any deals are struck. Mistrust creeps into agreements when one party has budgetary control over the others, yet is unwilling to disclose budget projections fully.

Recall the spaghetti analogy. Revenues make it possible to add other ingredients to the sauce and thereby influence intended outcomes. No one party should "buy ingredients," however, unless all agree to what they are and how they are to be used in the agreement recipe. Candid discussion and full disclosure are important.

Last but not least, the process of agreement making needs to include an analysis of those taken-for-granted policies of the other organization that may be at odds with your own institutional policies. Quite frankly, you may not be aware of standing policies in your own organization that could affect the workability of the agreement on the table. It is easy to overlook some of the seemingly peripheral people whose work may be greatly affected by the terms of the agreement. For example, institutional residency requirements can surprise you. The degree program on which the team has worked so diligently may not provide the student with enough hours in residence to qualify for one of your diplomas! Another concern is the coordination of financial aid. Who will monitor it–and how? Posting grades and issuing transcripts are among other important details that need to be worked out. Existing policies will probably guide the extent to which you can influence that part of the agreement.

Dozens of such considerations should be sorted out during the articulation process. Details make or break agreements. It is wise, therefore, to involve those who will ultimately be responsible for the logistics of the agreement as early in the planning stages as possible. The particular mix of others you consult will vary according to the nature of the agreement. Most typically they would include admissions, registration, financial aid, and business office personnel, who will remember to ask important questions the team may overlook. And they can help you think through logistical road blocks. When it comes to agreement making, the maxim "don't sweat the details" does not apply.

There is much to consider when pulling together an agreement. Governance issues are inherent. Is the faculty signed on? Will the board stand in the way? Is there a good fit with accrediting associations? Next are the curricular issues. Whose degree is this? How will we control quality? Facilities issues must address availability, accessibility, and costs. Resource issues examine the mainstays of human services and instructional support. Revenue matters must be hammered out. How much will students pay, and to whom and for what? How much will the partners contribute? What returns can be expected on the dollar? What are the budget projections? Who will manage the budget? Finally, there are policy issues. Are terms of the agreement in keeping with existing policies governing each partner's organization? Have all the affected people been consulted? It may take many hours and many meetings to answer these questions to everyone's satisfaction.

Once such matters have been resolved, the agreement can take effect. Depending on how your timeline was developed, you may

Details make or break agreements. It is wise, therefore, to involve those who will ultimately be responsible for the logistics of the agreement as early in the planning stages as possible.

have more than a little breathing room to collect your thoughts and turn to other matters. But eventually, your next step will be to assess the product of the agreement, and you will turn back again to your intended outcomes.

4. Has the agreement worked?

The real significance of any articulation agreement is in the assessment of its product. If learn-

If learners are served in a manner consistent with the intent of the articulation, then the agreement can be considered a success. But, that success must be measured in an ongoing fashion.

ers are served in a manner consistent with the intent of the articulation, then the agreement can be considered a success. But, that success must be measured in an ongoing fashion. An assessment measure captures a moment in time. It provides a snapshot of the program's effectiveness. A series of snapshots, however, helps determine whether the trend is in the right direction. It is important to confirm that what is working now continues to work over time.

It is also important to plan on using the evaluative data acquired to make appropriate changes to the program. For example, if the data indicate that graduates of the agreement program are not doing well on subsequent licensing exams, there are curricular implications. If the results of student surveys indicate frustration with library access, changes in library hours of operation may be warranted. It is useless to gather data and file it away. The commitment must be made to analyze and use it to improve the program and/or the terms of the agreement.

How are articulation/cooperative agreements assessed? These programs should be held as accountable as any of your other academic programs and can be assessed in the same ways. If your intended outcomes eventually become formalized in *measurable* terms, then you have an advantage. Tools for measuring outcomes range from standardized tests to in-class instructor assessment; from pre- and post-graduation surveys of students to surveys of employers; from assessments of selected students' portfolios to trend analyses of class performance over several years. Many different approaches may be suitable. It is best to let the intended outcome itself point toward preferred means of measurement. It is also smart to use existing data (as much as possible) in new ways

to answer measurement questions. Finally, it is important to identify multiple measures in order to draw conclusions about the efficacy of your agreement program.

For example, it is helpful to have the faculty collect comparison data on students involved in collaborative agreements and those "mainstreamed" on campus. Evidence of significant student success, or lack of it, compared to norms established in the traditional setting tells much about the quality of the program. Another measurement might be the degree of satisfaction among students, faculty, and support staff. Surveys can indicate whether satisfaction improves or worsens over time. A third measurement might be a survey of employers to determine whether needed skills were brought to the work place by graduates of the agreement program. Each of these measures is useful. But all three together create a more compelling picture of the success of the agreement.

What if the data indicate the agreement is not achieving its objectives? There are some administrators who hold that providing students with "access" to academic programs is a more important consideration than the quality of the programs. After all, the argument purports, students who have "something" are better served than students who have "nothing." This is a weak argument. Students who are served poorly are better off seeking service elsewhere. If the results of your assessments indicate that quality is insufficient to meet intended outcomes, it may be time to terminate the agreement.

To reiterate, it is the intended outcomes in the original agreement that should drive the assessment phase. Multiple measures should be used to evaluate effectiveness. And, most important, based on the data gathered in assessment, changes should be made to the program to improve upon it. Assessment and improvement should be cyclical and continuous. Responsibility for it should be assigned to the partners as the agreement is being crafted. Strict adherence to a plan yields more legitimate results and better informs the evaluators of their product.

5. What, if anything, can be done to improve the agreement?

The most ignored aspect of articulation agreements is review of the document. There is often a sense of relief and finality associated with the formal signing of the agreement–as though it were "finished." But the most valuable information comes later, after students have been cycled through the program once or twice. At that point there are assessment data to consider and subsequent program changes to analyze. A review of the document is called for before it is renewed.

Document review should have structure. A good approach is to engage the collaborators in the same dialogue, albeit in condensed fashion, that guided initial negotiations. Discuss intended outcomes to see whether the articulation did what it was supposed to do. Revisit the environmental concerns and see whether the strengths and opportunities still outweigh the weaknesses and threats. Examine processes critically; discuss problem areas openly. Then assess the assessment process. Were you able to measure your intended outcomes in meaningful ways? If not, how should measurement be approached in the future? Have you already made changes, either to the program or to the assessment approach? What changes still need to be made?

A renewed agreement subjected to this kind of review will be a stronger document and testimony to the success of collaborative efforts between your institution and others.

SUMMARY

This chapter proposes a five-step model for constructing cooperative curricular agreements. It is important first to clarify purposes for the agreement and determine whether it fits within the scope of the institutional mission. Second, the collaborative environment must be assessed to determine whether the key decision makers are appropriately involved, to establish a time frame and a timeline, to locate available facilities, and to consider the "pros" and "cons" of the project. Third, a process for establishing an agreement must be structured to address matters of governance, curriculum, facilities, resources, revenues, and policy conflicts. Fourth, the product of the agreement must be assessed and the data used for ongoing improvement of programming and the assessment techniques themselves. Finally, the assessment results must be used to reevaluate the terms of the agreement, revising or retiring it as necessary. These steps impose a structure on the drafting of off-campus agreements to ensure a better product for the collaborators.

Crafting agreements for alternative delivery of curricula can be likened to combining

PRINT REFERENCES

Commission on Institutions of Higher Education. 1991. *Assessment Workbook*. Chicago: North Central Association of Colleges and Schools.

Gronlund, N. E. 1995. *How to Write and Use Instructional Objectives* (5th ed.). Englewood Cliffs: Merrill.

Kearns, K. P. Summer, 1992. "From Comparative Advantage to Damage Control: Clarifying Strategic Issues Using 'SWOT' Analysis". *Nonprofit Management and Leadership* 3(1).

"Principles of Good Practice for Electronically Offered Academic Degree and Certificate Programs." October, 1995. *NCA Briefing* 13(3), special insert.

"Resources for Learning about Distance Education." December, 1995. *AAHE Bulletin* 48(4): 9–10.

Rogers, S. M. December, 1995. "Distance Education: The Options Follow Mission. " *AAHE Bulletin* 48(4): 4–8.

Rossman, M. H. and Rossman, M. E., eds. 1995. *Facilitating Distance Education*. San Francisco: Jossey-Bass Publishers.

Stark, J. S. and Thomas, A., eds. 1994. *Assessment and Program Evaluation*. Needham Heights: Simon and Schuster.

ELECTRONIC SAMPLER

http://edie.cprost.sfu.ca/~rhlogan/bm_dl.html
Long Distance Education Links to the Web. Ralph H. Logan.

http://www.atlantic.edu/studinfo/artic.html
Atlantic Community College Articulation Agreements.
Listing of some of the agreements this two-year college has with other institutions, including some in process.

http://www.bor.ohio.gov/transfer/atpolicy.html
Ohio Articulation and Transfer Policy. Ohio Board of Regents.

http://www.extension.ualberta.ca/atl/
Academic Technologies for Learning (formerly the Alternative Delivery Initiative). Faculty of Extension, University of Alberta.

http://www.thecb.state.tx.us/homepage/univ/distance/dlmphome.htm
Texas Higher Education Distance Learning Master Plan. Texas Higher Education Coordinating Board.

http://www.trsa.ac.za/main_campus/depts/cll/rpl-conf.htm
Recognition of Prior Learning Conference/Workshop, South Africa, 1996. Centre for Lifelong Learning of Southern Africa.

a good lesson plan with strategic planning principles. A well made lesson plan states specific goals and outcomes for the learners. Students are engaged in the learning environment and then evaluated to determine the extent to which they have learned. Further, the lesson plan itself is evaluated and modified as necessary. So it is with the partnership. Specific goals and intended outcomes are identified with the full involvement of all partners. The agreement is implemented. The program participants are evaluated, and the plan is revisited and modified as necessary.

Strategic planning begins with an analysis of the environment, an appraisal of the campus' strengths and weaknesses, and a listing of current opportunities for–and threats to–the institution. These discussions always include staffing and curriculum issues and should be closely attuned to fiscal resource implications. If resources are not directly and immediately tied to planning, the result is not strategic, but only preliminary. In strategic planning, one must link resources to objectives. Likewise, a good partnership agreement should analyze its environment, appraise its resources, and fully consider the fiscal implications of the proposed agreement. Its intended outcomes should be stated in clear and measurable terms and must also be linked to resources.

This model of partnering, then, combines the strategic element of planning (re-source allocation) with the deliberateness of the lesson plan (structure and evaluation). That combination begins the process of partnering. It lays a foundation upon which the bricks and mortar of an agreement can be assembled.

It is safe to assume that future articulation agreements between your institution and another are likely. Each one will be different. But the use of a planning model like this one provides needed structure and brings a comforting sense of familiarity to the process. Each prospective agreement can be seen as an opportunity. And each allows you to further refine the structure you have created to develop it. With each iteration, your collection of recipes grows, your menu of sauces is more inviting, and your reputation among the great chefs of agreement-making is assured. ◆

Enrollment Management

Recruitment/Retention Analysis Tools

Michael F. Middaugh and
Dale W. Trusheim

Financial Aid and Strategic Planning

Dale W. Trusheim and
Michael F. Middaugh

*E*nrollment planning is an integral part of the strategic planning process at any college or university. The authors describe specific strategies for acquiring more useful data to assist in the recruitment and retention of students.

Recruitment/Retention Analysis Tools

Michael F. Middaugh and Dale W. Trusheim

In his 1983 volume, *Academic Strategy*, George Keller emphasized the highly competitive nature of the higher education marketplace. In order to respond to that competition effectively, strategic planning must be rooted in an institution's accurate assessment of its niche within that marketplace. Nowhere is this more true than in shaping policy and programs to recruit and retain students. The integrity of the academic core curriculum, the depth and breadth of the full time faculty, a consistent tuition revenue stream (many institutions nationwide are 60 to 80 percent tuition dependent), and efficient utilization of facilities–all are directly or indirectly dependent upon a stable pool of students whose attributes match the mission of a given college or university. Whether it be an open admission community college, a major research university, or something in between, a college or university must have a clear vision of its mission, the clientele to be served, and the programs and services necessary for attracting and retaining that clientele. For purposes of planning, such a vision is imperative.

CORE PLANNING QUESTIONS

Effective enrollment management addresses a number of key planning questions about admissions and retention, including the following:

- What do we know about the relationship over time between applications for admission, offers of admission, and paid deposits for first time freshmen? For transfer students? How can these data be used to target admissions activity?

- What do we know about the institution's position in the admissions marketplace? Who are actual competitors for the kind of students we are currently enrolling? Who are competitors for other students whom we might wish to enroll? How do these groups of students perceive our institution? To what extent are those perceptions correct, and where incorrect, to what extent can they be modified?

- What proportion of entering freshmen are retained as matriculants in subsequent Fall semesters? What proportion of a given entering cohort of first time freshmen graduate within four years? Five years? Six or more years? What are the comparable data for transfer students?

- What do we know about satisfaction levels among students with regard to the institutional programs and services provided to them? What do we know about their satisfaction with the overall college experience at the institution? How are satisfaction levels different for those who remain at the institution compared with those who leave without graduating? How can this information be used to improve retention and graduation rates?

Michael F. Middaugh

is the Assistant Vice President for Institutional Research and Planning for the University of Delaware, Newark, Delaware. Middaugh is a member of SCUP's Professional Development Committee, was the Preconference Program Coordinator for the SCUP–31 Conference Committee, and has contributed to SCUP's quarterly, scholarly journal, *Planning for Higher Education*.

Dale W. Trusheim

is the Associate Director for Institutional Research and Planning for the University of Delaware, Newark, Delaware.

TABLE 1

Student Information System
Weekly Admissions Campus Summary Report

CAMPUS SUMMARY New Freshmen applicants, their SAT scores and PGI by admission status, major, and residency for the entering classes in the Fall of 1993 as of 09/22/93, the Fall of 1994 as of 09/17/94, and the Fall of 1995 as of 09/14/95

	ALL APPLICANTS			ADMISSION DENIED			OFFERED ADMISSION			ACCEPTED ADMISSION (AC)			RATIO OF OFFERED TO ALL APPLICANTS			RATIO OF ACCEPTED TO OFFERED		
	93	94	95	93	94	95	93	94	95	93	94	95	93	94	95	93	94	95
COUNTS																		
RES	1818	1800	1809	187	174	190	1604	1582	1588	1073	1038	1044	0.88	0.88	0.88	0.67	0.66	0.66
NON-RES	11,945	11,016	11,318	2875	2628	2700	8912	8270	8474	2152	1954	2128	0.75	0.75	0.75	0.24	0.24	0.25
TOTAL	13,763	12,816	13,127	3062	2802	2890	10,516	9852	10,062	3225	2992	3179	0.76	0.77	0.77	0.31	0.30	0.32
SAT VERBAL																		
RES	485	483	484	383	400	384	496	492	495	487	482	486	1.02	1.02	1.02	0.98	0.98	0.98
NON-RES	478	478	479	415	414	415	498	498	499	488	489	490	1.04	1.04	1.04	0.98	0.98	0.98
TOTAL	479	479	479	413	414	413	498	497	498	488	487	489	1.04	1.04	1.04	0.98	0.98	0.98
SAT MATH																		
RES	529	529	532	409	423	416	542	541	545	533	529	537	1.02	1.02	1.02	0.98	0.98	0.99
NON-RES	552	551	551	484	483	478	573	573	574	557	557	560	1.04	1.04	1.04	0.97	0.97	0.98
TOTAL	549	548	548	480	480	474	569	568	569	549	547	552	1.04	1.04	1.04	0.96	0.96	0.97
PGI																		
RES	2.37	2.40	2.43	1.21	1.26	1.30	2.50	2.52	2.56	2.43	2.46	2.50	1.05	1.05	1.05	0.97	0.98	0.98
NON-RES	2.43	2.43	2.46	1.79	1.78	1.81	2.63	2.63	2.66	2.56	2.57	2.62	1.08	1.08	1.08	0.97	0.98	0.98
TOTAL	2.42	2.43	2.46	1.76	1.75	1.78	2.61	2.62	2.65	2.51	2.53	2.58	1.08	1.08	1.08	0.96	0.97	0.97

BASIC CONCEPTS

Admissions planning. To determine where an institution wishes to go with its admissions policies and practices, a clear understanding of its present position within the marketplace is essential. A fundamental monitoring of admissions history is an important first step. Table 1 is a page from the weekly Admissions Monitoring Report in use at the University of Delaware. Conceptually, it is adaptable to any college or university. In this instance, it looks at admissions activity as of September 14, 1995, and compares it to similar points in the two preceding admissions cycles (September 17, 1994, and September 22, 1993). At any given point in the admissions cycle, this report allows comparison with the same point during preceding cycles. The table looks at several critical variables: total applicant pool, admission denials, admission offers, paid deposits (accepted admission), offer rate (ratio of offered to all applicants), and yield rate (ratio of accepted to offered). Within those variable categories, the table examines actual head counts, by Delaware resident/nonresident status (an important indicator at state related institutions), average SAT verbal scores, average SAT math scores, and predicted grade index (a mathematical prediction of freshman year grade point index based upon actual performance in core high school subjects).

Table 1 provides crucial data for strategic admissions planning. Suppose that the target size for an entering first time freshman class is 3,100 students. Knowing what the historical yield pattern has been for the past three years (the ratio of paid deposits to the number of admissions offers), it is possible to estimate the number of offers necessary to bring in the target class. Knowing the historical offer rate (ratio of offers to total applicants), it is possible to estimate the total number of applications needed to generate an acceptable offer pool. These estimates are essential for monitoring activity throughout the admissions cycle. Suppose that in early February the number of applications received is substantially lower when compared to early February in the two preceding cycles. A mid-course correction in the offer rate will ensure that the target class will be met by admitting students otherwise denied admission or put on a waiting list. The academic quality indicators (SAT scores and predicted grade index) allow weekly monitoring of

changes in the paid deposit pool to ensure that the mid-course corrections in offer rate are not deleterious to the overall quality of the entering class. If the decline in total applications holds throughout the cycle, the implications are obvious for expanded market penetration into new sources for quality applications.

Some institutions may wish to raise the academic profile of their entering freshman class. Table 2 is structurally comparable to Table 1, but arrays admission activity by SAT score intervals. If an institution wished to increase the number of enrolling freshmen with SAT scores above 1200, the same logical relationship between targeted deposits, offers, and applications described in Table 1 would apply here. Having set the target, it is possible to estimate how many offers to, and applications from, students with 1200+ SAT scores would be needed to realize the objective.

The total university summary displayed in Tables 1 and 2 is replicated for each of the eight undergraduate colleges at the University of Delaware. The analyses are provided for transfer students as well as first time freshmen. Where Delaware focuses on resident/nonresident measures, other institutions may choose to focus on gender, ethnicity, or some other variable related to institutional mission. The important principle here is the acquisition of critical information within a historical context that will allow for strategic decisions at appropriate points throughout the admissions cycle, thereby increasing the probability of an entering class that is academically and demographically consistent with the mission and revenue targets of the institution.

Having established the numerical patterns associated with admissions data, the next step in analysis is to define the behavioral context for those patterns. Why do high school students apply to certain schools and not others? Why do students who have received multiple offers of admission select one college or university over another? Many institutions attempt "prospect" research with varying degrees of success. One method is to approach those students who express an inter-

To determine where an institution wishes to go with its admissions policies and practices, a clear understanding of its present position within the marketplace is essential.

est in an institution (by requesting a catalog, viewbook, or through some other form of communication) but do not apply for admission. A survey to discover why the prospect failed to follow up might prove instructive; however, response rates to surveys of this kind are low and frequently do not justify the expenses incurred. Even more elusive and expensive are data from qualified students who live within the geographic area served by an institution but never express interest.

Institutions should not attempt these kinds of information gathering on their own. Colleges and universities that need to expand and/or deepen their market penetration, and for whom this sort of information would prove

TABLE 2

Fall 93, 94, and 95 Current First-Time New Students

INSTITUTIONAL RESEARCH AND PLANNING   94-95 WEEKLY ADM REPORT

FALL	TOTAL APPLICATIONS			TOTAL OFFERS			OFFERS AS PERCENT OF APPLICATIONS			TOTAL PAID DEPOSITS			PAID DEPOSITS AS PERCENT OF OFFERS		
	93	94	95	93	94	95	93	94	95	93	94	95	93	94	95
VERBAL SAT SCORES															
700-800	92	107	128	88	106	125	95.0	99.0	97.0	30	30	38	34.0	28.0	30.0
600-699	1003	851	1096	981	819	1056	97.0	96.0	96.0	248	215	307	25.0	26.0	29.0
500-599	3989	3841	3644	3681	3534	3341	92.0	92.0	91.0	1003	967	924	27.0	27.0	27.0
400-499	6362	5934	5930	4876	4486	4552	76.0	75.0	76.0	1645	1421	1531	33.0	31.0	33.0
300-399	1950	1807	2014	772	793	933	39.0	43.0	46.0	325	324	373	42.0	40.0	39.0
200-299	171	152	174	35	27	26	20.0	17.0	14.0	15	18	21	42.0	66.0	80.0
NO SCORE	159	125	141	50	30	34	31.0	24.0	24.0	26	17	18	52.0	56.0	52.0
AVERAGE¹	473	473	474	493	491	492				483	481	483			
MATH SAT SCORES															
700-800	704	632	765	672	610	744	95.0	96.0	97.0	144	159	199	21.0	26.0	26.0
600-699	3313	3023	3364	3052	2781	3085	92.0	91.0	91.0	763	638	805	25.0	22.0	26.0
500-599	5752	5338	4780	4689	4361	3906	81.0	81.0	81.0	1469	1281	1241	31.0	29.0	31.0
400-499	3082	3032	3190	1819	1819	2025	59.0	59.0	63.0	775	777	804	42.0	42.0	39.0
300-399	653	615	846	193	190	267	29.0	30.0	31.0	109	116	142	56.0	61.0	53.0
200-299	63	52	41	8	4	6	12.0	7.0	14.0	6	4	3	75.0	100.0	50.0
NO SCORE	159	125	141	50	30	34	31.0	24.0	24.0	26	17	18	52.0	56.0	52.0
AVERAGE¹	544	543	543	564	563	564				545	542	547			
COMB SAT SCORES															
1500-1600	9	12	17	9	12	17	100.0	100.0	100.0	1	2	1	11.0	16.0	5.0
1400-1499	100	108	131	99	106	128	99.0	98.0	97.0	36	30	40	36.0	28.0	31.0
1300-1399	405	388	463	394	375	456	97.0	96.0	98.0	88	102	126	22.0	27.0	27.0
1200-1299	1131	990	1210	1091	955	1165	96.0	96.0	96.0	271	231	310	24.0	24.0	26.0
1100-1199	2336	2183	2224	2208	2041	2078	94.0	93.0	93.0	524	479	539	23.0	23.0	25.0
1000-1099	3677	3354	3114	3241	2940	2685	88.0	87.0	86.0	986	797	802	30.0	27.0	29.0
900-999	3247	3083	2918	2424	2302	2206	74.0	74.0	75.0	876	834	773	36.0	36.0	35.0
800-899	1803	1747	1864	778	836	1042	43.0	47.0	55.0	367	375	460	47.0	44.0	44.0
700-799	614	622	778	166	164	215	27.0	26.0	27.0	102	100	114	61.0	60.0	53.0
600-699	191	160	214	23	31	40	12.0	19.0	18.0	15	23	28	65.0	74.0	70.0
BELOW-600	54	45	53	0	3	1	0.0	6.0	1.0	0	2	1	0.0	66.0	100.0
NO SCORE	159	125	141	50	30	34	31.0	24.0	24.0	26	17	18	52.0	56.0	52.0
AVERAGE¹	1018	1016	1017	1057	1054	1057				1028	1024	1030			
TOTALS	13,726	12,817	13,127	10,483	9795	10,067	76.0	76.0	76.0	3292	2992	3212	31.0	30.0	31.0

¹ Averages do not include students with no scores.

useful, would best be served by a reputable admissions marketing firm. Organizations, such as the American Association of Collegiate Registrars and Admissions Officers (AACRAO), can provide names of consulting firms.

A college or university can, however, gain invaluable strategic information by surveying its pool of accepted applicants to learn: (1) why students who were offered admission made the choice to enroll, and (2) why students who were offered admission but chose to enroll elsewhere, made that choice. The College Board has developed an instrument called *The Admitted Student Questionnaire*, more generally known as the ASQ, which can be purchased if funds are available. An institution can develop its own survey instrument, but would miss out on some of the analytical services and capabilities offered by the College Board. The survey can be administered to the full population of students offered admission, or to a sample. If sampling is used, appropriate stratification should ensure representative samples of enrolling versus non-enrolling students, as well as any other demographics important to a given college or university.

Any survey of the accepted applicant pool should garner several important pieces of information. Respondents should be asked to specify, by name, those institutions to which they sought admission, ideally in order of preference, and to indicate whether they were accepted, rejected, or wait-listed. This information identifies the competition and the focal institution's rank in the hierarchy of preferences. The survey should also list obvious characteristics of a college or university (range of academic programs, quality of faculty, physical facilities, campus appearance) and ask the respondent to indicate whether the characteristic is important to them and how the focal institution compares with others to which they applied. These questions will yield information regarding applicant perceptions of the institution, and where those perceptions position the institution with respect to competitors. While students' perceptions about a given institution may well be incorrect, they are nonetheless real. They must be addressed in order to improve the institution's perceived position in the admissions marketplace. If a college is perceived as a "party school" even though it has an active Phi Beta Kappa chapter and 60 percent of its seniors go on to graduate school, there is a genuine need to address the issue of academic rigor.

Similarly, it is useful to know where students are obtaining information about a college, whether the source is significant, and whether the information is favorable or unfavorable. If the admissions office learns that guidance counselors in the state's school districts are giving the institution unfavorable reviews, the strategic implications are obvious; build a better communication network with those counselors.

Finally, financial aid is often a key factor in the college selection process. The survey of accepted applicants should gather data about the amount and kind of financial aid being offered by competitors (merit/need based, grant, loan, work study), and specific attention should be given to financial aid packaging at institutions to which the focal college or university is losing students.

Having collected this information—whether from a commercially produced or locally generated instrument—an institution can identify its competitor pool, compare itself with that pool along a spectrum of institutional characteristics, discern which factors are important in a student's college selection decision, and identify critical sources of information students use in shaping their decision. Equipped with this knowledge, a college or university is ready to articulate a strategic plan for enhancing its current position or repositioning itself within the admissions marketplace.

Retention Planning. Presuming appropriate strategies are in place for recruiting students, the other half of enrollment planning is retaining and graduating those students. Students are recruited to an institution for the specific objective of earning a degree; effective enrollment planning includes systematic assessment of the extent to which this objective is realized. We recommend cohort survival analysis as the tool of choice for this assessment.

Each Fall semester, a new cohort of students enters an institution either as first-time freshmen or as transfer students. Each student is assigned a permanent identification number in the institution's data base. Cohort survival analysis is tracking student attendance patterns over time, using student identification numbers.

Presuming appropriate strategies are in place for recruiting students, the other half of enrollment planning is retaining and graduating those students.

Table 3 illustrates cohort survival. The table displays ten Fall cohorts and their persistence and attrition patterns recorded each Fall. For example, there were 3,394 students in the first-time freshman cohort entering the university in Fall 1984. Tracking those 3,394 student identification numbers over time, 2,839 were at the university in the second Fall, representing an 83.6 percent retention rate, or pessimistically, a 16.4 percent attrition rate; 2,538 or 74.8 percent were at the university in the third Fall, and so on. Ultimately 2,395 of those initial 3,394 students graduated from the university, for a 70.6 percent completion rate. Suppose a student who entered the university with the Fall 1984 cohort failed to return to the university in Fall 1985, but did in fact return in Fall 1986. This individual will always be reported as a member of the Fall 1984 cohort and, based upon the attendance scenario just described, would be part of the 16.4 percent attrition rate displayed for the second Fall—but would be part of the 74.9 percent persistence rate in the third Fall. The important concept here is the integrity and stability of the composition of the cohort.

Looking at the ten cohorts and the attendance patterns of each, it is possible to get reasonable estimates of freshman-to-sophomore, sophomore-to-junior, and junior- to-senior persistence rates over time. It is also possible to get a reasonable estimate of the length of time it will take for a student to graduate after the initial semester of entry. These data are important not just for state and federal reporting requirements; they are essential for solid enrollment planning. The data in Table 3 are also broken out at the University of Delaware by each of the eight undergraduate colleges, by gender, and by ethnicity, in each instance as a component for enrollment planning for groupings consistent with the institutional mission. Comparable tables are also available for transfer students. Developing reliable retention statistics is a critical component in an overall enrollment planning strategy.

While cohort survival data are essential to enrollment planning, so too are more contextual data that help explain why some students persevere while others leave without graduating.

While cohort survival data are essential to enrollment planning, so too are more contextual data that help explain why some students persevere while others do not graduate. Let us be totally candid about our bias: though commercial vendors produce withdrawing/non-returning student surveys, and institutions use them as well as home grown versions with varying degrees of success, it is our opinion that they are not an effective means of collecting data. Response rates to these surveys are low, and the student who has left has no vested interest in completing the survey. Those students who do complete the surveys usually cite personal or financial reasons for leaving, rather than providing more specific answers that could have policy implications. In our view, this is an expensive data collection strategy, with a low return on investment.

We advocate a different approach. At the University of Delaware, as at most colleges and universities, student satisfaction surveys are a routine part of the institutional research program. We use two different instruments: American College Testing Program's *Student Opinion Survey* and C. Robert Pace's *College Student Experiences Questionnaire*. The former assesses student use of, and satisfaction with, 23 programs and services typically found at most colleges and universities, and 42 institutional characteristics that assess student satisfaction with academics, admissions procedures, institutional rules and regulations, physical facilities, registration procedures, and the overall campus environment. The latter assesses student satisfaction with the quality of various aspects of the college experience including, interaction with faculty and other students, course learning, library experiences, and writing experiences. It also affords respondents the opportunity to estimate cognitive and attitudinal gains growing out of the college experience. These are but two of a number of student satisfaction instruments available from vendors. They are excellent, not only for reporting student satisfaction, but also for getting a reliable reading on the major discontentment factors that contribute to a student's withdrawal.

Student satisfaction surveys should be administered during the Spring semester to ensure a sufficient experience base, particularly for freshmen. They should be administered to a sample of sufficient size to be representative

TABLE 3

Enrollment, Dropout Rates and Graduation Rates for First-Time Freshmen on the Newark Campus (Total)

ENTERING FALL TERM		ENROLLMENT AND DROPOUT RATES						GRADUATION RATES			
		1ST FALL	2ND FALL	3RD FALL	4TH FALL	5TH FALL	6TH FALL	WITHIN 3 YRS	WITHIN 4 YRS	WITHIN 5 YRS	TOTAL
1984	N	3394	2839	2538	2437	695	123	9	1568	2218	2395
	% enrollment	100.0	83.6	74.8	71.8	20.5	3.6	0.3	46.2	65.4	70.6
	% dropout	0.0	16.4	25.2	27.9	33.3	31.0				
1985	N	3121	2632	2382	2291	768	139	10	1367	2062	2238
	% enrollment	100.0	84.3	76.3	73.4	24.6	4.5	0.3	43.8	66.1	71.7
	% dropout	0.0	15.7	23.7	26.3	31.6	29.5				
1986	N	3313	2842	2575	2483	802	128	10	1495	2242	2402
	% enrollment	100.0	85.8	77.7	74.9	24.2	3.9	0.3	45.1	67.7	72.5
	% dropout	0.0	14.2	22.3	24.8	30.7	28.5				
1987	N	3168	2764	2484	2398	723	140	10	1506	2170	2334
	% enrollment	100.0	87.2	78.4	75.7	22.8	4.4	0.3	47.5	68.5	73.7
	% dropout	0.0	12.8	21.6	24.0	29.6	27.1				
1988	N	3302	2849	2599	1519	731	140	12	1595	2283	2404
	% enrollment	100.0	86.3	78.7	76.3	22.1	4.2	0.4	48.3	69.1	72.8
	% dropout	0.0	13.7	21.3	23.3	29.6	26.6				
1989	N	2918	2510	2275	2190	659	112	18	1409	2007	2028
	% enrollment	100.0	86.0	78.0	75.1	22.6	3.8	0.6	48.3	68.8	69.5
	% dropout	0.0	14.0	22.0	24.3	29.1	27.4				
1990	N	2948	2475	2241	2167	652	0	10	1346	—	1346
	% enrollment	100.0	84.0	76.0	73.5	22.1	0.0	0.3	45.7	—	45.7
	% dropout	0.0	16.0	24.0	26.2	32.2	0.0				
1991	N	3213	2699	2428	2331	0	0	16	—	—	16
	% enrollment	100.0	84.0	75.6	72.5	0.0	0.0	0.5	—	—	0.5
	% dropout	0.0	16.0	24.4	27.0	0.0	0.0				
1992	N	2991	2553	2300	0	0	0	—	—	—	0
	% enrollment	100.0	85.4	76.9	0.0	0.0	00.0				0.0
	% dropout	0.0	14.6	23.1	0.0	0.0	0.0				
1993	N	3237	2743	0	0	0	0	—	—	—	0
	% enrollment	100.0	84.7	0.0	0.0	0.0	0.0				0.0
	% dropout	0.0	15.3	0.0	0.0	0.0	0.0				

NOTE: Because this report is run in October against the "live" SIS+ data file, the total graduation rate for 1989 may contain Summer 1993 graduates.

PRINT REFERENCES

Dolence, M. and Norris, D. 1995. *Transforming Higher Education: A Vision for Learning in the 21st Century.* Ann Arbor: Society for College and University Planning.

Middaugh, M.; Trusheim, D.; and Bauer K. 1994. *Strategies for the Practice of Institutional Research: Concepts, Resources, and Applications.* Tallahassee: Association for Institutional Research.

ELECTRONIC SAMPLER

http://apollo.gmu.edu/~jmilam/air95.html#index
> *Internet Resources for Institutional Research. AIR. (Association for Institutional Research). John H. Milam, Jr. (Information Management and Reporting, George Mason University.*

http://www.ed.gov/offices/OPE/
> *Office of Postsecondary Education, United States Department of Education.*

QUESTIONNAIRE RESOURCES

Admissions Planning Resources.
> *To obtain a copy of the Admitted Student Questionnaire (ASQ):*

The College Board
Admitted Student Questionnaire
45 Columbus Circle
New York, NY 10023-6992

> *For a fuller explanation of admissions monitoring reports, and for a sample of an institutionally-developed admissions marketing survey, the following volume is recommended, and can be obtained by writing to the Association for Institutional Research, 314 Stone Building, Florida State University, Tallahassee, FL 32306-3038:*

> Middaugh, M.F., Trusheim, D.W., and Bauer, K.B. *Strategies for the Practice of Institutional Research.* Tallahassee, Florida: Association for Institutional Research, 1994.

Retention Planning Resources.
> *To obtain specimen copies of the satisfaction instruments described in this chapter, contact:*

American College Testing Program
PO Box 168
Iowa City, IA 52243

College Student Experiences Questionnaire
c/o Dr. George Kuh
Center for Postsecondary Research and Planning
School of Education, Room 4228
Indiana University
201 N. Rose Avenue
Bloomington, IN 47405-1006

respondent pool is examined the following Fall semester and, using the identification numbers, is segmented into those students who returned for the Fall and those who did not return (excluding graduates), it is possible to test response patterns for significant differences between those who persevere and those who leave. We have found marked differences in satisfaction with such variables as financial aid practices. When the dissatisfied respondents were then examined for financial aid awards, the results enabled us to recommend specific strategies for overhauling the packaging strategies in the financial aid office. Other policy recommendations also grow out of these data, which are being collected at the peak moment of student satisfaction or dissatisfaction, not from a clouded retrospective view. We have found this practice to be most useful in shaping strategic recommendations for improving programs and services in support of enhanced retention.

SUMMARY

Michael G. Dolence and Donald M. Norris, in their 1995 SCUP volume, *Transforming Higher Education—A Vision for Learning in the 21st Century,* underscore the primacy of a learner-centered environment. While much of our foregoing discussion centered on the metrics associated with measuring retention and graduation, the contextual research strategies we described are essential to providing the optimal learner centered environment. A rich data base showing the extent to which students are satisfied with the quality of academic programs and services, and with the depth and breadth of their academic experiences, is essential in planning for the learner centered environment. Moreover, the data base provides a wealth of admissions recruiting information. Logic dictates that the happier students are with their college or university experience, the deeper their commitment to the institution, both before and after graduation. We have found the strategies described in this chapter to be useful in the overall planning process at the University of Delaware. We offer them as a starting point for readers who wish to develop recruitment and retention analysis tools tailored to the specific needs of their own institutions. ◆

of the student body. In the letter inviting students to complete the survey, we have found it useful to assure the respondents of confidentiality, but to ask them to provide their student identification numbers for future research. If the

This chapter discusses the increasing importance of financial aid and enrollment management and presents a broad framework to describe how financial aid awards can be related to enrollments. Finally, the authors highlight the importance of an effective and proactive financial aid operation in coming years.

Financial Aid and Strategic Planning

Dale W. Trusheim and Michael F. Middaugh

CORE PLANNING QUESTIONS

Today, perhaps more than at any time in the history of American higher education, academic planners need to understand and evaluate the relationship between institutional financial aid operations and enrollment management. The recent *Report to the Leaders of America's Colleges and Universities: Meeting the Challenge of Student Financial Aid*, produced by a distinguished task force and published under the auspices of the National Association for Student Financial Aid Administrators (NASFAA), highlights three most pressing concerns for higher education and financial aid:

- College costs continue to rise at rates higher than family income.

- Students are increasingly relying on loans to pay for college.

- Federal support for financial aid may be in jeopardy.

In addition, over the past several years, institutional financial aid budgets have soared while state and federal funds have declined. During the same time, competition in the admissions marketplace has increased, and many schools have undertaken sophisticated marketing analyses to evaluate the effectiveness of both admissions and financial aid operations.

These facts suggest that over the next decade, planners at higher education institutions must confront two critical issues:

- Can students and their families continue to **afford** our institutions?

- How can the financial aid program contribute to **effective** enrollment management?

Institutions of higher education have a critical stake in assessing successes and failures of financial aid because these outcomes impact institutional finances–both expenditures and revenues. The amount of institutional funds spent on financial aid is easily monitored; however, many institutions do not fully appreciate the important ramifications of financial aid for the institutional revenue stream.

Note, also, important differences between financial aid questions confronting small private liberal arts colleges, and large public research universities. Different institutions have different educational missions, different philosophies toward "building" a freshman class, different budgets, and quite different approaches to financial aid topics such as equity packaging, preferential packaging and purely "merit" scholarships. Competition between public and private universities is also an issue because of pricing differentials between the public and private sectors in American higher education.

Financial aid officers subscribe to the principles and practice of the National Association for Student Financial Aid, which

Dale W. Trusheim

is the Associate Director for Institutional Research and Planning for the University of Delaware, Newark, Delaware.

Michael F. Middaugh

is the Assistant Vice President for Institutional Research and Planning for the University of Delaware, Newark, Delaware. Middaugh is a member of SCUP's Professional Development Committee, was the Preconference Program Coordinator for the SCUP-31 Conference Committee, and has contributed to SCUP's quarterly, scholarly journal, *Planning for Higher Education*.

affirm the importance of financial aid distribution to needy students who might not otherwise be able to attend college. The needs of the student are paramount. However, there may well be tension between the needs of the student and the needs of the institution, and between issues of access and issues of institutional choice. The dimensions and levels of these debates vary from one school to another, and from one year to another, depending on leadership and a host of other variables.

This chapter focuses on key questions affecting enrollment managers and academic planners in their dealings with financial aid packaging and management information. We acknowledge from the outset that the full spectrum of issues confronting individual institutions may be quite different.

BASIC CONCEPTS

Financial aid. Financial aid is defined as any financial assistance (grant or scholarship, loan, work-study) from any source (institutional, federal, private, state) that students may use in addition to their own or parental contributions to pay for college. Typically, financial aid officers collapse awards into two types: scholarships or grants, and "self-help" funds such as loans and work-study programs.

Tuition discounting. This is a term defined as the ratio of institutional financial aid expenditures to the total tuition revenue in an annual budget cycle. The percentage typically ranges from five percent (in large state-supported institutions) to fifty percent (at some small private institutions).

Differential or preferential packaging. Preferential packaging is a relatively recent concept in financial aid awards. Students are rated according to some quality indicators (such as SAT scores or other indices that rank candidates) and financial need. Financial aid packaging is then adjusted according to candidate desirability. Students who are very high quality and low need may receive a more favorable financial aid package (more grant, less loan) than students who are lower quality with

a high financial need. This kind of financial aid strategy causes problems for some financial aid administrators because students with approximately equal levels of academic ability may be treated differently in the award distribution depending on financial need.

APPROACHES TO FINANCIAL AID ANALYSES

The starting point for any in-depth analysis of the relationship between financial aid and enrollment management is a clear sense of institutional mission and how financial aid should support that mission. The position of financial aid among overall institutional goals varies from institution to institution, resulting in different directions and focuses for the financial aid office. For example, some public state-supported institutions may devote all institutional scholarships to in-state students because the state legislature does not allow institutional funds to be awarded to out-of-state students. Consequently, the financial aid management approach in this situation is completely different from a private institution which does not distinguish state of residency.

Presuming, then, that an institution has clearly defined its mission and the position of financial aid within it, academic planners can begin by asking three basic questions:

- What effect does financial aid have on new student enrollment? On retention of currently enrolled students?

- What is the student/parent/institutional view of the effectiveness of the financial aid office?

- How useful to various stakeholders is the annual report from the financial aid office?

How quickly and accurately the director of financial aid operations can answer these questions will reveal much about the management information and reporting technology of any financial aid office. Can the officers respond to these questions in timely fashion? If not, the college or university may be in for rough sledding during the next decade.

Answers to these and similar policy questions require good data, good information retrieval systems, and timely and efficient management information reporting tools. Yet perhaps the most overlooked area in the assessment of financial aid operations is the development of effective management

> *T*he starting point for any in-depth analysis of the relationship between financial aid and enrollment management is a clear sense of institutional mission and how financial aid should support that mission.

information. All too often, financial aid officers are overburdened with the distribution of available aid funds, and the necessity of keeping abreast of rapidly changing federal and state aid regulations.

Another common complaint from financial aid professionals is that "off-the-shelf" software, even from the nation's leading commercial vendors, is not designed for management information reporting. The software is designed for efficient processing of transactions to individuals, not summary reporting of the overall picture. The fact that many financial aid databases stand alone, or are not integrated with other student information data presents another management problem. The kind of analysis necessary for evaluating the relationship of financial aid to enrollment requires a merge of admissions information and student term records for continuing (and withdrawing) students.

One of the first needs for an assessment of financial aid and enrollment management is a data base that contains the necessary data elements for statistical analysis. This requires the identification and extraction of the required data points or an integrated system that can be accessed.

But the lack of a data base with requisite data elements describes only the first half of the problem. Data accuracy is also critical for any program evaluation and policy decisions that may result from the analysis. Financial aid researchers at the institutional level note that obtaining high quality financial aid data is not an easy task. In the first place, a student's financial aid records may change from day to day depending on the student's acceptance, rejection, or modification of financial awards offered by the institution. On April 1, a student might be offered a $2,500 scholarship and a $2,500 Stafford loan. On April 30, the student might elect to borrow only $1,500. On May 31, the student might receive a grant from a state agency in the amount of $1,000 and further downsize the loan amount to $1,000. Obviously, snapshots of the financial aid files taken on these three days would present three different pictures.

That financial aid data files may not accurately describe all the data elements presents a further complication. As noted above, most financial aid software focuses on individual transactions. The effective analysis of financial aid programs requires that individual

financial aid funds be accurately identified with respect to kind of aid (academic grant, athletic or other merit scholarship, loan, work-study) and source and type of aid (merit-based/need-based, state funds, private/outside funds such as the National Merit Scholarship, Lion's Club, federal government). Since timing and accuracy of data collection is an issue for retrieving management information, the institution must carefully decide on the best time to make an "official" reporting extract of financial aid information.

There are basically two large financial aid areas that need to be explored. The first pertains to freshmen (and transfer) admissions. Assessing the impact of financial aid upon freshmen admissions would clearly require a data set that merged financial aid information and admissions variables for new freshmen and transfers. The second major area involves financial aid for the entire undergraduate population. The scenario here asks for an analysis of all currently enrolled students and attempts to describe the situation for all currently matriculated students. A subset of this analysis involves the effort to determine the relationship between financial aid and student retention.

The appropriate time to select data for these two questions is not definitive. Freshmen admissions questions might be asked around the time of the official student enrollment extract for the fall term. Prepared to report data to IPEDS, it would therefore yield the most up-to-date information available for an analysis of the new freshmen class. The same time period could be chosen for the data extract for the entire student body. However, some researchers prefer a more retrospective data file for the analysis. Often, the financial aid award and distribution files continue to change throughout the academic year. Researchers might therefore want to extract data from the previous academic year (Fall 1994 through Spring 1995 in the Fall of 1995) to have the complete story on financial aid during the past academic year. The timing of this kind of data extract also makes it possible to explore the effect of aid on student retention. A suggested

One of the first needs for an assessment of financial aid and enrollment management is a data base that contains the necessary data elements for statistical analysis.

minimum list of variables that would be included in a data extract appears in Table 1.

ANALYSIS AND DISPLAY OF PLANNING INFORMATION

Despite financial aid's obvious importance to enrollment management and institutional fiscal health, there is a surprising dearth of published research to help individual institutions accumulate information for planning purposes. Much of the published research appears as large-scale descriptive reports of the total numbers of students receiving aid and how much they receive (for example, see the U.S. Department of Education statistical series or the results from various National Postsecondary Student Aid Study reports). Or it may be sophisticated multivariate statistical analyses

---

TABLE 1

Financial Aid/Admissions Extract

Demographic Variables	Financial Aid Variables
Student identification number	Financial need
High school GPA	Family income
SAT or ACT scores	Total financial award
Age	Total scholarship or grant amount
Gender	Total work-study amount
Ethnic origin	Total loan amount
Admissions index (if available)	Amount of unmet need
State origin	Independent/dependent status
Other admissions variables	

Overall Financial Aid Extract

Demographic Variables	Financial Aid Variables
Student identification number	Financial need
Cumulative GPA (if available)	Family income
SAT or ACT scores	Total financial award
Age	Total scholarship or grant amount
Gender	Total work-study amount
Ethnic origin	Total loan amount
State origin	Amount of unmet need
Department and major	Independent/dependent status
Earned credit hours	

---

such as the work done by Chapman and Jackson (1987), Cabrera and Castaneda (1992), or St. John (1989, 1990, 1992).

The problem for individual institutions, therefore, is twofold. First, are student record and financial aid data available to undertake a descriptive study? Second, which model(s) or techniques can institutions use to analyze the effects of financial aid on enrollment? James Scannell (1992) recognized these limitations in his publication *The Effect of Financial Aid Policies on Admissions and Enrollment*. He recommends that the institutional focus be "on the strategic deployment of institutional resources to meet a particular institution's enrollment goal" (p. 65). To make strategic decisions, institutions need to know where they currently stand. Scannell offers a variety of helpful templates that individual institutions might employ to document the outcomes of the financial aid award process.

There are three main components of financial aid analysis an institution should undertake. The first is research in the area of new student admission, including admitted students who did enroll and those who did not. Research involving all currently enrolled students (including freshmen) makes up the second. The third area pertains to consumer satisfaction (student and parent) and institutional assessment of the success of the financial aid effort. We address each of these areas below.

Freshmen admissions and financial aid. One of the first steps in an analysis of the relationship of financial aid to new student admissions is to trace all possible outcomes for aid and non-aid applicants who do and do not enroll. Figure 1 shows one way of presenting this information in a simple and straightforward fashion. The purpose of this research is threefold: first, to compare yield ratios in a sequential fashion throughout the aid process; second, to determine precisely which students receive financial aid; and third, to investigate areas where a possible redirection of aid funds might improve admissions yield.

Financial aid researchers (or other institutional staff) would need to fill in the various cells of the financial aid flow chart with actual numbers of students who fall into each category or cell. This information would only be presented for applicants who were offered admission. Each cell should contain two items of information: the total number of students in the cell, and the yield ratio for that number. (Yield ratios are calculated by dividing the number of enrolling students by the total number of applicants.)

Although the numbers in Figure 1 are illustrative only, they present a clear picture of

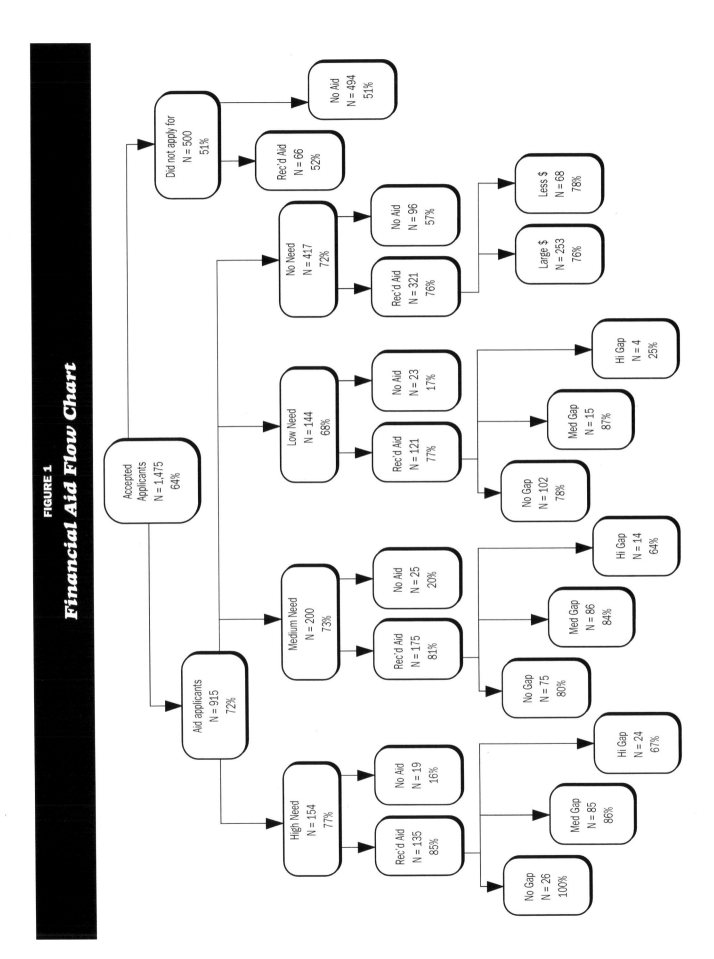

FIGURE 1

Financial Aid Flow Chart

what the admissions/financial aid flow might be at a single institution. The chart contains a substantial amount of information. It shows, for example, percentages of applicants who apply for aid and percentages of applicants who do not. It displays the percentages of students who have high, medium, low, or no need, as well as the non-aid applicants who might receive aid (either through merit scholarships or unsubstantiated Stafford loans). For example, a data presentation such as this underscores the importance of financial aid for high-need students. In this illustration, 85 percent of the high-need students who receive aid enroll, compared to only 16 percent of the high-need students who do not receive financial aid. This chart also shows the strong impact of aid for students who apply for assistance but who do not demonstrate financial need: 76 percent of students who did not have need but who received some "merit" aid enrolled, compared to 57 percent of the no-need applicants who did not receive awards. The chart further allows institutions to investigate the impact of different award gaps on admitted applicants, assuming that this practice is followed.[1]

It is also very important to note that this method of data presentation is quite valuable when done systematically and annually. Planners can assess whether yield rates within specific groups are increasing or decreasing, or whether the percentage of students in higher need groups is increasing substantially from year to year. As aid award strategies evolve or change from year to year, the data presentation allows planners to monitor the effects of these adjustments. If we assume that a college or university elected to transfer financial aid funds from low-need to high-need students and, further, to implement a medium gap award policy instead of one that attempted to meet full need, the results of this strategy would have to be monitored to determine the policy's success, as well as to make necessary mid-course adjustments. The main benefit of this kind of data presentation is that it allows the institution to see exactly how admissions and financial aid interact for admitted applicants to the freshman class.

A recent development in financial aid is the use of econometric modeling to forecast actual enrollment and to budget financial aid.

In assessing the impact of financial aid on admissions, it is important to compare two groups of students: enrolling students and non-enrolling students. Table 2 provides illustrative data on these two groups by level of need, but also adds several other important variables:

- Average of the total aid award (grants, loans, and work study);
- Average award of only institutional dollar expenditures;
- Percentage of financial need met;
- Percentage of grant and scholarship funds in the total aid package;
- An indicator of whether the student has declared the institution as first choice; and
- Yield ratios.

In addition, each summary statistic is broken down by SAT level. This kind of presentation allows planners to explore discrepancies in the aid packages offered to enrolling students and non-enrolling students, and also demonstrates SAT levels which might benefit from expanded contributions of institutional financial aid. For example, if the yield rate is much stronger at lower SAT levels (say, 1100 to 1199) than higher SAT levels (say, 1400–1600), and it can be determined that nonenrolling students in the lower range received significantly less favorable financial aid awards, institutions might want to consider different award strategies. Questions about the strategic manipulation of aid funds would remain unanswered without the kind of data presentation shown in Table 2, which documents the actual distribution of financial aid dollars.

A recent development in financial aid is the use of econometric modeling to forecast actual enrollment and to budget financial aid. In brief, this kind of modeling requires an econometrician or statistician (often, an external consultant), who develops a model to predict overall new student enrollment and the amount of financial aid necessary to achieve the predicted goal. This is not the place to discuss econometric modeling in detail, but it does represent an effective and useful way to plan a freshman class. Econometric modeling has been enthusiastically endorsed by several users (Massa, 1995).

Currently enrolled students. Too often, perhaps, financial aid research looks primarily at the impact of aid on new students. It is equally

---

[1] The specific cut points that group students in various need categories and various financial aid categories can vary from school to school. High, medium, and low-need groups are usually defined by specific monetary ranges. It may be better to use a percentage basis for the need-met categories: e.g., medium gap defined as 50 percent to 99 percent of need met; high gap defined as less than 50 percent of need met.

TABLE 2

Admissions and Financial Aid Outcomes by SAT Range: Illustration

HIGH NEED ($7,000+)

ENROLLING

SAT – Total	Average Aid $	N	Average College Funds ($)	N	% of Need Met	% Grant	1st Choice %	Overall Yield %
1400-1600	7800	4	3000	4	84	70	50	80.0
1300-1399	7766	8	2333	3	85	73	50	67.0
1200-1299	6783	12	1000	1	85	73	38	75.0
1100-1199	7312	13	2265	6	84	64	85	86.7
1000-1099	6248	13	5250	2	69	64	62	59.0
400-999	6817	30	2334	9	76	57	74	68.2

NON-ENROLLING

SAT – Total	Average Aid $	N	Average College Funds ($)	N	% of Need Met	% Grant	1st Choice %
1400-1600	5380	1	4000	1	42	100	0
1300-1399	3563	4	1000	1	48	74	0
1200-1299	3813	4	2000	1	45	78	25
1100-1199	3563	2	0		43	74	50
1000-1099	3696	9	0		40	67	57
400-999	3099	14	0		61	51	25

HIGH NEED ($3,500-6,999)

ENROLLING

SAT – Total	Average Aid $	N	Average College Funds ($)	N	% of Need Met	% Grant	1st Choice %	Overall Yield %
1400-1600	6381	4	2500	3	92	75	57	57.1
1300-1399	5200	3	2238	3	96	69	67	50.0
1200-1299	4431	14	2040	10	74	85	63	73.7
1100-1199	4729	18	2329	14	84	56	44	62.1
1000-1099	4614	32	1286	10	86	59	63	84.2
400-999	4975	21	1530	13	87	48	81	72.4

NON-ENROLLING

SAT – Total	Average Aid $	N	Average College Funds ($)	N	% of Need Met	% Grant	1st Choice %
1400-1600	6325	3	2000	1	92	58	0
1300-1399	4700	3	1500	2	77	72	33
1200-1299	5475	5	1500	2	78	51	40
1100-1199	4177	11	1750	2	71	50	18
1000-1099	4842	6	1200	2	89	50	17
400-999	4662	8	986	3	88	43	50

HIGH NEED ($1-3,499)

ENROLLING

SAT – Total	Average Aid $	N	Average College Funds ($)	N	% of Need Met	% Grant	1st Choice %	Overall Yield %
1400-1600	7600	1	4230	1	100	100	100	25.0
1300-1399	3908	5	1200	6	100	62	83	60.0
1200-1299	3840	7	1656	10	98	76	80	62.5
1100-1199	3605	3	2517	20	99	55	85	71.4
1000-1099	3548	2	3845	21	97	51	71	53.8
400-999	3841	4	1285	41	97	41	85	67.2

NON-ENROLLING

SAT – Total	Average Aid $	N	Average College Funds ($)	N	% of Need Met	% Grant	1st Choice %
1400-1600	4000	3	3000	1	100	100	0
1300-1399	2313	4	1500	2	71	79	25
1200-1299	2983	6	1000	3	88	60	33
1100-1199	2705	8	1200	3	89	33	33
1000-1099	2469	18	1000	7	100	64	44
400-999	1071	20	500	10	88	52	50

as important to continue monitoring the distribution of aid among currently enrolled students. Table 3 presents a way to think about the relationship of financial aid to all enrolled students. (As with earlier charts, these data are illustrative only.) Table 3 simply reports the number of majors at a college or university and the associated percentage of the total undergraduate enrollment. It then shows the number of students in the major who receive financial aid, the average award, the total amount of scholarship dollars invested and, finally, information about the academic standing of the aid recipients. The final two columns show the ratio of aid recipients to all majors: a high percentage indicates that this specific major is well-subscribed; a low percentage indicates that students within this major do not receive much financial aid. The last column shows the ratio of the aid received to the total financial aid distribution–useful for determining which majors or departments are being underwritten by financial aid.

Note that although Table 3 presents information disaggregated to the major level, other institutions may choose to group the data in larger units, for example, departments. It is also important to note that the data are reported only for currently enrolled freshmen, sophomores, and juniors, since the senior class will be graduating and all institutional scholarship funds will probably be reinvested in the next freshman class. Holding out the seniors from Table 3, therefore, allows planners to see how much scholarship aid will be available

TABLE 3
Institutional Scholarship Award Distribution by Major
Freshmen, Sophomores, and Juniors Only:

Major	N of Majors	% of Total Enrolled	N of Awards Rec'd	Average Award	Total Dollars	Average Cumulative GPA: Aid Recipients	Average SAT of Aid Recipients	Ratio of Aid Recipients to Majors	Departmental Percentage of All Aid
General Agriculture	10	1.2	4	$4,348	$17,392	2.85	1030	40.0	1.8
Accounting	35	4.1	11	$4,500	$49,500	2.69	1050	31.4	5.1
Business Administration	40	4.7	5	$2,005	$10,025	2.99	1040	12.5	1.0
Management	22	2.6	10	$2,350	$23,500	2.62	1102	45.5	2.4
Electrical Engineering	45	5.3	22	$3,492	$76,824	2.88	1145	48.9	8.0
Applied Music-Voice	5	0.6	5	$3,086	$15,430	3.15	1104	100.0	1.6
Music	8	0.9	1	$6,000	$6,000	2.75	1280	12.5	0.6
Philosophy	5	0.6	1	$1,417	$1,417	2.73	1160	20.0	0.1
Physics	12	1.4	3	$4,877	$14,631	2.39	1275	25.0	1.5
Political Science	17	2.0	7	$2,850	$19,950	2.84	1187	41.2	2.1
Psychology	56	6.5	33	$1,000	$33,000	3.15	1150	58.9	3.4
Biochemistry	33	3.9	8	$3,070	$24,560	3.22	1111	24.2	2.6
Biological Sciences	112	13.1	39	$3,417	$133,263	3.13	1170	34.8	13.9
Chemistry	75	8.8	26	$3,868	$100,568	2.96	1082	34.7	10.5
Computer & Info Sciences	39	4.6	8	$4,046	$32,368	3.17	1128	20.5	3.4
Criminal Justice	21	2.5	3	$2,321	$6,963	3.07	1119	14.3	0.7
English	43	5.0	4	$3,000	$12,000	3.11	1038	9.3	1.2
Communication	11	1.3	4	$2,345	$9,380	3.00	1073	36.4	1.0
Political Science	37	4.3	5	$1,467	$7,335	2.83	1020	13.5	0.8
Economics	32	3.7	17	$5,710	$97,070	2.92	1110	53.1	10.1
Teacher Education	76	8.9	29	$3,674	$106,546	3.00	1020	38.2	11.1
History	55	6.4	21	$4,542	$95,382	3.03	1160	38.2	9.9
Sociology	66	7.7	15	$4,573	$68,595	3.22	1090	22.7	7.1
TOTAL	**855**	**100**	**281**	**$3,422**	**$961,699**	**2.84**	**1155**	**32.9**	**100.0**

because of senior graduation, and it also depicts the probable situation for underclassmen.

Planners can use this information to target new students into undersubscribed majors or continue to build some of the academically stronger areas at the institution. The key purpose of the analysis is to describe the existing distribution of financial aid awards and relate it to enrollment targets for the coming year. This same table can be broken down into subgroups (ethnic status, gender) for help in planning for diversity and other goals.

Financial aid program evaluation. There are any number of ways to conduct program evaluations for financial aid operations. Keeping in mind that it is impossible (because of financial limitations or legal restrictions) for financial aid officers to "please" all clients, it is still possible to obtain useful evaluations of how the office is conducting business. These reviews should take place on a systematic basis, perhaps as often as every other year.

One starting place is the institutional guide for financial aid self-evaluation, available from the National Association for Student Financial Aid Administrators (NASFAA, 1996). According to NASFAA, the guide was designed "as in in-house tool to assist financial aid administrators in evaluating the efficiency and effectiveness of their administration of financial aid programs, as well as compliance with federal laws and regulations" (p. ii). Systematic and repeated administration of this self-study should be helpful in highlighting departmental strengths and weaknesses.

Other techniques that can be used for program review include survey research, focus group interviews, and departmental process or functioning reviews. Random samples of students and parents who interact with the financial aid office can be contacted by telephone or mail to request information about their experience with the financial aid office. If the survey respondent can be identified (by name or student ID number), researchers have the capability of merging information from the aid files to control statistically for items such as the amount of aid awarded or percentage of need met. Incorporating institutional financial aid data with attitudinal information permits more sophisticated and in-depth research studies. It may also be the case that financial aid administrators are doing their job by not awarding large scholarships to certain categories of students, even though competitors make significantly higher offers. These parental and student surveys should focus on questions about the accuracy and timeliness of financial aid communication or the efficiency of financial aid services.

Often surveys are conducted along with a small number of focus group interviews, which provide a much richer, though less universally applicable, collection of comments and insights into a department's operations. Institutional researchers may be available to help set up focus group formats and assist with the professional conduct of this kind of research.

Finally, it may also be useful to conduct departmental process and functioning reviews: internal examinations of organizational charts; paper flow with respect to processing, filing, and efficiency; and the accuracy and availability of good management information. It can reveal the need for updated computing equipment and additional computer programming support for management information. A department process review can be conducted with an internal institutional consultant or, budget permitting, a consultant who is expert in financial aid operations and information retrieval.

*I*t may also be useful to conduct departmental process and functioning reviews: internal examinations of organizational charts; paper flow with respect to processing, filing, and efficiency; and the accuracy and availability of good management information.

ACTIONABILITY ISSUES

One way to force data to influence policy is to see whether they are available to answer strategic questions. If the following questions, falling under the three major themes identified above, were posed to the chief financial aid officers, how quickly and accurately could a response be delivered?

- What effect does financial aid have on new student enrollment? On retention of currently enrolled students? Additional preliminary questions include: Who receives institutional financial aid? What effect does financial aid have on matriculation probabilities? How much aid is spent on special interest groups? Is this money being spent wisely? How is

PRINT REFERENCES

Cabrera, A.; Nora, A.; and Castaneda, M. 1992. "The Role of Finances in the Persistence Process: A Structural Model." *Research in Higher Education* 33(5): 571–594.

Chapman R. G. and Jackson, R. 1987. *College Choices of the Academically Able Students: The Influence of No-Need Financial Aid and Other Factors.* New York: College Entrance Examination Board.

Massa, R. 1995. "How Much Is Enough?: The Strategic Use of Institutional Aid." Paper presented at the 1995 National Association of Student Financial Aid Administrators Annual Conference, San Antonio, TX.

National Association of Student Financial Aid Administrators. 1996. *Self-Evaluation Guide for Institutional Evaluation in Title IV and Other Federal Programs, 12th ed.*, 1995–1996 and 1996–1997. Washington, DC: NASFAA.

Report to the Leaders of America's Colleges and Universities : Meeting the Challenge of Student Financial Aid. 1995. Washington, DC: National Association of Student Financial Aid Administrators.

St. John, E. P. 1989. "The Influence of Student Aid on Persistence." *Journal of Student Financial Aid* 19(3): 52–68.

St. John, E. P. 1990. "Price Response in Enrollment Decisions: An Analysis of the High School and Beyond Sophomore Cohort." *Research in Higher Education* No. 31(2): 161–176.

St. John, E. 1992 "Workable Models for Institutional Research on the Impact of Student Aid." *Journal of Student Financial Aid* 22(3): 13–26.

Scannell, J. J. 1992. *The Effect of Financial Aid Policies on Admissions and Enrollment.* New York: College Board.

Also of use are any issues of the *Journal of Student Financial Aid*, Washington, DC: National Association of Student Financial Aid Administrators.

ELECTRONIC SAMPLER

http://finaid.org/nasfaa
   NASFAA (National Association of Student Financial Aid Administrators).

http://www.ed.gov/index.html
   Ed Home. United States Department of Education.

http://www.ed.gov/NLE/sfa.html
   Bibliography on Student Financial Aid. National Library of Education.

http://www.ed.gov/offices/OPE/
   United States Department of Education, Office of Postsecondary Education.

http://www.finaid.org/
   FinAid: The Financial Aid Information Page.NASFAA (National Association of Student Financial Aid Administrators). Mark Kantrowitz.

this determination made? Does financial aid support the retention of students?

- What is the student/parent/institutional view of the effectiveness of the financial aid office? Moreover, how satisfied are students and their parents with the quality of information and service received from the financial aid office?

- How useful is the annual report from the aid office? Does a single annual report provide information in timely fashion, or should more routine management infor-

mation reporting be put in place? Additionally, how much institutional revenue is spent on financial aid? How much net revenue do these expenditures generate? What is the institution's tuition discount rate? Has this changed over time? What are projections for the next three years? What is the trend line in institutional financial aid awards? Is this line outpacing net revenues, or is it increasing faster than tuition increases? Is the chief aid officer an integral part of budget planning?

RECOMMENDATIONS

Given the new demands soon to be placed on financial aid programs, some recommendations for greater success in enrollment management can be made. First, financial aid operations should be supported with new technology to improve service, data management, and information storage and retrieval. Many financial aid officers spend most of their time dealing with individual students, processing individual transactions, and keeping current with changing regulations. Thus, it is important to assist the financial aid office with computer programming support necessary to generate effective management information. A review of current financial aid reports and paper flow might lead to more efficient ways of processing the bulk of information financial aid officers must handle.

Second, planners should ask the aid officials to develop financial aid plans for best, worst, and probable outcomes for a given year. Even while recognizing that there is more art than science in predicting the behavior of college-bound high school seniors and college students, it is critical for the fiscal health of an institution to monitor carefully the financial aid expenditure budget and its impact on tuition revenue. Using the kind of enrollment management reports presented above, it is possible to track institutional fund expenditures and to project expenditures from students who have not yet replied. A major and unexpected shift in yield in either direction may have heavy and damaging budgetary impact for years to come.

Third, it is not sufficient to see financial aid offices as nothing more than distributors of available resources. In coming years, chief aid officers must, through effective information management, take the lead in constant monitoring of the effectiveness of the financial aid program. Including the director of financial aid on the budget team may be appropriate for many institutions. ◆

Human Resources Planning

Human Resources Planning

Carol Everly Floyd

𝒯his chapter analyzes basic mission and quality issues that become the framework for human resources planning. Then, moving to specifics, the first subsection addresses faculty recruitment and retention; the second focuses on faculty roles, responsibility, and accountability.

Human Resources Planning

Carol Everly Floyd

CORE PLANNING QUESTIONS

A new focus on connecting human resources planning with basic institutional mission commitments is being reinforced by emerging expectations on the part of accrediting bodies and governmental funding sources. Institutions, therefore, are focusing more sharply on fitting their concepts of faculty effectiveness and productivity into their institutional missions and goals. Institutions are linking student outcomes assessment with what faculty do, explaining how commitments to diversity and affirmative action are being kept, and making specific connections between recruitment/retention practices and institutional quality.

Regional and specialized accrediting bodies, as well as state higher education boards, are broadening the challenge to higher education to demonstrate ongoing improvement and quality assurance. Although some concepts and practices date back to the 1970s, faculty development is receiving newly concentrated attention as an area in which to demonstrate continuous quality improvement. The scope of faculty development activity has broadened from its original focus on improving the skills of individual faculty to include both reformulation of the curriculum to incorporate new concerns, and creation of more career options. The core planning questions about human resources include:

- How will the academic culture adjust to the emerging calls for enhanced quality and accountability?
- How rapidly will faculty roles change in response to a learner-centered policy agenda?

- To what extent can faculty development become linked to organizational development?

BASIC CONCEPTS

Faculty recruitment and retention. Institutions have historically thought about faculty recruitment and retention in fairly simple terms: a strong faculty combined with staffing flexibility. They sought well-prepared faculty, expected probationary faculty to present a strong record, and expected tenured faculty to be responsive to institutional needs and productive within their disciplines. Some flexibility was provided by faculty turnover and the use of part-time faculty; however, institutions have always been concerned about limited opportunities for introducing new blood and over concentration of resources in the senior ranks.

In the future, institutions will be recruiting faculty to serve an increasing number of non-traditional college students in an increasingly complex labor market. Without doubt, full-time regular faculty will be more difficult to recruit, in most fields, than in the 1980s and early 1990s because significantly more faculty hired during higher education's boom years have retired. But the number of new hires needed is very elusive because of uncertain patterns of retirement behavior and institutional hiring preferences. Some incentives encourage early retirement while the removal of a mandatory retirement age encourages those who are so

Carol Everly Floyd

is Assistant to the Provost for the University of Illinois at Springfield, Springfield, Illinois. Floyd is Associate Convener of SCUP's Academic Planning Academy, a member of SCUP's Publications Advisory Committee, and was formerly the Associate Editor of *Planning for Higher Education*, SCUP's quarterly, scholarly journal.

inclined to stay. Institutional hiring of faculty, especially full-time regular faculty, may be constrained by decreasing revenue. This is especially so in public state institutions when economic downturn leads to declining tax revenue. Uncertain patterns of student demand for various fields of study present another problem.

Institutions are likely to have difficulty recruiting full-time faculty in engineering, accounting, and quantitative-oriented business fields. Relatively few doctorates are awarded in such fields and there is fierce competition from both academic and nonacademic employers. On the other hand, hiring well-prepared faculty will be less difficult for the humanities, where students have continued to pursue the doctorate in large numbers and where degree holders typically find nonacademic employment unappealing.

New external expectations help institutions focus on the importance of an institutional academic culture that nurtures excellence and continuous self-improvement in both students and faculty. Consequently, institutions give increasing attention to such issues of faculty recruitment and retention as the status of minority and female faculty, the employment of part-time faculty, and fair and equitable compensation.

The academic culture is complex; no one should assume new faculty know what to do or how to do it.

Minority and female faculty. Many institutions have difficulty attracting and retaining minority and female faculty in numbers consistent with the national market. In many departments female and minority faculty are too few to meet diversity goals. The retention rate of such faculty through tenure and promotion tends to be lower than for white male faculty, contributing to a "revolving door" scenario frustrating to both probationary faculty member and academic department.

Although issues of compensation and supporting resources must be addressed, the primary difficulties on most campuses lie in the academic culture and informal institutional socialization. The academic culture is complex; no one should assume new faculty know what to do or how to do it. New faculty sometimes receive confusing and easily misinterpreted messages. Spelling out messages clearly, especially expectations for tenure and promo-

tion, is especially important for minority and female faculty. Difficulties encountered by minority and female faculty include: less graduate school socialization, weak mentoring relationships, fewer networking opportunities, and greater demands to serve on committees and advise students. Institutions can address such problems by creating incentives for senior faculty to work with junior faculty, conducting orientation for new faculty, and scheduling yearly meetings of the faculty member, chair and dean. All should be done in a way that respects the diversity of department members (Tierney and Rhoads, 1993; Tack and Patitu, 1992).

Questions about appropriate ways to diversify the faculty are being addressed in an increasingly complex environment. Some affirmative action procedures are subject to question on political and legal grounds. In the wake of the University of California Board of Regents' decision to strike down all its affirmative action policies in July, 1995, many institutions are carefully examining specific affirmative action policies and procedures while simultaneously affirming their commitment to diversity. In this environment, institutions are beginning to do focused studies of the connection between objectives, means, results, and outcomes for various population subgroups. Analysis focused on advantages and disadvantages of particular policies contributes to reasoned policy discussion.

Part-time faculty. Although over reliance on part-time faculty has always been regarded negatively by planners, systematic attention to approaches for proper use of part-time faculty is a recent development. Maintenance of institutional quality now requires that such appointments be used carefully and for clearly educational rather than solely budgetary reasons. Part-timers should maintain office hours for students, should be provided office space and other support services, and should be involved in some public service or research activity. Institutions should be able to demonstrate that all faculty members are prepared and supported in their efforts to provide high quality instruction (Gappa and Leslie, 1993).

The new qualitative expectations relating to use of part-time faculty clearly have direct financial implications of space and support services, and less direct implications for compensation. The tug of war between qualitative improvement and financial constraints will need to be addressed. Part-time faculty can be expected to continue to play a significant role at most institutions, especially when they bring subject matter and experience not otherwise available, in fields where evolving priorities require flexible staffing patterns, and to meet short-term or emergency needs.

Market and equitable salaries. As institutions of higher education compete in a national labor market, they must pay "market" salaries to attract and retain faculty. At the same time, salaries must reflect fairness and equity. The first consideration urges significant differentiation based on perceptions of salary levels by discipline and also by subdiscipline. The second emphasizes evaluation of contribution and meritorious performance.

Both market and merit will remain significant factors in setting salaries at time of hire and in salary administration. Institutional refinements in both areas will be necessitated by continuing external pressure from the national academic marketplace and internal pressure for fairness and equality based on individual merit and contribution to campus mission priorities. Special market adjustments on many campuses in "hot" fields in recent years have, in many instances, drawn strong negative reactions from a fairness or equity perspective. Similarly, very high salary increases for the few raise questions of favoritism or bias (Moore and Amey, 1993).

Periodic performance reviews of faculty, based on well-understood criteria and administered in a well-documented way, should increase fairness and equity in salary administration. Criteria should be developed with significant faculty participation and should emphasize institutional criteria, but include college/school or departmental criteria as well. A sound evaluation system creates an accountability system for administrators, discouraging inappropriate decisions and increasing the perception of fairness and equality (Lozier and Dooris, 1989). More specifics on faculty evaluation are discussed below, especially teaching and scholarship foci and rewards for excellence in teaching.

In summary, the application of concepts of quality assurance and continuous improvement to the areas of recruitment and retention of faculty creates several benefits. It results in

the identification of methods to incorporate fully all segments of the faculty into the institutional academic culture; provides adequate support services, fosters individual faculty development, evaluates faculty performance, and compensates faculty fairly and equitably.

Faculty roles, responsibilities and accountability. Intense discussions are underway within the national higher education community about faculty roles, responsibilities and accountability—all within the framework of institutional mission commitments and priorities. This has resulted in the refinement of many existing and new planning concepts, as well as the reconfiguration of others. Planning practice has moved away from a narrow focus on work loads into analysis of a number of institutional issues. Such discussions help institutions frame their responses to external and internal challenges that they use resources more productively and be more accountable. Resolutions of these broader issues have major implications for the mix and balance of faculty duties, and evaluation and rewards for faculty performance.

The "research and development" efforts that are providing new planning concepts on faculty resources are the Pew Higher Education Research program ("Testimony," 1992) based at the University of Pennsylvania, the National Center for Higher Education Management Systems (NCHEMS) projects (1995), and the American Association of Higher Education (AAHE) Forum on Faculty Roles and Rewards (1995). The first two draw heavily from the disciplines of economics and management, while the latter draws upon more traditional higher education research. These projects converge in their emphasis on consensus building within institutions and the rebuilding of collegial bonds that have atrophied over the past forty-five years. Both the Pew/Pennsylvania program and the AAHE forum emphasize rebuilding collegiality within departments initially and then across departments, since departments are recognized as the gateway to change and to improved productivity in the academic culture.

> *The application of concepts of quality assurance and continuous improvement to the areas of recruitment and retention of faculty creates several benefits.*

Faculty workload should be generally understood to include all activities that take the time of university faculty members and are directly related to institutional and/or professional duties, responsibilities, and interests. In short-hand fashion, faculty workload involves teaching, research and service. Scholarly activity includes performance/creative activity for fine arts faculty. Service includes institutional, professional, and public service.

Because workload studies consistently show that faculty devote an average of 50 to 60 hours per week to professional activities (very few report less than 40 hours; some report over 70), planning should focus on how faculty work time is distributed rather than on time spent.

Because workload studies consistently show that faculty devote an average of 50 to 60 hours per week to professional activities (very few report less than 40 hours; some report over 70), planning should focus on how faculty work time is distributed rather than on time spent. The question is whether allocations of faculty activities are consistent with institutional missions and priorities, and thus meet the needs of students and other beneficiaries of university programming.

The broad context for faculty planning includes institutional mission commitments, the relationship between scholarship and teaching, and departmental units rather than individuals. Specific topics deserving examination include: ensuring a strong core for the undergraduate and graduate curriculum, enhancing the mutual benefits of the scholarly/teaching connection, expanding the range of faculty development activities, differentiating faculty responsibilities, strengthening evaluation methods for teaching and scholarship, and improving rewards for excellent teaching.

Institutional mission commitments. Faculty involvement in scholarship is important at any institution to foster faculty currency within the discipline/profession and to update instructional content. American higher education has long stressed that college teaching is informed and strengthened by faculty scholarship. Increasingly, community college faculty are being encouraged to engage in scholarly activity.

The mix of faculty professional activities should vary depending upon the institutional mission and the academic goals and priorities that derive from it. Faculty work loads at in-stitutions that offer substantial graduate teaching and related research activity should show an increased emphasis on scholarship compared to institutions offering baccalaureate degrees only. That emphasis should increase further if an institution offers several doctoral or professional degrees, and should be especially pronounced at universities whose primary emphasis is doctoral education and research.

Institutions should also examine patterns relating to kinds of scholarship conducted at the institution. In his report, *Scholarship Reconsidered* (1990), Ernest Boyer identifies four kinds of scholarship: discovery, application, integration, and teaching. Boyer believes that most institutions devalue any scholarship except discovery and urges institutions to broaden their definition. Institutions would be well served by faculty discussions that evaluate the soundness of Boyer's categorization (especially the "teaching" category), and apply more precise definitions of them to campus patterns. It can be argued that institutions whose strongest mission is in teaching should give particular attention to the scholarship of application, integration, and teaching because of a closer connection with the instructional function and less strain on resources.

Relationships between teaching and scholarship. The conduct of scholarly activity and dissemination of results should closely relate to university instructional programs because teaching and research are complementary, not competitive. Each is stimulated and strengthened by the other, contributing to greater effectiveness and efficiency in both areas.

The interconnection between teaching and scholarship should be even stronger at the graduate level where seminars prevail and where students explore their field and research interests in depth. The output of a student's doctoral research and that of the student's doctoral supervisor will often come from a "joint development" process in which the research process and the research training process have common elements. Student involvement in scholarly activity should also be a significant element in most master's programs. Scholarship extends even to the undergraduate level: many institutions are developing programs of research participation for selected undergraduates.

Of course, complex tradeoffs between time devoted to scholarship and time devoted to teaching are sometimes encountered. But this is a matter of adjusting time commitments to complementary, not competing, activities.

Focus on departmental units. The focus on departmental units recognizes that departments are the fundamental unit of university organization as the "producers" of instruction, research, and public service. Departments should, therefore, be held accountable for making whatever changes are necessary in the departmental academic culture to support a pattern of faculty roles and responsibilities consistent with institutional mission.

Planning for management of human resources should focus on outputs of faculty activity rather than on minute measurement of faculty time. Recent elaboration of this perspective emphasizes concepts of faculty citizenship in departments aimed at getting a mix of "faculty team" activity necessary to achieve desired student learning outcomes and other programmatic achievements. This approach relies heavily on faculty consensus development at the departmental level. It begins with leadership that impels faculty to look upon their own individual professional roles as a part of departmental and institutional citizenship more than they have in recent years.

MANIPULATION AND DELIVERY

With the above as a more general framework, analysis can move to more specific foci.

Ensuring strong curricula at both the undergraduate and graduate levels. Faculty review of both undergraduate and graduate curricula should focus on reexamining the core courses in order to reinvigorate the common body of knowledge within a discipline or professional area. This review is likely to result in a reconceptualization on a firmer base, lengthening the core in relation to more specialized courses. Such a reconceptualization would improve the quality of both undergraduate and graduate education and enable a department to meet student needs more effectively and efficiently.

Increasing the mutual benefits of the scholarship/teaching connection. More explicit attention can be given to the way in which faculty relate their scholarly activities to other aspects of institutional mission, especially instruction and student advising. Departmental approaches can be developed that would emphasize these interconnections when faculty are hired, when expectations are set, and when evaluations of performance are made. Prospec-

tive faculty should be encouraged in the interview process to talk about the connections between their ambitions and the institutional mission, between their teaching and scholarship, and to address the opportunities for participation of undergraduate and graduate students in their scholarship.

Expanding the range of faculty development opportunities. Institutions should have a variety of activities or units designed to assist faculty in fulfilling their professional responsibilities and enhancing their skills and capabilities. These include instructional support units, faculty exchange programs, faculty mentoring programs, and teaching/learning workshops. Planning should begin with evaluation of any existing units, assessing general effectiveness and overall results. The importance of faculty development activities should be emphasized as one part of institutional development to meet a constantly changing set of institutional challenges; no indication of individual shortcoming is involved.

Institutions would be well served by integrating the concepts and funding for faculty development with sabbaticals in order to maximize flexibility for renewing faculty vitality and meeting institutional goals.

Differentiating faculty responsibilities. Higher education institutions are beginning to formalize approaches to faculty responsibility patterns based on the intuitive understanding that different faculty make different contributions and that members' interests evolve along the length of their careers. Institutions can negotiate workload weights at the time of hire and alter workload weights from time to time by mutual consent within parameters consistent with the institutional mission. The strength of this approach is that it considers individual faculty and preferences, but its fluidity may lessen the clarity of institutional standards and expectations.

Strengthening evaluation methods for faculty teaching and scholarship. Institutions should test the validity of, and refine methods for, evaluating faculty teaching and scholarly activity. Useful assessment must examine the full

> *D*epartments should be held accountable for making whatever changes are necessary in the departmental academic culture to support a pattern of faculty roles and responsibilities consistent with institutional mission.

scope of faculty activities while using broadly acceptable analytical procedures and definitions (Braskamp and Orly, 1994). In the past, evaluation of teaching has either ignored or overemphasized student evaluations of in-class delivery. Ordinarily, the review of scholarly activity has focused somewhat on the specifics of peer review, but has been strongly influenced by sheer volume of publication.

The AAHE Forum on Faculty Roles and Responsibilities emphasizes development of a more systematic review of teaching, especially through peer review, as a way of strengthening the status of teaching relative to scholarly activity. One such method incorporates the review of a teaching portfolio. Clarification is needed on the degree to which evaluations of such portfolios are based on professional academic judgment.

Improving rewards for excellent faculty teaching. An effective faculty reward system must fit closely with academic mission commitments and faculty choices among various kinds of professional responsibilities. How well are evaluations connected to faculty salaries and other compensation? Unless such systems appropriately reward those faculty who give a particularly strong emphasis to instruction and excel at it, faculty will not be motivated to concentrate their efforts on instruction. This suggests an ongoing dialogue about fine tuning the reward system, and vigilance to see that stated norms are upheld in practice. Further analysis might be made of the effectiveness of any formal awards that recognize excellent teachers (including monetary or non-monetary awards). The most effective combination of monetary and non-monetary awards will vary from campus to campus.

Emphasizing research about teaching. Higher education institutions should especially encourage and reward faculty research and other scholarly activity dealing with all aspects of instruction, including classroom teaching. Especially strong institutional affirmations will be necessary for the commitment to be credible to faculty. The historical pattern of the last 30 years reveals that research with pedagogical elements has not been valued at most institutions involved in graduate education.

> *Higher education institutions should especially encourage and reward faculty research and other scholarly activity dealing with all aspects of instruction, including classroom teaching.*

Application of principles to liberal arts colleges and community colleges. Most of the national discussion on faculty roles, responsibilities, and accountability has been concerned over whether graduate institutions are paying appropriate attention to undergraduate education and teaching. Little attention has been paid to applying these principles to small independent liberal arts colleges of very modest means and community colleges. More attention is deserved, since faculty involvement in scholarship is important at all institutions as a way to foster faculty currency within the discipline/profession and to update instructional content. On each campus, the question becomes "What kinds of scholarly activities are appropriate—and how much scholarly activity is appropriate—in light of institutional mission commitments?" A real challenge of resources is seen in circumstances that require faculty to teach four or five courses per semester.

ACTIONABILITY

An institutional planning framework should require the formulation of a faculty roles and rewards policy as an explicit part of planning at the institutional, college/school and departmental level. Such a policy recently established at Virginia Commonwealth University requires that:

- A system of work unit accountability become the focus of planning and evaluation;

- Faculty work roles be flexible, keyed to the work unit's mission and consistent with promotion and tenure criteria;

- Standards of excellence be the basis for evaluation of all faculty and work units; and

- The institution implement a fair and consistent system of merit-based rewards.

It may be difficult to direct full institutional attention to planning issues on faculty resources in the absence of a major external crisis. External motivation may come from the press, reporting class shortages attributed to low faculty teaching loads and too much faculty research. Thus the student is hampered in the pursuit of a degree. Although higher education boards in some states are directly pushing for increases in teaching loads, others are trying to get institutions to address a number of human resource issues connected with faculty roles, responsibilities, and accountability.

If institutions are slow to address these issues within consultative channels on campus, they are likely to find themselves facing more detailed external expectations and deadlines imposed by accreditors and state boards.

Institutions must also plan for the costs of implementing improved faculty support systems and faculty development activities. Institutions will need to become more like other knowledge-intensive sectors of the economy, allocating significant sums for professional support and development closely connected with institutional mission commitments.

RECOMMENDATIONS AND CAVEATS

1. As human resource planning focuses on the academic core of the institution, it must closely involve faculty and operate within a consensus-building framework. The greater the level of faculty involvement in planning, the greater chances for success.

2. Although this chapter talks about culture and socialization primarily in terms of one campus, higher education is strongly influenced by the national cultures of the disciplines and professions that frame graduate school socialization and heavily influence the operations of the national labor market. The split loyalties of faculty members (to their institution and to their discipline/profession) makes this national organization involvement very significant. Only the combined planning efforts of institutions and national professional organizations can provide a base for human resource planning consistent with institutional mission and societal needs.

3. Departments must be recognized as the gateway to change in the academic culture, and to increased institutional effectiveness and efficiency. Institutions should strive to ensure that departmental units have an institutional mandate to plan for faculty roles and responsibilities, institutional support to conduct that planning, and rewards for successfully completing it. The institution ultimately relies on the integrity and professionalism of faculty themselves at the departmental level where instruction takes place and from which other creative contributions emerge.

4. This chapter does not address the growing national discussion about the extent to which tenure practices in their current

PRINT REFERENCES

Alvino, Kathleen M., ed. 1995. *Strategic Planning: A Human Resource Tool for Higher Education*. Washington, DC: College and University Personnel Association (CUPA).

American Association for Higher Education (AAHE). 1992. "Forum on Faculty Roles and Responsibilities." Activities reported in issues of *AAHE Bulletin*, continuing, and at Annual Conference of Forum. Washington, DC: AAHE.

Boyer, E. L. 1990. *Scholarship Reconsidered: Priorities of the Professoriate*. Princeton: Carnegie Foundation for the Advancement of Teaching.

Braskamp, L. A. and Orly, J. C. 1994. *Assessing Faculty Work: Enhancing Individual and Institutional Performance*. San Francisco: Jossey-Bass Publishers.

Edgerton, R. interviews R. Chait, J. Gappa and R. E. Rice. 1995. "From Tenure to… New Pathways: Reframing the Debate." *AAHE Bulletin* 47(10): 3–7.

Gappa, J. and Leslie, D. 1993. *The Invisible Faculty: Improving the Status of Part-Timers in Higher Education*. San Francisco: Jossey-Bass Publishers.

Hammon, L. H. and Hartman, M. 1989–90. "Planning for Faculty Development at a Comprehensive State University." *Planning for Higher Education* 18(4): 31–46.

Johnstone, D. B. 1993. "Enhancing the Productivity of Learning. The Short Version." *AAHE Bulletin* 46(4): 3–8.

Lozier, G. G. and Dooris, M. J., eds. 1989. *Managing Faculty Resources*. New Directions for Higher Education No. 63. San Francisco: Jossey-Bass Publishers.

Moore, K. M. and Amey, M. J. 1993. *Making Sense of the Dollars: The Costs and Uses of Faculty Compensation*. ASHE-ERIC Higher Education Reports 5. Washington, DC: George Washington University.

National Center for Higher Education Management Systems (NCHEMS). 1995. *Faculty Workload and Productivity*. Presented to Third AAHE Conference on Faculty Roles and Rewards. January 19, 1995.

Tack, M. W. and Patitu, C. L. 1992. *Faculty Job Satisfaction: Women and Minorities in Peril*. ASHE-ERIC Higher Education Reports 4. Washington, DC: George Washington University.

"Testimony from the Belly of the Whale." 1992. *Policy Perspectives*, Pew Higher Education Research Program 4(3): A1–A8.

Tierney, W. G. and Rhoads, R. A. 1993. *Enhancing Promotion, Tenure and Beyond: Faculty Socialization as a Cultural Process*. ASHE-ERIC Higher Education Reports 6. Washington, DC: George Washington University.

Wergin, J. F. 1994. *Analyzing Faculty Workload*. New Directions for Institutional Research No. 83. San Francisco: Jossey-Bass Publishers.

ELECTRONIC SAMPLER

http://HEDSFTP.FANDM.EDU/
  (HEDS) *Higher Education Data Sharing Consortium*.

http://www-lsdo.ucdavis.edu/ssworkload.html
  Faculty Workload Report. Division of Social Sciences, University of California, Davis. Barbara Metcalf (Dean).

http://www.aahe.org/
  AAHE (*American Association for Higher Education*).

http://www.aahe.org/ffrrnew2.htm
  AAHE *Forum on Faculty Roles & Rewards*. AAHE (*American Association for Higher Education*).
  A particularly valuable part of of the AAHE website.

form serve either institutional or individual faculty interests. AAHE announced in March, 1995 a New Pathway Project to "deepen the emerging national discussion about tenure and to cast it in broader terms" (Edgerton, 1995). Anticipated foci include re-envisioning faculty careers and developing creative employment arrangements. Faculty professional organizations and collective bargaining representatives have expressed concerns about how the purposes and protections of tenure are to be maintained while pursuing such an agenda.

5. Institutional success in attracting and retaining minority and female faculty is likely to increase in the next decade as institutions in the 1990s have given greater attention to fostering a more diverse and inclusive institutional culture and more effective institutional socialization. Such success is dependent on maintaining a strong institutional commitment at all levels, starting with the board of trustees and senior administration and including all departmental units. This includes regular monitoring of movement toward goals, reassessing concentration of efforts, and identifying new initiatives.

6. The use of part-time faculty, and institutional support for them, has become a regular topic in campus planning discussion (emerging either from uncritical acceptance or condemnation).

7. Refined planning analysis of market and equity factors in salary administration will be necessary on most campuses. Salary administration is an increasing source of frustration for both administrators and faculty. Formal and informal grievances about possible inequities on grounds of gender and race have increased. Senior faculty are frustrated at salary compression as junior people are hired at higher salaries. The delicate institutional balancing act on salaries becomes more and more complex.

8. The treatment of faculty development in this chapter has been limited primarily to development in the teaching and scholarly roles narrowly defined. Some commentators (notably Schuster and Wheeler, 1990) see this breadth as falling very short of the aims of both theorists and practitioners in the 1970s to offer a broader range of activities fully integrated with two other elements—personal development and organizational development. A greater emphasis on faculty and institutional vitality involves increasing career preparation for prospective faculty in graduate school, providing career consulting services to mid-career faculty, promoting faculty health and wellness, providing employee assistance programs (EAP) appropriate to academia, and designing attractive options for early retirement.

9. Preparing prospective faculty for the teaching role is an increasingly important aspect of doctoral preparation at many graduate schools and it needs to be an even higher priority (Schuster and Wheeler, 1990). Such preparation was initially limited to student teaching assistantships at graduate schools. Gradually, the variety and range of such preparation activities has increased. It is increasingly common for departments to offer courses on college teaching and actively supervised teaching internships. Graduate school deans have worked with multiple departments to offer additional teaching opportunities not feasible for any one department,

10. Institutions of higher education will need to respond in coming years to a number of external forces (social, political, and economic environment) that will affect faculty roles and responsibilities (Wergin, 1994).

11. Larger and more sustainable productivity gains probably lie in measures that focus directly on increasing student learning rather than on increasing workloads of faculty and other professional staff. So observed Bruce Johnstone, former chancellor of the State University of New York, emphasizing that a direct focus on student learning leads to an re-examination of the curriculum, pedagogy, and technological support. He identifies more individually paced mastery learning and expeditious completion for full-time traditional age students as areas for exploration (Johnstone, 1993). ◆

Planning for Information Technology

Institutional Informational Technology Resource Assessment

Linda Fleit

Planning for Information Technology

Susy S. Chan

Information technology (IT) is not an end in itself. It is only vital when it serves institutional goals and objectives–when it actually produces results. Our institutions need that kind of excellent IT and all its related products and services. If IT is to be a useful partner in planning for an improved educational climate, it must subject itself to ongoing evaluation and assessment. This chapter discusses the assessment process, illustrating that it begins by asking the right questions.

Institutional Information Technology Resource Assessment

Linda Fleit

High quality assessments are difficult in any discipline, but perhaps especially so in the area of information technology (IT). The ingredients necessary for a good IT assessment–objectivity, knowledge, and wisdom–are hard to come by, especially in combination. A useful assessment takes time. The process can make people uncomfortable, bringing together a wide range of campus personnel, perhaps for the first time. Nevertheless, such assessment is critically important, and institutions that do not face its challenges likewise miss out on its returns, both present and future. Successful planning is impossible without it.

On one hand, there is the promise and potential of technology. Virtually every goal and objective a college or university espouses can be affected in positive ways by information technology. Whether it is using computers and networking to strengthen current and new educational programs, to provide individualized learning experiences for students, to attract and retain students best able to benefit from the institution's educational experience, to enhance the quality of student life, or to emphasize sound planning and increased financial strength, information technology has an important, substantive role to play.

Working against these positive forces, however, is the fact that technology is very

expensive. No matter how quickly hardware prices decline, no matter how much better the price/performance ratio is this year than last, no matter how much more one can buy for one's dollar, the total cost of information technology on a typical college campus is huge. It is taking an increasingly large bite out of the institution's budget. As financial pressures continue to mount for most colleges and universities, the bite seems more and more voracious.

What makes the situation even more compelling is the fact that higher education is itself increasingly being held accountable for the management of its resources. Parents, state governments, trustees, and others are all asking very hard questions these days. Where are the campus dollars going? Are tuition money, grant and foundation dollars, and government funding being spent sensibly? How well, really, are college students being educated? Is college today still "worth" attending, and if so, at what price? What is the real purpose of a college education in today's society?

The positive potential of IT on one hand and its great expense on the other, make it difficult to find the right balance and to

Linda Fleit

is President of Edutech International, Bloomfield, Connecticut.

create the most appropriate plans for the institution to follow. Asking questions about technological accountability, as many institutions do, is a good start toward finding the balance. However, just asking the questions—even the right questions asked in the right way—is not sufficient. There must also be answers, based on knowledge and understanding of what technology is about. In a climate of accountability, information technology and its related services are often at a big disadvantage. IT has to compete with campus priorities whose benefits may be more immediate or more obvious. There are still many people on campus who question, if not the activity level, at least the value of what is going on with IT, and whether the campus could be choosing better investments for its limited resources. In this context especially, an IT assessment should be done—not just as a way to reduce costs—but with solid appreciation for the high potential of IT benefits.

There are still many people on campus who question, if not the activity level, at least the value of what's going on with IT, and whether the campus could be choosing better investments for its limited resources.

How does all this relate to planning? An assessment forms the very basis of planning, by providing the starting point for the future. While planning efforts are always focused on deciding our destination, assessments describe where we are starting from and allow us to plot the appropriate course. An assessment, properly done, brings consensus on the current situation, proves invaluable in identifying and analyzing institutional strengths and weaknesses, and gives us the jumping-off point for all future activities.

WHAT AN ASSESSMENT IS (AND IS NOT)

Consider first the nature and definition of what is to be assessed. One of the traps institutions often fall into is thinking that the only task in assessing information technology is to give a performance review to the department responsible for delivering information technology resources and services. While that is one component, it is far from the whole issue. The real value in an IT assessment is that it creates understanding of how the whole institution is dealing with technology. A thorough assessment looks at the whole picture, including how and how well users employ technology, how communications about technological issues are disseminated, how the administration is promoting and funding technology, and how technological innovation is being rewarded.

An IT assessment should also incorporate a wide variety of technologies, often supported through different departments. Computers and computing are included, to be sure, but so should be video technology, voice and data communications, imaging, and all the increasingly ubiquitous instances of electronic tools and devices.

As an important planning tool, an IT assessment serves several purposes. First, it is a diagnosis. Of course, there are institutions where information technology is everything wonderful, all services run beautifully, everyone on campus feels they have sufficient resources, and everyone is working in perfect harmony on IT issues. At least, I think such institutions are out there—somewhere. In most, however, IT is a source of some consternation. And, almost always, the exact cause of the consternation is not clear. Is it too much demand? Too little money to spend? Too much prima donna behavior in the computer center? Too few in the top administration who understand IT? All of the above? Diagnosing the situation and identifying root causes for the consternation is one of the most important aspects of an IT assessment. It is not a blame tool, however; that is not the point at all. The point is to figure out what's wrong, to identify factors that are contributing to a less-than-highest-quality computing environment, and then to use that information to attack the problems. It does not really matter how the problems got there, or who made what decisions that may have led to them. What matters is the diagnosis—upon which a cure can be based.

Second, an IT assessment is preventive medicine. Like taking vitamins or working out regularly on the treadmill, performing an IT assessment can prevent major problems from developing. For instance, realizing through an assessment that the IT department should be putting together formal plans for each project, relying heavily on user participation, may prevent the next major technological initiative from going seriously awry. An assessment is an anticipatory mechanism; it finds whatever should be changed to enhance the institution's dealings with IT, and it detects signals that trouble is brewing.

Third, an assessment obtains a comparative measure, asking the questions, "How well are we doing? How well *could* we be doing? How well are other institutions doing?"

Finally, an IT assessment achieves consensus on the important issue of measuring quality. IT people themselves traditionally have measured those things which are most relevant to them and which are most easily quantified: lines of programming code written per day, number of CPU cycles, percentage of mainframe downtime, number of microcomputers in public labs. But when all those numbers seem satisfactory, or fall within the "right" ranges, it may be difficult to understand why the users don't seem happy. Users, in fact, may be using entirely different measurements. They may be measuring (at least subconsciously) the quality of IT services by how much technical jargon the computer people use when they talk to others, not how much disk space is available. One of the important things we are beginning to realize now is that the traditional quantitative measures used by IT people do not get to the heart of the issue for the users. What is needed, and what an IT assessment promotes and provides, is an agreement among IT people, users, and the administration about what constitutes success.

It is important to remember what an IT assessment is not. It is not an audit. The purpose is not to look for areas of control or potential mischief; the emphasis is not on compliance, asset protection, reliability and accuracy of data, or any of those audit-oriented subjects. The questions are more strategic; the answers are meant to provide insight into the broad array of services offered, the way they are administered and delivered, and the relationship between the department and the larger institution. The assessment is designed to elicit information, not just data. The answers are to be weighed, judged, and open to interpretation. Many answers will be more subjective than objective; none will be stated numerically.

Whereas the focus of an audit is on efficiency and control, the focus of an IT assessment is on effectiveness, assessing the quality and quantity of technology resources, the department's responsiveness, and policies that promote usefulness.

KEY ASSESSMENT AREAS AND QUESTIONS

There are ten ingredients for "doing IT right"– ensuring that an institution of higher education is investing an appropriate amount in IT

and getting the most benefit in return. These ingredients, in order of importance, are:

- The right IT governance structure, including reporting relationships and committees;

- A planning process;

- Sufficient and qualified support staff to match the institution's technology goals and objectives;

- An information architecture built on the principles of data integration, easy access within security constraints, and functionality;

- Publicized standards for hardware, software, acquisitions, networking, and procedures;

- A network which connects all computing devices, everywhere at the institution, capable of high-speed transmission of voice, data, and video;

- Software that includes integrated software for administration, classroom software for students, and research software for faculty, some purchased and some created in-house;

- Microcomputer-based end-user tools for data access and manipulation;

- Ongoing training and support for everyone, including end users, technical staff, top administration, faculty, and students; and

- Proliferating hardware as it becomes smaller, faster, and cheaper.

The point of an IT assessment is to gauge how well the institution is doing in assembling these ingredients. The questions, therefore, should fall into categories that correspond to the ingredients list. I suggest using the following categories as a starting place, and I have included a few of the many possible questions in each category.[1]

Governance. Does the IT department report to the right level within the institution? Does it report to a person knowl-

*I*t is important to remember what an IT assessment is not. It is not an audit. The purpose is not to look for areas of control or potential mischief; the emphasis is not on compliance, asset protection, reliability and accuracy of data, or any of those audit-oriented subjects.

---

[1]For an expanded and more detailed list of questions, see CAUSE Professional Paper #12, *Self-Assessment for Campus Information Technology Services.*

edgeable about computing issues and able to provide substantive guidance and support? Is there support from the president for information technology institution-wide? Does the IT department get enough of the right kind of attention? Are IT activities supported and governed by the right set of committees? Has the institution achieved the right balance of centralization and decentralization so that the entire community is being well served in the most cost-efficient ways? Are the expectations of the end users realistic, given the institution's funding of information technology, the capabilities of current technology, and their own perceptions of what their investment needs to be (education and training, participation in planning and setting priorities, providing specifications, review and evaluation of deliverables)? Are the users' perceptions about both the quality and quantity of computer services favorable? Do the users hold the department's staff members in high esteem? Does the department have influence with decision makers? Is the person in charge of information technology services thought of as a part of the institution's "management team?" Do annual reports show the results and costs of computing activities measured against the plan for the year? Is the priority-setting process for the department objective and well understood? Is it controlled by the users and accountable to the administration? Is everyone clear on how new technology initiatives are justified? Is funding at an appropriate level to support the institution's technology goals? Does the level of institutional funding for IT accurately reflect its level of importance? Do information technology services receive a steady percentage of the institution's budget from year to year?

Planning. Is there a multi-year plan for computing and telecommunications in place for the whole institution? If so, was it drawn from institutional objectives, even if those objectives are not fully articulated? Was the planning process participative and collaborative? Is the plan updated on a regular basis, say, once a year? Are there formal, written project plans (in which

*I*s the IT department a regular participant in other planning activities, such as new building construction or building renovation, capital campaign planning, and enrollment management?

users have participated) for every major project that the IT department undertakes? Is the IT department a regular participant in other planning activities, such as new building construction or building renovation, capital campaign planning, and enrollment management?

Support staff. Do all or most of the IT staff members have experience in higher education? Are the "politics" of higher education institutions an accepted part of the work environment? Do the staff members who work directly with end users understand the users' work environments, including goals and objectives? Do all staff members have enough technical expertise? Does everyone in the department have excellent interpersonal communication skills, both oral and written? Do staff members see themselves as productive work partners with their users? Do they have high self-esteem without being arrogant or unapproachable? Is morale in the department good? Is a service orientation promoted and understood throughout the department? Does the computer center make use of student workers whenever feasible?

Information architecture. Is the system architecture sufficiently flexible to promote end-user computing and control? Is the right combination of mainframe, microcomputer, and minicomputer used to provide solutions to end users? Are data definitions consistent and understood by all those who create and access data?

Standards. Are there hardware, software, and procedural standards that both computer staff and users are encouraged to meet? Are programs always written the same way, using reusable codes and libraries whenever possible? Are there choices within the standards so users can retain some local control? Is ethical computing widely promoted by department staff?

Networking. Is the campus network ubiquitous and able to handle high-speed and high-volume traffic? Is it easy to send email anywhere? Can everyone get to the Internet from their desktops? Does the planning for new buildings and other spaces always include networking considerations?

Software. Are there formal ways of determining which applications should be supported by purchased software—which should be developed in-house, and which should be a combination of the two? Is the backlog of service requests, especially for applications programming changes and enhancements, at a reasonable level? Is it short enough to avoid a "hidden" demand or guilt on the part of users in asking for something? Are fourth-generation tools, such as non-procedural programming languages, relational data base management systems, and software engineering tools, either in use already or planned for the near future? Are they, or will they be, accessible both by administrative and academic users? Is there a "research and development" function within the department to assure that technical innovations and recent developments are not overlooked?

End-user tools. Are the department's products and services moving toward a distributed computing environment? Is the department's philosophy supportive of self-sufficiency for end users? Are there tools, such as a report writer, download software, and a query capability available to promote end-user computing? Does the department have a customer outreach function? Are there ways to let academic and administrative users know about new technological innovations in their areas and new sources of materials and information? Are users regularly canvassed to determine how the department can be helpful to them?

Training and support. Is there a training strategy for users? Does it make the best use of a variety of resources, including self-paced instruction, classroom training, one-on-one assistance, and video? Is there a formal IT staff training and an education program? Is it reviewed on a regular basis to make sure it is up-to-date and serving genuine staff needs? Is it geared toward the higher education environment? Are staff members cross-trained so that service areas are not vulnerable to someone's absence? Is there well-written and accurate user documentation for every service area in the department?

Hardware. Are there enough microcomputers for everyone? Is there a replacement policy? Is there a capital budgeting process for information technology to minimize unexpected costs and to provide for orderly growth? Are hardware usage statistics checked regularly against capacity on items such as mainframe response time and disk storage? Are there established ways of dealing with both under- and over-utilization?

These questions are by no means exhaustive, and are presented here to give an idea of the range of issues covered in an assessment.

DOING THE ASSESSMENT

There are a variety of ways an IT assessment can be done. The IT department can do its own assessment, for instance (Fleit, 1994). Or a team of administrators and faculty can do it. Many institutions, on the other hand, decide to work with outside professional colleagues, or even to hire consultants for the job.

As a former computer center director, I favor having the IT department do its own assessment, especially if there is reason to believe the department is in trouble. We who are or have been in this position know the shock of being told by our supervisor that an outside consultant has been called in to do an assessment. Your main task becomes trying to maintain an objective, non-defensive, "good-soldier" posture. At the same time you must explain every decision you've ever made to a group of outsiders who haven't a clue about your actual circumstances. The worst part is knowing that the review is being conducted because there is some perception, real or imagined, that your department has some very serious problems it can not solve on its own.

If a self-assessment is not possible, the institution might consider a committee or task force assembled for this purpose, made up of a representative sampling from across campus. An important advantage of a committee approach is that it sets the stage for the collaboration necessary for subsequent planning efforts. As mentioned earlier, there does need to be a mixture of objectivity, knowledge, and understanding of IT's potential in order to obtain the most relevant and effective results. If objectivity is not possible, then outsiders need to be called in to do the assessment, either by using colleagues from other campuses or professional consulting firms.

The essential task is to formulate and agree on the questions to be asked. They should be phrased to make it easy to evaluate the results. Note that all the questions listed

We who are or have been in this position know the shock of being told by our supervisor that an outside consultant has been called in to do an assessment.

PRINT REFERENCES

Allen, D. 1995. "Performance Anxiety." *Computerworld*, February 15, 1993.

"Asking the Users: How Are We Doing?" 1991. *The EDUTECH Report*, May 1991.

"Be Your Own Consultant: Review Computer Services." 1989. *The EDUTECH Report*, April 1989.

Bromley, M. L. 1984. *Departmental Self-Study: A Guide for Campus Law Enforcement Administrators*. Hartford: International Association of Campus Law Enforcement Administrators (IACLEA).

EDUTECH. 1986. "What Makes A Computer Center Great?" *EDUTECH Report* (December).

EDUTECH. 1988. "Ten Reasons Why Computer Centers Fail." *EDUTECH Report* (August).

Evaluation Guidelines for Institutional Information Technology Resources. 1995. Boulder: Higher Education Information Resources Alliance.

Fleit, L. H. 1994. *Self-Assessment for Campus Information Technology Services*. CAUSE Professional Paper #12. Boulder: CAUSE.

Green, K. C. 1995. *Campus Computing 1994: The Fifth National Survey of Desktop Computing in Higher Education*. Encino: Campus Computing.

Hawkins, B. L., ed. 1989. *Organizing and Managing Information Resources on Campus*. McKinney: Academic Computing Publications.

McLaughlin, G. W. and Howard, R. D. 1991. "Check the Quality of Your Information Support." *CAUSE/EFFECT* (Spring): 23–27.

Meyer, N. D. January, 1991. "IS Gets a Physical." *CIO Magazine*, January 1991.

Norton, D. P. and Rau, K. G. A. 1982. *Guide to EDP Performance Management*. Wellesley: Q.E.D. Information Sciences, Inc.

Peters, T. J. and Waterman, R. H. 1982. *In Search of Excellence*. New York: Warner Books.

Robbins, M. D.; Dorn, W. S.; and Skelton, J. E. 1975. *Who Runs the Computer? Strategies for the Management of Computers in Higher Education*. Boulder: Westview Press.

What Presidents Need to Know About Evaluating Institutional Information Resources. 1995. Boulder: Higher Education Information Resources Alliance.

ELECTRONIC SAMPLER

http://cause-www.colorado.edu/

   CAUSE. *(the association for managing and using information resources in higher education)*.

http://cause-www.colorado.edu/information-resources/ir-library/abstracts/pub3012.html

   Self Assessment for Campus Information Technology Services. CAUSE. Linda Fleit.

http://cause-www.colorado.edu/member-dir/corp-profiles/edutech.html

   Providing Information Technology Services to Higher Education. Edutech International.

http://www.cio.com/CIO/

   CIO Magazine: The Magazine for Information Executives.

http://www.educom.edu/program/nlii/keydocs/massy.html

   Using Information Technology to Enhance Academic Productivity. NLII (National Learning Infrastructure Initiative). William F. Massy and Robert Zemsky.

http://www.igc.apc.org/aaup/

   AAUP (American Association of University Professors).

http://www.thejournal.com/contents/current.html/

   Technological Horizons in Education Online. T.H.E. Journal.

above are answered "yes" in the best of all possible worlds; "no" answers stand out immediately. While it would be difficult to make the case that any "no" answer automatically spells trouble, a question answered with a "no," "maybe," or anything less than "yes," suggests further scrutiny. A large number of negative answers probably indicates that the institution has serious IT problems, or is at least approaching them. On a more positive note, if all, or even most, answers are "yes," then IT is probably in good shape. The greater the number of positive answers, the more assurance everyone has that things are going well, and will continue to go well.

The job then becomes to solicit a wide range of views from current IT users, potential IT users, top administrators and deans, academic department heads, front-line staff, students, and, of course, the members of the IT department. Although it may be necessary, especially on a large campus, to use questionnaires, personal interviews are much more effective for eliciting useful information.

Data for comparisons with other institutions are available from a variety of sources, including CAUSE in Boulder, Colorado; NACUBO in Washington, DC; and Campus Computing in Encino, California. A word of caution, however: comparisons can be very tricky; it is difficult to determine similarities and differences among institutions being compared. Data definitions tend to vary, as do the ways in which items are counted. These comparisons tend to be more useful on an aggregate level.

The assessment itself should take about two weeks, perhaps longer in large institutions. Compiling the results takes a bit longer, especially if done by an outsider. Not much, if any, research is required to answer the questions in this kind of an assessment, since they are much more qualitative than quantitative. They deal with issues that people can respond to directly, from personal experience. The assessment is not particularly difficult in terms of information gathering.

WORKING WITH THE RESULTS
Once the results of the assessment are in hand, it is time to begin developing substantive plans. With a common baseline for everyone, the process of formulating a vision for the future and designing the roadmap to reach that vision can be expedited.

If the assessment has turned up trouble spots, short-term plans may be needed before long-range planning can be done. For instance, one of the most common items uncovered in an IT assessment is the lack of the right committee structure to lead the institution forward in its use of IT. An institutional "Information Technology Policy Committee" may be needed, as well as various user groups. Before long-range planning is done for IT, the right committees should be assembled and charged.

The IT assessment represents ground zero from which to launch the planning process. As we have said, next to governance, planning is the most important ingredient in doing technology right. In developing a strategic plan for information technology that is comprehensive, consensus-driven, forward-thinking, and appropriate to the institution's resources, mission, and goals, an IT assessment is an invaluable tool.

FINAL THOUGHTS

Technology is all about partnerships: the president in partnership with the institution's chief information officer, the IT department in partnership with the users, the technology vendor in partnership with the campus buyer. Like all partnerships, they are two-sided and have to be nurtured in order to thrive. Each partner has to understand what he or she brings to the table, and what he or she can expect in return. Insofar as a well-done IT assessment can bring clarity to partnerships and contribute an objective rendering of the institution's IT picture, it is a vital tool. It is not a weapon. It is a communications and planning device to help strengthen the partnership.

Technology is not an end unto itself. It is only vital when it serves institutional goals and objectives—when it actually produces results. Our institutions **need** that kind of excellent information technology and all its related products and services.

What are the ingredients for excellence? On the whole, two characteristics mark an institution's information technology environment: (1) it assists in the effort to provide and improve quality education, and (2) it assists in lowering the cost of administering and delivering that education. In other words, information technology, by contributing directly to the goals of its institution, helps make the institution both more effective and more efficient.

It is incumbent upon us, whether we are higher education information technology professionals, or users of information technology services, to strive for excellence. In order to see how well we're doing in reaching that goal, ongoing evaluation and assessment is critically important.   ◆

A learner-centered academic environment in the information age calls for innovative applications of information technology. As more traditional planning approaches may serve the needs for specific information technology initiatives, a more comprehensive, holistic approach is necessary to achieve long-term institutional results. Strategic thinking, process reengineering, and the re-examination of academic goals, delivery, and vision, should incorporate the role and benefits of information technology in the student's pursuit of learning.

Planning for Information Technology

Susy S. Chan

CORE PLANNING QUESTIONS

Higher education planners face unique challenges in information technology planning. The ever-evolving nature of information technology, coupled with its visible impacts on people and processes, the escalating expectations from constituents across the institution, and high costs of such investment, heighten the importance of information technology planning.

The pervasive use of information technologies has forced many industries to move from a factory model of industrial economy into the information economy, characterized by easy access and distribution of information. There are abundant examples showing how this transformation reshaped the marketplace, restructured industries, and reengineered core business processes for effective competition.

Michael G. Dolence and Donald M. Norris (1995) suggest that a parallel transformation will take place in higher education. Their vision captures the opportunities available for learners through transforming the academic enterprise into a learner-centered environment of the information age. The traditional (factory) model of higher education has centered on faculty scholarship, classroom teaching, and certification process. In an information age, colleges and universities should emphasize real-time access to vast information resources and "anywhere, anytime" learning through asynchronous communications and network technology. The information age model challenges the paradigm of academic enterprise bounded by the institution, faculty interests, and academic disciplines.

William Massy and Robert Zemsky (1995) concur with this observation. Universities and colleges capable of adapting to change and addressing traditional barriers will be able to take full advantage of their information technology investment. This requires a redefinition of academic productivity and redesign of learning process in light of the learner's interests. Information technology is likely to reshape many traditional academic support services, because learners will demand different cost structures and service delivery models. Maintaining the status quo will weaken higher education as a whole. Planning for information technology, therefore, must be approached in the broadest context of transformation.

Universities and colleges are facing the reality of decreased fund-

Susy S. Chan

is Associate Professor, Director of Center for Information Resource Management for the School of Computer Science, Telecommunications and Information Systems, and Former Vice President for Planning and Information Technology—at DePaul University, Chicago, Illinois. Chan is also the Theme Coordinator for the SCUP-32 Conference Committee and a previous member of SCUP's Publications Advisory Committee.

ing from traditional sources, increased public demand for accountability, heightened consumer expectation for more sophisticated services and data access, a continually evolving network organization structure, and increasingly technologically sophisticated workers and their demand for support (Ernst, Katz, and Sack, 1994). These trends drive higher education institutions to take

Such a holistic view demands that deans and department chairs cultivate a capacity for strategic thinking, organizational change management, and innovative use of information technology.

a holistic approach to changes in organization design, process, information access, technology, and training of people. Transformation-guided strategic planning, therefore, needs to start with strategic thinking and a knowledge of how to deploy this holistic set of strategies–a frontier for most academic managers. A solid understanding of the transformation process and supporting strategies must take place first.

In most cases, planners can still apply four types of planning–strategic, operational, budgetary, and major initiatives. Each type serves different objectives (Badagliacco, 1992). There is an acute need to link information technology planning to institution-wide strategic planning. However, most reported experiences were focused on other kinds of planning.

Regardless of the kind of information technology planning, it is important to develop strategies for organization, work process, information, and technology as a coherent set. Such a holistic view demands that deans and department chairs cultivate a capacity for strategic thinking, organizational change management, and innovative use of information technology. A linear process of planning will no longer be sufficient. A holistic model is needed to support fast-paced, multidimensional change in an information age (Dolence and Norris, 1995).

Within this broad context, academic planners typically face the following questions at the beginning of the process:

- What is the institution's vision regarding the use of information technology? Is it to be a leader, early follower, or late follower? Each position has financial and organizational implications.

- How does the investment, deployment, and management of technology and information support the institutional mission?

- What are the benefits and opportunities of distributed network and information access? What should be done first? Who would be the beneficiaries?

- Is the institution ready for advanced technology and user ownership of data and technology?

- Are the institution's information technology resources adequately provided, effectively organized, and efficiently managed to support strategic initiatives?

- How are major investments financed? How does the institution know it is making the right investment?

- How could technology and infrastructure be properly upgraded? How could obsolescent technologies be migrated into new platforms?

- What changes in process, organizational structure, and skills of people—in the institution and the information technology organization—are necessary to optimize the investment of new technology?

BASIC CONCEPTS

Four types of planning. Three types of planning (strategic, operational, and initiative-based) differ in scope, information requirements, and processes. Strategic planning offers the broadest scope, emphasizing strategic thinking, visioning and long-term directions. Its process is broad-based and requires general information, while planning for major information technology initiatives is undertaken to achieve specific objectives; a kind of planning that provides detailed analysis about benefits, resources, timetable and deliverables. A fourth type, financial or budgetary planning activities, usually accompanies one of the first three types of planning.

Strategic planning. An institution-wide information technology plan should link closely with an institution's multi-year strategic plan, or as an integral part of institutional priorities, resource allocations, program delivery, and expected outcomes. A strategic information technology plan should have a clear vision about how information technology applications could enable the institution to achieve its mission. For example, distance learning technology will enable a nursing program to reach new student markets, enhance teacher-learner interaction, and generate new revenues. However, information technology is-sues have not received adequate attention in institutional strategic planning at most cam-puses. The Pennsylvania State University's Office of Computer and Information Systems conducted a benchmark study (1995) of five "best-in-class" large, research universities re-garding their information technology resource management and support. Based on the benchmark results, there is very little formal institution-wide planning for information technology; the existing strategic planning processes generally do not adapt to critical information technology issues. This reflects a need to address information governance as well as the institution's knowledge about the impact and importance of information tech-nology on the academic enterprise.

Operational planning. An information technol-ogy division or a senior manager within the area can develop a short-term plan to imple-ment technology and service goals. Such a plan usually has a one to three year time ho-rizon, addresses strategies and resources, and provides a timetable for implementing ongoing services and new initiatives. Its scope ranges from service improvement (help desk), infra-structure maintenance and investment (insti-tution-wide cabling and networking), new services (electronic library services), technol-ogy enhancement (voice response systems for telephone registration), new system develop-ment (a new human resource system), to fa-cility upgrades (student microcomputing centers). An operational plan for an informa-tion technology division should have a com-prehensive and institutional scope, but it is usually approached from the perspective of the service division. The value of operational plan-ning is to set implementation priorities, timelines, and resource commitment. Key to effective operational planning is the clarifica-tion of outcome measures and deliverables.

Major initiative planning. Multi-year or large information technology projects also call for formal planning. Such projects are expensive and often exceed budgets or timelines. Rigor-ous project planning is critical in ensuring successful completion. A cross-functional team approach has become a preferred way of imple-menting major information technology initia-tives. Academic planners need to develop knowledge about complex project planning

and management, emphasizing project objec-tives, solutions, and benefits to the institution. Such projects should also include a timeline with milestones, resource requirements, team members, and user involvement.

Financial-budgetary planning. Enhancement and investment in information technologies are generally costly and require an institution to make a multi-year commitment. A new information system for integrated student ser-vice using distributed network technology could easily cost several million dollars over five years. It is necessary to present a detailed budgetary analysis showing multiple scenarios which could compare the costs for adopting the new systems, while maintaining current fragmented processes, to the costs for a reen gineered process, such as one providing stu-dents with direct access to their grades, sched-ules, bills, and other personal information. The analysis should identify funding sources and methods, maintenance costs over time, ben-efits, and anticipated cost savings or payback schedule. Outsourcing strategies, through partnering with vendors, should be explored to achieve cost savings or service improve-ment. The typical twelve- to eighteen-month cycle for budget planning and review does not make allowances for rapid technology changes and needs. Capital funding, based on some formula or life-cycle of different categories of technology, provides greater flexibility in planning and allo-cation.

INTEGRATED PLANNING MODELS

Traditional planning approaches do not address the fast-paced change initiated by information technology. However, models that integrate organization, pro-cess, information, and technol-ogy issues are emerging. One example is the learning action plan proposed by Maricopa Community Colleges (Baltzer, 1994). This model puts informa-tion technology planning in the context of or-ganizational culture, customer communities, and technology assessment. The model con-tains six components, supporting strategies, tools, and tactics. The components include:

*A*cademic planners need to develop knowledge about complex project planning and management, emphasizing project objectives, solutions, and benefits to the institution.

aligning of the information technology division with the institution, creating a shared vision, articulating strategic principles, designing the information technology organization structure, applying a process reengineering approach, and providing continuous feedback for services and priorities through customer input. A holistic approach creates incentives for institutional learning.

Pennsylvania State University's benchmark study identified four guiding principles practiced by research universities:

- Use policy, budget, and strategy measures to maximize the benefits of information technology through a clear information technology governance structure and reporting relationship, early adoption of a process reengineering approach, the balance of centralized and decentralized needs, and use of life-cycle funding to support the rapid pace of technological change.

- Encourage early implementation of information technology infrastructure and standards to implement institution-wide connectivity.

- Emphasize customer service in order to integrate technology into the institutional culture through faculty development and information technology training.

- Develop standards, security, and architectural planning to create a supportive environment for change.

PLANNING FOR IT ORGANIZATIONAL CHANGE

Transformation has to occur in the information technology organization in order for it to facilitate change elsewhere. Obsolete technologies, ineffective organizational design, escalating user expectation, rapid technology advancement, and limited institutional experience in process reengineering, challenge the information technology organization and its

Transformation has to occur in the information technology organization in order for it to facilitate change elsewhere. Obsolete technologies, ineffective organizational design, escalating user expectation, rapid technology advancement, and limited institutional experience in process reengineering challenge the information technology organization and its members to embrace constant changes.

members to embrace constant changes. Such transformation requires careful planning. Restructuring formerly fragmented information technology resources into a coherent structure is one of the approaches under consideration. It helps to flatten the organization, emphasizes cross-functional processes, and directs the information technology division's attention to customer services (Chan, 1995). Successful restructuring demands a commitment to staff development. The debate on a centralized versus decentralized IT organization can be viewed in terms of resources and services. A centralized IT organization, without the turf wall between academic and administrative computing, can achieve greater efficiency and productivity. For large institutions of decentralized culture, services will need to be aligned more closely with the customer base through shared reporting and accountability.

DATA SELECTION AND CAPTURE

Information technology planning, like any other planning process, should start with an assessment to identify institutional strengths, weaknesses, infrastructure, capacity, and customer satisfaction, along with institutional needs regarding information technology. These assessment data form the basis for growth, upgrades, and financial impact projection. In Chapter 8, Linda Fleit addresses assessment issues and strategies. A more detailed discussion of the framework can be found in her *Self-Assessment for Campus Information Technology Services* (Fleit, 1994).

The Higher Education Information Resources Alliance (HEIRAlliance, 1995) recently updated its guidelines and examples of what the information technology environment might look like at an information resource-intensive institution. The text of both the guidelines and the supplementary document can be retrieved from the CAUSE Web server <http://cause-www.colorado> or <edu/collab/heira.html>. This set of guidelines encompasses information technologies (computing and voice, video, and data communications), information services, and information itself. It addresses a growing area of common concern for both libraries and information technology organizations—access to and delivery of information through computing and communications technology (electronic information resources).

Planners can use various methods to capture data:

- Focus groups, committees, periodic surveys, and task-based feedback cards assess user satisfaction and needs. The choice of method should be determined by the question to be answered. A broad annual survey of use satisfaction gauges a general response by user groups. A short feedback card for each project and task will generate more formative information for improvements.

- Financial and budgetary information on hardware, software, new services, support, and infrastructure should address both initial investment, maintenance, and replacement in view of the life-cycle of each category of technology. Projections and comparative data may be obtained through vendors and comparable institutions or industry.

- Performance data on quality and effectiveness come from resource allocation behavior (information technology budget as a percent of institutional operating budget), user satisfaction measures (percent satisfied with timeliness of service), cost ratios (costs per user for bundled software license), and operating efficiencies (percent uptime for network and email service, number of users supported by each help desk staff). For specific measures on performance and for planning purposes, it may be useful to collect data from the industry in areas such as help desk staffing, network support, and number of subscribers per port for dial-in service. These measures are well established and less affected by industry type.

- Policies and procedures are part of this assessment. Most colleges and universities are struggling with the need to create policies to cope with the changing environment. Data can be gathered through both observation and interviews with people who deliver, manage, and use the services.

- Information on current and projected application portfolios is crucial for architectural planning. It is usually scattered or kept only in the technician's head. Review of documentation and group interviews could help reconstruct the technical information.

- Both CAUSE and NACUBO provide benchmarking data. The CAUSE ID Survey provides comparative data on budgets, staffing, policies, practices, and services for participating member institutions. It is a useful source on services and funding practices, such as how many institutions use chargebacks to recover costs for network services. Since 1992 the NACUBO Benchmarking Project has collected cost data on information technology and telecommunications activities and functions. These benchmarking data are often fraught with problems in definition and comparability. As the Penn State (1995) experience revealed, it is extremely difficult to establish common definitions to measure information technology resources and services, even within a small set of similar institutions. The focus on numeric input data is better shifted toward outcomes and on framing evaluation questions.

MANIPULATION & DELIVERY

A written plan with clear goals, objectives, strategies, budgets, timelines, and expected outcomes with frequent updates is essential. Specific data can be displayed in multiple formats. Like all effective planning information, the choice of presentation format and level of details on information technology plans should be determined by the objective of the communication and knowledge of the audience. Because of the technical nature of the subject matter, greater attention should be devoted to effective presentation of planning data and recommendations. The following are some examples:

- Architecture and infrastructure data are best presented in graphs showing logical layers, geographical and physical distribution and configuration.

- Financial and budgetary data should be presented in spreadsheets; diagrams; pie charts; and summaries of benefits, costs, and choices. The resource allocation should be tied to objectives and benefits.

Like all effective planning information, the choice of presentation format and level of details on information technology plans should be determined by the objective of the communication and knowledge of the audience.

- Staffing and operating performance data should be presented in trends and ratios to show stability and improvement.

- User feedback and satisfaction data are best presented by service groups or customer groups in trend analysis to capture the change over time.

- Electronic presentation via *Power-Point*™ or HTML allow integration of complex data.

- Major projects should always be presented in a summary form with project objectives, benefits, approaches, timelines, and estimated budgets.

- Use electronic means, such as email, to solicit user feedback.

ACTIONABILITY ISSUES

In selecting an appropriate planning model, academic planners should always be mindful about unique institutional characteristics and needs. Research universities, community colleges, and liberal arts colleges have vastly different needs and technology solutions. Generalizations about the planning processes at different institutions are prone to oversimplification because planning depends heavily upon the personalities of the leadership and the specifics of traditions of those institutions. However, these three kinds of institutions can be differentiated by their degree of centralization, the participants in planning, and the central focus of the planning process (Smallen, 1992). The nature of decentralization and power among the three institutional types differs substantially and is reflected in their planning processes.

In selecting an appropriate planning model, academic planners should always be mindful about unique institutional characteristics and needs.

- At research universities, decision making is generally decentralized, with considerable power vested in the schools, research centers, and sometimes the individual departments. In such an environment, planning for information technology is generally a decentralized, though highly coordinated process. The situation at public universities may be further complicated by statewide or systemwide technology planning groups, determined by funding source, and research grants. Developing and enforcing architecture, standards, and policies presents a challenge for planners. The economy of scale and large information technology staff enable these universities to develop some of the most innovative technology applications.

- Community colleges are principally funded by state allocations and have highly centralized decision making processes that focus on the teaching mission of the institution. A more top-down approach to information technology planning is common. There is also greater success in integrating information technology planning and institutional strategic planning. Several large community college systems, such as the Maricopa Community Colleges and Miami-Dade Community College, emphasize the use of network technology and distance learning to reach the learning needs of growing student populations.

- Private liberal arts colleges focus on teaching, small class size, and faculty student interaction, but also maintain an emphasis on research. Because of their size and small information technology staffs, these colleges are often unable to take advantage of economies of scale in undertaking new initiatives. Outsourcing, collaboration, and a clear focus on institutional mission become more important strategies.

It is also necessary to clearly define the users, constituent groups, and participants of the planning process. Executive sponsorship and participation of key users are critical for information technology planning at all levels, as there is heightened attention on technology investment and its impact. The most effective process would be one that is linked with strategic planning. Technology solutions are presented as part of institutional directions. At large complex universities such integration is difficult to achieve. A formal planning process that involves many committees and constituent groups may not be productive, especially when there is no centralized information technology division to advocate strategies and priorities. It would be appropriate to organize special groups and processes to facilitate ongoing review of policies, priorities, and technology directions. These groups should include representatives of faculty, administrators, staff, and students. Representatives from the student government bodies will become increasingly vocal about their learning needs, information policies, and technology fee assessment. Their active participation in information technology planning should be considered.

Information technology plans need to provide a clear argument about benefits to the institution and user, requiring deans, department chairs, and faculty committees to make special efforts to be imaginative about what technology applications could accomplish in terms of academic mission and program objectives. These benefits must be presented in nontechnical language. In light of process reengineering, institutions are also interested in identifying cost savings to be achieved through streamlined or redesigned processes and technology solutions. There is a high expectation that new processes can be delivered at a lower cost and new technology solutions can therefore be funded out of this saving. Planners need to do a thorough analysis to support or counter these expectations. Reengineering often impacts people and work assignment. The analysis has to include a human resource view.

RECOMMENDATIONS

Academic planners may consider the following actions in initiating and supporting planning for the information technology area:

- Because of the high costs in IT investments, there should always be rigor and discipline in the planning and implementation process, deliverables, milestones and accountability.

- Executive sponsorship is critical for enabling and sustaining process change and financial commitment.

- The use of consultants and committees are instrumental in achieving leverage, objectivity, and buy-in.

- Effective communication throughout the planning and implementation phases is necessary in order to set appropriate user expectation.

- A balance between governance and decision making in the planning for information technology will help to keep momentum for visible results and acceptance of standards.

PRINT REFERENCES

Anandam, K., ed. 1989. "Transforming Teaching with Technology: Perspectives from Two-Year Colleges." *EDUCOM Strategy Series on Information Technology*. Washington, DC: EDUCOM and Academic Computing Publications.

Badagliacco, J. 1992. "Planning for Information Technology Resources: The Methods." In *Computing Strategies in Liberal Arts Colleges*, edited by M. Ringle. New York: Addison-Wesley.

Baltzer, J. 1994. *The Learning Action Plan: A New Approach to Information Technology Planning in Community College*. Boulder: CAUSE.

Chan, S. S. 1995. "Strategies for Restructuring IT Organizations." *CAUSE/EFFECT* 18(3): 13–19.

Dolence, M. and Norris, D. 1995. *Transforming Higher Education:: A Vision for Learning in the 21st Century*. Ann Arbor: Society for College and University Planning.

Ernst, D. J.; Katz, R. N.; and Sack, J. R. 1994. *Organizational Technological Strategies for Higher Education in the Information Age*. Boulder: CAUSE.

Fleit, L. 1994. *Self-Assessment for Campus Information Technology Services*. CAUSE Professional Paper #12. Boulder: CAUSE.

Graves, W. H., ed. 1989. *Computing across the Curriculum: Academic Perspective*. EDUCOM Strategy Series on Information Technology. Washington, DC: EDUCOM and Academic Computing Publications.

Hawkins, B. L., ed. 1989. *Organizing and Managing Information Resources on Campus*. EDUCOM Strategy Series on Information Technology. Washington, DC: EDUCOM and Academic Computing Publications.

HEIRAlliance. 1995. *Evaluation Guidelines for Institutional Information Resources*. Boulder.

Lynch, B. P., ed. Summer, 1995. *Information Technology and the Remaking of the University Library*. New Directions for Higher Education No. 90. San Francisco: Jossey-Bass Publishers.

Massy, W. F. and Zemsky, R. 1995. *Using Information Technology to Enhance Academic Productivity*. Washington, DC: EDUCOM, Interuniversity Communications Council, Inc.

Office of Computer and Information Systems, Pennsylvania State University. 1995. "Observations on Benchmarking Information Technology Support." *CAUSE/EFFECT* 18(1): 20–28.

Ringle, M., ed. 1992. *Computing Strategies in Liberal Arts Colleges*. New York: Addison-Wesley.

Smallen, D. 1992. "Planning for Information Technology Resources: The Issues." In *Computing Strategies in Liberal Arts Colleges*, edited by M. Ringle. New York: Addison-Wesley.

ELECTRONIC SAMPLER

http://cause-www.colorado.edu/
CAUSE (the association for managing and using information resources in higher education).

http://cause-www.colorado.edu/collab/heirapapers/hei0400.html
What Presidents Need to Know About the Payoff on the Information Technology Investment. HEIR Alliance Executive Strategies Report # 4.

HEIR is the Higher Education Information Resources Alliance of ARL, CAUSE, and Educom. It has published many other valuable reports.

http://educom.edu/

ELECTRONIC SAMPLER

EDUCOM (transforming higher education through information technology).

http://www.educom.edu/program/nlii/keydocs/massy.html
Using Information Technology to Enhance Academic Productivity. NLII (National Learning Infrastructure Initiative). William F. Massy and Robert Zemsky.
A white paper from the Wingspread Enhancing Academic Productivity Conference in June 1995.

http://www.educom.edu/web/pubs/review/teachLearnIndex.html
Teaching and Learning Index from Educom Review.

http://www.state.va.us/cim/cim.html
Virginia Council on Education Management.

http://www.thejournal.com/2hot/what.html
Technological Horizons in Education Online. T.H.E. Journal.

http://www.scup.org
SCUP's Planning Pages. SCUP (Society for College and University Planning).
SCUP, the publisher of this book, has information about SCUP's events and publications including its highly regarded journal, *Planning for Higher Education.* The URLs cited in this book are accessible through "SCUP's Planning Pages."

http://www.utahsbr.edu/tech/intror.htm

Information technology plays multiple roles in enabling an interactive knowledge network. As more traditional planning approaches may serve the needs for specific information technology initiatives, a more comprehensive, holistic approach is necessary to achieve long-term institutional results. From the information technology and service provider's perspective, the transformation starts from re-aligning its organization with institutional goals. From the institution's perspective, strategic thinking, process reengineering, and the re-examination of academic goals, delivery, and vision, should incorporate a clear definition of the roles and benefits of information technology in facilitating active and interactive pursuit of learning activities by the student.

ADDITIONAL READINGS

Both EDUCOM and CAUSE have publications addressing information technology strategies. These publications form a good basis for current issues and exemplary practices at different colleges and universities.

- *EDUCOM Strategy Series on Information Technology* provides an in-depth look at academic strategies (Graves, 1989; Anandam, 1989) and practices at community colleges (Anandam, 1989), liberal arts colleges (Ringle, 1992), and large institutions (Hawkins, 1989). These source books, although published several years ago, still provide a good insight on organizational and process issues.

- CAUSE has a professional series on a variety of current topics and best practice. The most useful source is from the online resource on current publications, CAUSE conference proceedings, and various CAUSE online discussion groups. ◆

- Staffing readiness with skill sets required for supporting new technology and organizational transformation should be part of the planning assumptions.

- There should be reasonable process reengineering commitment and experience in order to optimize returns of information technology investment.

- Commitment to training and development as part of implementation strategies is part of a holistic model.

In conclusion, a learner-centered academic environment in the information age calls for a transformation process and innovative applications of information technology to facilitate the learning process and delivery.

Student Services

Student Development:
An Integrated Approach
to the Age Old Pursuit

Diana L. Sharp and
G. Gary Grace

Planning the
Co-Curricular
Component

Gretchen Warner Kearney and
Stephen P. McLaughlin

he academic and affective realms of student development have been separated in the higher education environment for centuries. The authors look at the need to integrate both realms of student development and offer practical methods for incorporating student development outcomes into the planning process.

Student Development: An Integrated Approach to the Age Old Pursuit

Diana L. Sharp and G. Gary Grace

CORE PLANNING QUESTIONS

Student development has been viewed by some as an unsystematic byproduct that happens by chance. Although this has been invalidated by a growing body of literature, student development is still often considered elusive. Institutional planners and researchers have had difficulty understanding where student development fits into the planning and evaluation processes. Some of this confusion is inherent to the field, where a variety of labels have been used for what seem to be similar functions, and multiple theories and models have been used to develop activities and influence research. Student development functions have grown considerably over the years; however, their growth has been accompanied by a struggle for recognition and acceptance as a field. The organizational structure of higher education has also aggravated the confusion by ignoring differences between campus subcultures and often separating the intellectual from developmental growth of students. Such issues affect the academic planning processes. The core planning questions facing student development include:

- How can the evolving nature of student development and its subcultures contribute to effective, integrative academic planning?

- How can student development outcomes become an integral component of learner-centered higher education?

BASIC CONCEPTS

Labels related to student development. The labels for student development functions and subsequent organizational models are not as discrete as those in other fields. Some literature suggests that student development is concerned primarily with the impact of college on students (Pascarella and Terenzini, 1991). Others, like Creamer (1980), state that student affairs work comprises services that support the instructional mission of the institution and are intended to help students. These functions are known by many different names, including student personnel services, student affairs, and student development (Crookston, 1980). The philosophical underpinnings of one institution's "student development" and another institution's "student services" may be the same, while the array of service units reporting to each organization might be vastly different

Diana L. Sharp

is Executive Assistant to the Assistant Chancellor for Student Affairs for the University of Wisconsin-Parkside, Kenosha, Wisconsin.

G. Gary Grace

is Assistant Chancellor for Student Affairs for the University of Wisconsin-Parkside, Kenosha, Wisconsin.

in role and scope. Whatever they have been called, and regardless of which organizational units report to the area, there are three conceptual models that exemplify the organizational approach used at most institutions: functional services (units offering specific support functions that students need), environmental-interaction (units focusing on the interaction between aspects of the organization and student lives), and human development (units that focus on the holistic growth of students–intellectually, personally, spiritually, and physically). Many institutions use aspects of all three models in an eclectic organizational scheme.

The lack of a uniform organizational approach to student services leads to ambiguity about their purpose and philosophy. Some practitioners use the terms and organizational schemes interchangeably; others argue that there is purposeful distinction in the various labels. In any case, the organizational concepts and the philosophical orientations behind the labels are fuzzy and are influenced mostly by institutional tradition and practice. The models used in isolation or in combination at an institution reflect different assumptions as well as specific planning needs for the institution.

> *The historical roots of student development add to confusion about student-oriented services and their rightful place within the planning activity of the organization.*

Historical separation of affective and intellectual development. The historical roots of student development add to confusion about student-oriented services and their rightful place within the planning activity of the organization. As Rudolph (1962) points out, presidents and faculty in the middle- and late-1800s made efforts to rid themselves of responsibilities for student records, advising, and discipline. This movement gave way to the creation of separate freshman advising programs and special offices to handle a myriad of student matters, while the responsibility for the academic program remained with the president and faculty. By World War I, the separation of the intellectual and affective domains of students was evidenced by distinct offices for academic and social matters at most colleges and universities. The *Student Personnel Point of View* (ACE, 1937) served as a response to this separation, articulating a philosophy that affirmed the importance of the "whole person," a philosophy that "imposes upon educational institutions the obligation to consider the student as a whole—his intellectual capacity and achievement, his emotional make up, his physical condition, his social relationships, his vocational aptitudes and skills, his moral and religious values, his economic resources, and his aesthetic appreciations" (p. 49). This philosophy put "the emphasis… upon the development of the student as a person rather than upon his intellectual training alone" (p. 49). Over the past sixty years, this philosophy has had far-reaching impact on student affairs work, and the document has been nationally reaffirmed in 1949 and 1987 (NASPA, 1989).

The reintegration of academic and student affairs called for in *The Student Personnel Point of View* was aggravated by many post-World War II events, including the rapid expansion of colleges and universities necessitated by the introduction of the GI Bill and the accommodation of the "baby-boom" generation. Other student development changes occurred as a result of campus protests in the 1960s and the emergence of human development theory as a programming consideration for meeting the needs of college students. Some critics argue that student and academic affairs have never attained the integrated approach to education of the whole person envisioned in *The Student Personnel Point of View*.

It is clear that this brief history contains unresolved issues that have implications for student development within the broader context of institutional planning. Since much of institutional planning has been devoted to academic planning, it is important to note the organizational separation of responsibility for affective development from intellectual training. Some attempts at reintegration have been made, but there is still a schism at many colleges and universities between the intellectual (academic) and affective (social) development of college students. This gulf may be narrowed as our accreditation bodies, governing and legislative bodies, and the public-at-large hold our institutions more accountable for what happens to students at college and their learning outcomes. Recent emphasis on accountability and assessment of college and student outcomes may offer the most real opportunity in recent times for institutions to bring academic and student development together into a co-ordinated whole.

Student development subcultures. The existence of distinct cultural subgroups within colleges and universities also brings complexity to the prospect of planning and student development. Bergquist (1992) describes four distinct cultures within the academy:

- *Collegial*—represented most by the faculty and their emphasis upon rationality, is concerned with values of research and scholarship and the dissemination of knowledge.

- *Managerial*—values fiscal responsibility and supervisory effectiveness as it is used to achieve specified institutional and individual goals.

- *Developmental*—involved in program, service, planning and research activities that support cognitive, affective, and behavioral maturation of all students, faculty, administrators and staff.

- *Negotiating*—consists of individuals who find meaning in equitable and egalitarian policies and value the use of fair bargaining for the distribution of resources in ways that benefit the institution at large.

According to Bergquist (1992), rational planning can find root and support in at least three of the four student development subcultures, namely, collegial, developmental, and managerial. However, student development appears most often in the developmental culture.

Differences will exist when individuals from these varying subcultures try to work together or communicate without understanding the inherent cultural influences. Student development professionals focus on process-based growth of the whole student, while academic professionals emphasize content-based knowledge. Student development professionals are typically trained as generalists to work in vertical cross sections of the organizational structure. Academicians are typically trained as specialists in their disciplines and viewed as entrepreneurs in a more horizontal hierarchy. While student development professionals might emphasize qualitative methodologies for planning and research, academics might see more value in quantitative approaches. Each views and relates to their world based on their academic cultural heritage.

The inevitable value conflicts and differences of meaning between these roles and the cultures they represent requires a level of planning and strategy that captures a "rational sequence of activities that moves from research to development to packaging before dissemination takes place" (Bergquist, 1992, p. 199). Bergquist further observes that planning of this kind is massive, requiring meaningful relationships between and among the participants from each culture and active coordination of logical sequences of planning activity.

Role and scope of student personnel services. Student affairs professionals are involved in a wide variety of administrative support functions—from the recruitment of potential students, through the delivery of services upon entrance to the university, to their placement in jobs upon graduation (Garland, 1985). Often, the breadth of roles and responsibilities in student affairs contributes to an ill-defined identity on campus and to confusion about the stance student affairs professionals take vis-à-vis the academic mission of the institution. Student affairs exists for the purpose of contributing to the mission and goals of higher education (Hurst and Morrill, 1980). Although the role of student affairs professionals in the achievement of educational goals may differ from their academic counterparts in the classroom, the role must be compatible with and supportive of the overall educational mission. Hurst and Morrill(1980, p. 4) describe the primary roles of student services professionals as:

- To study and understand the student, environment, and the outcomes of their interaction in order to identify potential mismatches and needed interventions.

- Growing out of the first role, to facilitate student resource development by providing students with the skills, attitudes, and other resources they need to take advantage of and profit from the learning environment.

- To promote environmental resource development by restructuring and interventions designed to create the optimal environment within which human development may occur.

> *Often, the breadth of roles and responsibilities in student affairs contributes to an ill-defined identity on campus and to confusion about the stance student affairs professionals take vis-à-vis the academic mission of the institution.*

General theories of student development. For most of the twentieth century, student affairs professionals have employed both theories and models of student development to carry out the fundamental roles described by Hurst and Morrill. While student affairs professionals have focused primarily on human development theories over the years, they have also embraced a variety of other theories—from personality theory to systems theory—to help explain role expectations of college students and relationships among a host of variables under consideration (Moore and Upcraft, 1990). The genesis of student development grew from theories about personal growth and development. Psychological theorists using such theories as identity development (Erikson, 1968), integration and differentiation (Sanford, 1962), and vectors of development (Chickering, 1969), have influenced the way student affairs professionals think about college students. Theories of career development, such as that postulated by Holland (1966), have helped guide the work on vocational assessment and career choice.

Miller and Prince (1976) first defined student development as "the application of human development concepts in postsecondary settings so that everyone involved can master increasingly complex developmental tasks, achieve self-direction, and become interdependent." Drum (1980) later conceptualized student development as a process in which an individual undergoes a number of changes toward more complex behaviors that result from mastery of the increasingly demanding challenges of life. Drum describes a multidimensional model that charts development of three major life systems: (1) cognitive development (changes in how students think, solve problems, seek and evaluate knowledge), (2) development of self (changes in how students relate to the questions of essence and responsibility as well as how a sense of personal identity emerges), and (3) social development (changes in how students relate to friends and others, such as ethnic groups). Drum's dimensions are not assumed to be independent (substantial change in one dimen-

sion may result in change in another dimension); the dimensions are based upon several central developmental assumptions, such as "human development is characterized by growth toward more complexity, internal integration, and finer discrimination" (Morrill, Hurst, and Oetting, 1980, p. 25).

Specific theory-based student development. Beginning in the 1970s, the use of theory shifted to specific aspects of student development. Intellectual development theories such as Perry's (1970) and moral development theories (Kohlberg, 1971) were used to help explain reasoning and cognitive development of college students. Peer group influences (Newcomb and Wilson, 1966) were studied to understand the interpersonal aspects of the campus environment more fully. Ecological perspectives focused on the relationship between college students and their environment (Walsh, 1978). Astin (1985) conceptualized involvement theory to focus attention on why students learn best in a collegiate setting characterized by investment of physical and psychological energy in the academic experience. Schlossberg, *et al.* (1989) theorized student success as a function of the degree to which students are made to feel they matter at the institution. Tinto's (1987) work on freshman integration into college life suggested that student departure from a campus can be studied in distinct stages: separation, transition, and incorporation. Multiple theories expanded the general theories that informed the student development profession. Given the diversity of student bodies and the complexity of the campus environment, student affairs professionals could never depend on only one or two theories to guide their work. Various theories and models have been applied by practitioners to develop services and programs that maximize student development.

What do all these emerging theories actually mean for student affairs practitioners? Developmental theories can provide useful frameworks for understanding students and their needs, goals, attitudes, and problems, offering a context from which to design, implement, and evaluate programs and activities to serve students. Theoretical perspectives provide student affairs professionals with a rationale for their work and a framework for gathering and interpreting data in the field. As Brown and Barr (1990) observe, student affairs

Given the diversity of student bodies and the complexity of the campus environment, student affairs professionals could never depend on only one or two theories to guide their work.

professionals who have developmental perspectives often approach tasks differently from professionals who lack that perspective. Because many of the responsibilities of student affairs professionals can be approached from either a task orientation or a task and process point of view, the "whole person" can be considered in addition to the "how" and "why" of each task. It is this "whole student" perspective, centered on the learner instead of on the institution, that is advocated as the institution translates theories and practices into assessable student development outcomes.

How does student development translate into measurable outcomes in the higher education environment? Winston and Miller (1994) developed a practical model for assessing student development outcomes. They identify the themes traditionally identified in student development (academic, cultural, emotional, intellectual, moral, physical, purpose, and social-interpersonal) and offer examples of outcome variables that planners or researchers might pursue under each category:

- Evidence of academic literacy in the academic category;

- Cultural, racial, ethnic, and religious tolerance; intercultural exchange; and cultural literacy in the cultural component;

- Sexual identity, interdependence, personality characteristics, and life coping skills in the emotional category;

- Commitment in relativism (Perry, 1970, 1980) in the intellectual domain;

- Spiritual development (Fowler, 1981), stages of moral judgment (Kohlberg, 1973), and transcending moral relativism (Gilligan, 1980; Kohlberg and Kramer, 1969) in the moral category;

- Salubrious lifestyle (Winston and Miller, 1987) in the physical domain; and

- Intimacy, empathy, citizenship, and civility in the social-interpersonal component (Winston and Miller, 1994).

Using their model as a roadmap, and their themes as the guide, higher education professionals can collaboratively design, implement, assess, and revise programs and activities aimed at student development outcomes for their particular student body. As Bergquist (1992) advocates: the integration of academic and student affairs professionals, operations, and philosophies in the planning and assessment processes is imperative if institutions are serious about realizing student development outcomes. The overall institutional plan must be grounded with measurable and achievable student development goals that are tied to programs and activities throughout the institution. The regular assessment of student development outcomes could then feed new information into the planning processes and program development at the institution.

DATA SELECTION, COLLECTION AND MANAGEMENT

Data selection and collection. Most campuses collect student information related to admission, enrollment, retention and graduation. These quantitative data are captured through pre-admission testing, admission applications, registration forms, financial aid forms, orientation and other surveys, such as the Cooperative Institutional Research Program (CIRP) under the sponsorship of The American Council on Education. Data items are usually specific to the campus operation collecting the data (academic records for advising; financial background for financial aid packaging). Additional data fields may be collected if they are included in a pre-packaged software program or if a functional area has agreed to collect or store data items for another area's use. Federal and state regulations, institutional or systemwide policies, research interests of individuals or organizations, program reviews, auditing requirements, and other concerns often drive the collection of related data. Many of these data items are translated into reports that exist at most institutions, but may not be well circulated or understood. Some of the data items may not be in print, but may be available in electronic form.

Institutions usually have an array of instruments for collecting the data that they have historically identified as "necessary" for operations. These instruments may be developed by the institution, imposed by state or federal laws, or may come from a variety of vendors. Commercial surveys can be used to collect environmental-interaction data, student satisfaction data, and outcomes assessment data. Many

The overall institutional plan must be grounded with measurable and achievable student development goals that are tied to programs and activities throughout the institution.

vendors provide validity and reliability measures and normative data for campus comparisons. Strengths and limitations of the more popular instruments and their usage are often documented in journal articles or books, or can be obtained from professional organizations or accreditation groups.

Most professional organizations can provide the names and addresses of national, regional or local consultants who offer data collection instruments. Published resources for instruments include the *Mental Measurements Yearbook* (Conoley and Kramer, 1992), *Tests in Microfiche* (Educational Testing Service), *Tests in Print* (Mitchell, 1983), and *Student Services/Involvement Assessment Instruments, Institutional Effectiveness Assessment Instruments* (Clearinghouse for Higher Education Assessment Instruments, 1993). There is also an online Bibliographic Retrieval Service of the Educational Testing Service that provides access to their instruments. Vendors such as the American College Testing College Level Assessment and Survey Services (Iowa City, IA), Noel Levitz (Iowa City, IA), or Socratek (St. Paul, MN) are just a few of the many organizations that currently supply survey instruments related to student development.

Although a campus may collect a plethora of information, the items currently collected may not be sufficient to assess student development. Much of the information captured by campuses reflects the functional approach to student services (number of students per counselor, for example). Student development planning needs functional information, but also must be supported by environmental-interaction (student satisfaction with counseling received) and human development related information (life coping skills acquired in the counseling program).

Winston and Miller (1994) urge campuses to look beyond what is already collected. Because of the complexity of influences on student development, they suggest "using qualitative and quantitative methods and both direct and unobtrusive (institution records) measurements" (p. 10). Once student development outcomes are established, determining a variety of ways to measure them improves the opportunity to get a more complete picture of what is happening with students and a well-informed method of evaluating campus practice related to student development (Winston and Miller, 1994).

Qualitative research used in conjunction with quantitative measures may enhance information collected in student development and environmental-interaction areas. Focus groups (Krueger, 1988), diaries (Benjamin, 1990) and interviews (Siedman, 1991) can assist in the identification of assessment criteria and add new dimensions to particular strengths and weaknesses that may not be discernible from quantitative studies. Other qualitative methods suggested by Hanson (1991) include observable performance measures such as work samples or oral presentations, consensus rendering techniques that bring different constituent groups together to analyze whether and how an outcome has been achieved, or simulations such as in-basket exercises or case studies.

The data collection system process development. DeVellis (1991) suggests that before an institution picks assessment tools or designs the data collection processes, it needs to accomplish the following:

- Develop a concise definition of the outcomes to be measured;
- Determine the data needed to assess those outcomes;
- Determine the scale of measurement (such as Likert-type or Guttman-type);
- Have data items reviewed and evaluated by experts;
- Pilot the instrument with a representative group of students;
- Evaluate the pilot results for internal consistency, reliability, and scale structure;
- Optimize the scale based on these results; and
- Conduct a validity study of the final instrument.

The American College Personnel Association Commission IX published a useful guide for identifying instruments to assess certain constructs of student development (ACPA, 1990). Turning to the literature in student develop-

*S*tudent development planning needs functional information, but also must be supported by environmental-interaction... and human development related information.

ment research may offer campuses additional insights as they develop assessment criteria.

Research timing should be appropriate to the criteria being assessed. Baseline data must be collected early enough to reflect true starting points for students. Outcome data are captured after students have had significant academic and extracurricular experience and the time to incorporate new dimensions into their lives. The context of institutional life should also be taken into consideration. Information collected immediately following a campus crisis may be reflected in the data. Data collection approaches taken too late in the academic term may be a followup nightmare for the researcher; students are often too preoccupied with upcoming exams to respond, and once exams are completed, they quickly exit campus life.

DATA MANIPULATION AND INFORMATION DELIVERY

A combination of systematic data collection processes is necessary to bring student characteristics, environmental-interaction and satisfaction, and student development data together in the analysis process. Every method of data gathering has its strengths and weaknesses. The reliability and validity of the data can be derived from correlation of similar findings across a collection of approaches rather than one specific instrument–resulting in a full array of data by which the criteria for student development can be appropriately analyzed.

Functional approach. The functional approach uses reports every campus is familiar with: enrollment or admissions data broken out by student demographic characteristics or academic programs, or cost comparison information. Campuses tend to display functional data in very similar terms: retention charts, prospective student pool breakdowns, and audit indicators related to cost per student indices. Functional models focus on cost, time, and number of students served. Graphs or charts to display the data are typically offered in a common comparison basis related to the functional area (cost of leadership development activities over a five-year period, number of top quartile high school students who live in each residence hall, or the number of students of color involved in student government).

Environmental-interaction. Environmental-interaction models focus on satisfaction and environmental fit. Most campuses have formal reports on student satisfaction such as class evaluations or campus service unit/program evaluations. Informal reports on environmental-interaction or satisfaction include, but are not limited to, complaint letters, student newspaper columns, and personal interaction with constituents such as parents, students, alumni and colleagues. Graphs and charts are frequently used to display this data (such as the number of students highly satisfied with health services compared by services offered in that unit). Environmental-interaction data collection is gaining new strength as campuses look beyond satisfaction data to determine the underlying cause of student satisfaction or environmental fit. Data in this area can be displayed by using Moos' (1979) three dimensions (relationship, personal growth, and clarity of expectations) to help the institution know the "extent to which people are involved in a setting, the extent to which they support and help one another, and the extent to which they express themselves freely and openly… the basic goals of the setting… and the extent to which the environment is orderly and clear in its expectations, maintains control, and responds to change" (p. 15–17).

Comparing the reasons students leave the institution, or other factors, by each dimension may offer a new view of campus culture. Banning's (1978) *Campus Ecology: A Perspective for Student Affairs* is a good resource for information on ecological or environmental studies related to behavior-setting theory, personality types and model environments, subculture approaches, need-press culture theory, and transactional models. Banning's work considers the effect learners have on the institution as well as the effect the institution has on the learners.

Developmental models. Developmental models focus on the long term assessment of outcomes based on student development theory. Cross-sectional designs (sampling various cohorts by class standing) and longitudinal designs (following a certain group of students over time) are typically used for developmental

A combination of systematic data collection processes is necessary to bring student characteristics, environmental-interaction and satisfaction, and student development data together in the analysis process.

PRINT REFERENCES

American College Personnel Association (ACPA) Commission IV. 1990. *Clearinghouse list of environmental and student development assessment tools.* Bowling Green: Department of Student Affairs and Higher Education, Bowling Green University.

Astin, A. W. 1985. *Achieving Educational Excellence: A Critical Assessment of Priorities and Practices in Higher Education.* San Francisco: Jossey-Bass Publishers.

Banning. 1978. *Campus Ecology: A Perspective for Student Affairs.* Cincinnati: National Association of Student Personnel Administrators.

Benjamin, M. 1990. *Freshman Daily Experience: Implications for Policy, Research, and Theory.* University of Guelph Student-Environment Study Group.

Bergquist, W. H. 1992. *The Four Cultures of the Academy.* San Francisco: Jossey-Bass Publishers.

Brown, R. D. and Barr, M. J. 1990. "Student Development: Yesterday, Today, and Tomorrow." In *Theoretical Perspectives on Students*, edited by L. V. Moore. *New Directions for Student Services* No. 51. San Francisco: Jossey-Bass Publishers.

Chickering, A. W. 1969. *Education and Identity.* San Francisco: Jossey-Bass Publishers.

Clearinghouse for Higher Education Assessment Instruments. 1993. *Student Services/Involvement Assessment Instruments, Institutional Effectiveness Assessment Instruments.*

Conference on the Philosophy and Development of Student Personnel Work in College and University. 1937. *The Student Personnel Point of View. The American Council on Education Series I*, Volume 1(3). Washington, DC: American Council on Education (ACE).

Conoley, J. C. and Kramer, J. J., eds. 1992. *The Eleventh Mental Measurements Yearbook.* Lincoln: Buros Institute of Mental Measurements.

Creamer, C. G. 1980. "Issues in Student Development: From Models to Reality." In *Student Development in Higher Education: Theories, Practices and Future Directions*, edited by D. E. Creamer. San Francisco: American College Personnel Association.

Crookston, B. 1980. "Student Personnel: All Hail and Farewell." In *College Student Personnel Development Administration and Counseling*, edited by J. Eddy, J. D. Dameron, and D. T. Borland. Washington, DC: University Press of America.

DeVellis, R. F. 1991. *Scale Development: Theory and Applications.* Newbury Park: Sage.

Drum, D. 1980. "Understanding Student Development." In *Dimensions of Intervention for Student Development*, edited by W. H. Morrill and J. C. Hurst. New York: John Wiley & Sons.

Educational Testing Service. (updated quarterly). *Tests in Microfiche.* Princeton.

Erikson, E. H. 1968. *Identity: Youth and Crisis.* New York: Norton.

Fowler, J. W. 1981. *Stages in Faith: The Psychology of Human Development and the Quest for Meaning.* San Francisco: Harper & Row.

Garland, P. 1985. *Serving More Than Students: A Critical Need for College Student Personnel Services. ASHE-ERIC Higher Education Reports* No. 7.

Gilligan, C. 1980. "Restoring the Missing Text of Women's Development to Life Cycle Theories." In *Women's Lives: New Theory, Research, and Policy*, edited by D.G. McGuigan. Ann Arbor: University of Michigan, Center for Continuing Education of Women.

Hanson, G. 1991. "The Call to Assessment: What Role for Student Affairs." In *Puzzles and Pieces in Wonderland: The Promise and Practice of Student Affairs Research*, edited by K. J. Beeler and D. E. Hunter. Washington, DC: National Association of Student Personnel Administrators.

model assessments. The analysis of developmental data may be more complex as quantitative and qualitative data are merged to obtain a broad view of each of the developmental outcome criteria. The display of developmental data is often organized by developmental outcome criteria. Text combined with graphs, charts, and samples from interviews or diaries offer analysis snapshots of student groups under each of these criteria. The effectiveness of programs, services, curricula and other student interventions may be rated by the degree of influence on the holistic development of students or the influence of targeted programs on specific aspects of student development.

Cross functional approach to research. Since student development is not the sole province of any one group on campus, data analysis is best performed by a lateral cross-functional team involved in planning, data collection, analysis, implementation and review melded with student development theory models. Such an approach should help minimize philosophical differences regarding the assessment of student development, allowing concerns to be addressed throughout the process by team members. Ideally, it could unite the best thinking of the institution with the data needed to continue to improve programs and better meet the needs of an ever-evolving student clientele.

RECOMMENDATIONS FOR PLANNING FOR STUDENT DEVELOPMENT

Five recommendations are offered to improve the collaboration between academic and student development planning. First, student development goals must be integrated with the mission of the university, and particularly with instructional programs. Research in a variety of fields points to the intellectual and student development changes traditional and non-traditional aged college students experience. The affective side of the student's growth cannot be ignored. It must be recognized and planned for, just as academic programs and lessons are planned and recognized to expand the intellectual horizons of students. The impetus for this integration may flow from processes such as accreditation, accountability reports, or outcome assessments. These processes are excellent opportunities to begin bridging the gaps between intellectual and affective planning.

Second, although it may be unreasonable to assume that after more than a century of separation the intellectual and affective realms of student development can be easily integrated, there is no reason to ignore the positive impact of collaborative research and planning that may lead to a reunion. Planners and researchers need to bring together personnel from all backgrounds to perform broadly based assessment and provide input into processes that will offer the institution and its students opportunities for holistic improvement.

Student services and academic professionals must assess the aspects of planning in which they excel. Student services professionals are usually quite adept at reassessing and revising programs, activities, and plans to meet the varied issues (and crises) that each new semester brings. Academic planners may be more adept at long term planning and goal development. Each individual and each profession brings a wealth of talent, skill, and vision to the collaborative planning process. Planning professionals need to recognize multiple perspectives in the planning process.

The implicit assumptions behind subcultures and professional training need to be recognized; they affect collaboration and coordination efforts. Explicit and conscientious communication processes must be used to overcome negative influences. Planners must model an inclusive environment for institutional and programmatic planning and development. In this way, the holistic learner-centered plan can become integrated within the broad-based strategic planning and operational functions of an institution.

Third, planners need to move from roles typically focused at the upper administrative level to become expert consultants at the production/process/program stage. Here, together with those who implement programs, they could collaborate on structuring strategic questions, program designs, and evaluation schemes. Planners must share their expertise "in dialogue" with those closest to the students; those in front-line operations must share their expertise with planners. Both must work hand-in-hand to plan for, implement, and assess programs that help achieve desired student development outcomes. Ideally, students should also be included in this dialogue.

Fourth, planning processes need to be reshaped to include implementation strategies and continual re-evaluation as a part of the plan. As each new generation of students crosses the threshold into our classrooms and

PRINT REFERENCES

Holland, J. 1966. *The Psychology of Vocational Choice*. Waltham: Blaisdell.

Hurst, J. C. and Morrill, W. H. 1980. "Student Environmental Development as the Conceptual Foundation for Student Affairs." In *Dimensions of Intervention for Student Development*, edited by W. H. Morrill and J. C. Hurst. New York: John Wiley & Sons.

Kohlberg, L. and Kramer, R. 1969. "Continuities and Discontinuities in Childhood and Adult Moral Development." *Human Development*, 12(2): 93–120.

Kohlberg, L. 1971. "Stages of Moral Development." In *Moral Education*, edited by C. M. Beck, B. S. Crittenden, and E. V. Sullivan. Toronto: University of Toronto Press.

Kohlberg, L. 1973. "Continuities in Childhood and Adult Moral Development." In *Life-span Developmental Psychology: Personality and Socialization*, edited by P. Baltes and K. Schaie. New York: Academic Press.

Krueger, R. A. 1988. *Focus Group Interviews: A Practical Guide for Applied Research*. Newbury Park, CA: Sage.

Miller, T. K. and Prince, J. S. 1976. *The Future of Student Affairs*. San Francisco: Jossey-Bass Publishers.

Mitchell, Jr., J. V., ed. 1983. *Tests In Print: An Index to Tests, Test Reviews, and the Literature on Specific Tests* (3rd ed.). Lincoln: Buros Institute of Mental Measurements.

Moore, L. U. and Upcraft, M. L. 1990. "Theory in Student Affairs: Evolving Perspectives." In *Evolving Theoretical Perspectives on Students*, edited by L. Moore. *New Directions for Student Services* No. 51. San Francisco: Jossey-Bass Publishers.

Moos, R. H. 1979. *Evaluating Educational Environments*. San Francisco: Jossey-Bass Publishers.

Morrill, W. H.; Hurst, J. C.; and Oetting, E. R. 1980. *Dimensions of Intervention for Student Development*. New York: John Wiley & Sons.

National Association of Student Personnel Administration. 1989. *Points of View*. Washington, DC.

Newcomb, T. M. and Wilson, E. K., eds. 1966. *College Peer Groups: Problems and Prospects for Research*. Chicago: Aldine.

Pascarella, E. T. and Terenzini, P. T. 1991. *How College Affects Students: Findings and Insights from Twenty Years of Research*. San Francisco: Jossey-Bass Publishers.

Perry, W. G. 1970. *Forms of Intellectual and Ethical Development in the College Years*. New York: Holt, Rinehart and Winston.

Rudolph, F. 1962. *The American College and University: A History*. New York: Vintage Books.

Sanford, N., ed. 1962. *The American College*. New York: John Wiley & Sons.

Schlossberg, N. K.; Lunch, A. Q.; and Chickering, A. W. 1989. *Improving Higher Education Environments for Adults: Response Programs and Services from Entry to Departure*. San Francisco: Jossey-Bass Publishers.

Seidman, I. E. 1991. *Interviewing as Qualitative Research: A Guide for Researchers in Education and the Social Sciences*. New York: Teachers College Press.

Tinto, V. 1987. *Leaving College: Rethinking the Causes and Cures of Student Attrition*. Chicago: University of Chicago Press.

Walsh, W. B. 1978. "Person/Environment Interaction." In *Campus Ecology: A Perspective for Student Affairs*, edited by J. Banning. Cincinnati: National Association of Student Personnel Administrators.

Winston, R. B., Jr. and Miller, T. K. 1994. *A Model for Assessing Developmental Outcomes Related to Student Affairs Programs and Services*. NASPA Journal, 32(1): 2–19.

ELECTRONIC SAMPLER

http://vocserve.berkeley.edu/

NCRVE (National Center for Research in Vocational Education). University of California, Berkeley.

NCRVE is the nation's largest center for research and development in work-related education. Headquartered at the University of California at Berkeley since 1988, NCRVE has played a key role in developing a new concept of vocational education as the center works towards fulfilling its mission to strengthen education to prepare all individuals for lasting and rewarding employment, and lifelong learning.

http://www.acpa.nche.edu/

American College Personnel Association.

http://www.naspa.org

Student Affairs on the Internet. NASPA (National Association of Student Personnel Administration).

http://www.siu.edu/staffair/saihome.html

Student Affairs on the Internet. Southern Illinois University. David D. Shinn.

This is a project to understand the Internet's use and potential for student affairs.

Using any of the Web search engines, you can search for "student affairs" or "student development" and locate dozens, if not hundreds, of student affairs and student development Web pages from around the world.

http://www.wiu.edu/users/micpc/index.html#top

CPC (Curriculum Publications Clearinghouse). Department of Elementary Education and Reading, Western Illinois University

CPC exists through a funding agreement with the Illinois State Board of Education's Department of Adult, Vocational and Technical Education for the purpose of producing and distributing state-developed materials on a cost-recovery basis.

planning model that effectively integrates all pieces of the planning puzzle cannot be found. The assumption that turbulence will be eliminated by proper planning is also a myth. Planning in student development is a fluid process, not a static product. It is muddied by individual growth and development and an ever-changing mix of students. Linear plans are not effective and are conspicuously absent from modern theory in student development. Multidimensional circular or spiral models may be more appropriate for planning in student development. The conceptual model of units (functional, environmental-interaction, or human development) typically drives the data collection and planning processes. It needs to be tempered by the inclusion of differing views and models as planning for the planning process begins. Planners can help initiate the inclusion of differing views and help their institution take advantage of the variety of models available.

The interplay between model-building and evolving theories of student development has implications for current administrative software systems. Most student record system designs are insensitive to student developmental dimensions. Data elements seldom include student behavioral characteristics associated with student development. Only recently have co-curricular transcripts and similar developmental features appeared in software systems. Most of these new designs are add-ons to the administrative software and are not supported by most vendors.

The argument comes full circle: institutional planning gets back only what is put into the planning process. The integration of intellectual and affective realms will only take place one step at a time. Institutional planners have the opportunity to embrace or ignore the opportunity on their doorstep. ◆

residence halls, we need to be prepared for their new challenges. Student development and institutional planning are ever evolving processes that cannot remain static, cannot rely on yesterday's snapshot. Institutional planners are needed to help implementers predict and prepare for the future. The forward thinking higher education institution of the future will lead the paradigm shifts, not simply react to them.

Finally, all models by definition are incomplete, but some are useful. The perfect

*C*o-curricular programming has been shown to have a positive impact on student educational attainment, persistence to graduation, and career success. Because the co-curriculum supplements and supports classroom learning, it is vital that student affairs and academic affairs planners work together to develop, implement, and assess the effectiveness of these programs. The authors discuss ways in which this can be accomplished.

Planning the
Co-Curricular Component

Gretchen Warner Kearney and Stephen P. McLaughlin

CORE PLANNING QUESTIONS

What is the co-curriculum? Before exploring ideas for integrating the co-curricular component within the academic planning process, we must define the term "co-curriculum" (or "extracurriculum" in some institutions). According to Stage and Manning (1992, p. 65), "the co-curriculum includes any activity that takes place outside the college classroom." Or in the words of MacKinnon-Slaney (1993, p. 35), "co-curricular activities can be viewed as experiential learning augmenting the cognitive and theoretical perspectives of the classroom."

Co-curricular activities and services are generally thought to include student clubs and organizations; sports and cultural activities; leadership, wellness, and multicultural programming; experiential and service learning (volunteer work, internships); and student employment This definition is broadened to encompass direct academic support services such as tutoring, group study and mentoring programs, academic advising, counseling, and services for students with physical and learning disabilities. Co-curricular programming and services are typically located within the student affairs divisions of colleges and universities, although in some institutions academic support components such as tutoring, mentoring, academic advising, student disability services, and career/student employment services report through academic affairs.

At least some of the cultural and athletic programs offered on many campuses are either planned through academic affairs or are a joint responsibility of the academic and student affairs divisions. An example of one such collaborative venture is a holiday program entitled "Let Us Light Candles," a narrated musical performance presented by the University of Wisconsin-Parkside Office of Student Life in collaboration with three academic departments–English, Music, and Dramatic Arts. This program is used throughout the chapter to illustrate various aspects of co-curricular planning.

Why is the co-curriculum important? The theoretical basis for the importance of the co-curriculum comes from a number of research sources. Tinto's model of student persistence, discussed in his book *Leaving College* (1993) has generated a large body of research that overwhelmingly documents the importance of student co-curricular involvement. This research correlates students' satisfaction, success in college, and ultimately persistence to graduation with both their social and their academic integration into the life of

Gretchen Warner Kearney

is the Director, Office of Educational and Career Development for the University of Wisconsin-Parkside, Kenosho, Wisconsin. Warner Kearny became a member of SCUP's Academic Planning Academy in 1995 and is currently Convener of that academy.

Stephen P. McLaughlin

is the Dean of Students for the University of Wisconsin-Parkside, Kenosha, Wisconsin.

the college. Many studies have found that involvement outside the classroom can positively affect students' critical thinking ability and other forms of cognitive development (Terenzini, 1993).

Pascarella and Terenzini (1991) analyzed twenty years of research on the topic and conclude that "extracurricular involvement has a positive impact on educational attainment" (p. 624). They explain that students who are involved in co-curricular activities often enter college with higher educational aspirations than other students, and that these active students form peer groups to reinforce their aspirations. They also present evidence that extracurricular involvement, especially when students are placed in leadership roles, has a moderately positive impact on career success after graduation from college. Student-faculty interaction outside the classroom is a related factor that positively impacts student values and attitudes, career choice, student persistence, and cognitive development. One way in which this kind of interaction can be achieved is through participation in co-curricular events.

Co-curricular planning differs from other kinds of planning in its emphasis on qualitative measures deriving from student development theory and the learning outcomes process.

> *Co-curricular planning differs from other kinds of planning in its emphasis on qualitative measures deriving from student development theory and the learning outcomes process.*

Movement in this area has been away from production-centered planning, which has traditionally focused on such quantitative measures as student/faculty ratio, number of library volumes, total institutional budget, and faculty workload.

What nationwide trends are affecting co-curricular planning? Because co-curricular programs focus on students and student needs, it is not surprising that the rapidly changing demographics of today's college-going population are having a significant impact on program planning. The white, traditional-aged student who lives in a campus residence hall and enrolls in classes full-time is rapidly becoming a thing of the past. A more likely matriculant today is an older female minority student who commutes to campus, works off-campus, and balances a variety of time-consuming family responsibilities. Garland and Grace (1993)

present a concise profile of today's college students: over half are women, almost half attend college part-time, more than 20 percent are minorities, the median age is 28, and an ever-rising number have a disability or are academically underprepared.

To respond to these new, diverse groups of students, co-curricular initiatives, as well as other student services and academic programs, will increasingly have to be restructured to address their various levels of social and academic preparation, needs, and expectations. Program design and implementation will have to stress flexibility, accessibility, presentation in new formats (at off-campus sites such as corporations, shopping malls, and training centers, and through information technology), and specialized content focused on particular student groups. Academically underprepared students, for example, require an increasing variety of special support services and intervention strategies including tutoring, group study opportunities, mentoring, developmental course sequences, intrusive academic advising, and career counseling.

What are the most common obstacles to co-curricular planning? A number of obstacles to planning are inherent in the fact that, at most institutions, the co-curriculum is housed primarily within the domain of student affairs. As such, it is often perceived as an unnecessary luxury, a frill that can easily be eliminated without consequence when budgets get tight. As explained in Chapter 10, the prevailing assumption on many campuses is that student affairs professionals are responsible for students' social development (including discipline, personal issues, and other support functions), while the faculty control the direction of students' intellectual growth—a task more central to the college's mission of teaching and learning. Over time this assumption has led to the development of a conceptual gap between individuals who do co-curricular planning, and those who engage in academic (curricular) planning. Many institutions have thus failed to forge linkages between students' co-curricular experiences and what occurs within the classroom—a failure that has had a negative impact on students' personal development as well as their academic experience (Seldin and Associates, 1990).

Another obstacle arises when the lines of planning responsibility are blurred. In the case of "Let Us Light Candles," planning is done jointly by three separate academic departments and the student life division. Co-curricular programming frequently calls for such collaborative efforts between student and academic affairs planners. Unfortunately, they often result in poorly conceptualized and executed programs when no one from either area takes sufficient initiative to carry out the planning process thoroughly or cooperatively. Exacerbating the problem is the fact that the academic affairs and student affairs planning cycles are commonly out of synch. On campuses where students are enrolled in classes year round, student affairs programs and planning are conducted on an ongoing, twelve-month basis. In contrast, many academicians and faculty operate on a nine-month calendar.

Co-curricular programs are generally held on weekends, in the evenings, and during lunch hours when students with tight schedules (and little time to spend on campus) can attend. In the case of academic support programs, services must be made available on an emergency or short-term basis in response to student need. Tutoring, testing, academic advising, and career counseling are ongoing support services and are generally offered throughout the summer and between semesters as well as during the academic year. These delivery modes may not coincide with course schedules or with the academic calendar, which is often published years in advance and is relatively unchanged from one year to the next. In order to be effective, co-curricular planning needs to be collaborative, systematically including both academic and student affairs personnel. Later in the chapter recommendations are examined for facilitating this kind of interaction.

BASIC CONCEPTS

Environmental factors. Co-curricular planning is not linear in nature—that is, it does not always flow logically in a neat, stepwise pattern. Rather, because of the diverse nature of today's students and the often overlapping functional boundaries between academic and student affairs as they pertain to the co-curriculum, the process needs to be flexible and synergetic. Before beginning to plan, careful consideration should be given to both the internal and external environments of the institution as they might affect program effectiveness. These environmental influences

could include faculty, staff, student governance groups, community and alumni organizations, and informal power structures that exist at the institution. Resistance to planning is still high on many campuses, and it can be easy to underestimate the degree of resistance any particular plan might engender (Norris and Poulton, 1991). Therefore, it is vital that any planning effort be centrally coordinated, that it receive financial and political support from institutional leaders, and that it be accomplished within the context of the institution's mission statement.

Other factors to consider include resource availability, institutional size (Can it support the type and scale of the proposed program?), and the residential or commuter character of the campus. It is much more difficult to attract students to co-curricular programs at nonresidential institutions since most students who commute to two- and four-year campuses have jobs, families, and other responsibilities. Many planning models are based on the assumption that most students live on campus even though the opposite situation prevails today. Nonresidential students are primarily interested in an educational, not social, experience.

In order to attract commuting students, it is helpful to tie co-curricular programming to classroom experiences or related academic topics. It is often most successful to schedule programs and activities during the lunch hour, immediately before or after class times, or during an established "activity hour" during which it is agreed that no classes will be held. Offering educational programs that can be enjoyed by the entire family and providing on-site child care are strategies to attract older, commuting students.

Finally, although in theory the co-curriculum serves all students attending an institution, the growing diversity of today's student population precludes any one program meeting all needs. Before beginning to plan a program, careful thought should be given to which student group(s) will be targeted and why these groups have been identified.

Co-curricular planning model. Co-curricular planning is usually internally-directed,

*R*esistance to planning is still high on many campuses, and it can be easy to underestimate the degree of resistance any particular plan might engender.

focusing on the needs and development of students at a particular institution. It is often accomplished over a short time frame. Thus, while some of the elements of strategic and long-term planning processes may be applicable, operational or tactical planning models that focus on the shorter term, are more appropriate. Stage and Manning (1992) advocate the use of Russell's (1982) model for recreational and co-curricular programming. Six basic elements form the model:

- Needs assessment;
- Determination of program objectives;
- Generation of program possibilities;
- Program development;
- Program implementation; and
- Program evaluation.

The growing diversity of today's student population precludes any one program meeting all needs. Before beginning to plan a program, careful thought should be given to which student group(s) will be targeted and why these groups have been identified.

Depending upon the kind of co-curricular program under consideration, a cross-disciplinary planning team with representatives from both student and academic affairs should be formed to work together through all stages of the process. This team should also include student representatives from the target group(s) toward which the program is focused. From the outset, this strategy should increase support (personal and financial) for the program, reduce existing political tensions, and assist in integrating co-curricular programming within the academic affairs planning cycle.

Needs assessment. The first phase, is best accomplished through **collection of both quantitative and qualitative data**; a process that may be time-consuming but will give a much more balanced, accurate, and useful profile of the needs of the target population than any one kind of data alone. This phase needs to be accomplished in conjunction with stage six, evaluation or outcomes assessment. Together, the two constitute an ongoing system of co-curricular planning and evaluation. Because most student outcomes are influenced by a wide variety of programs, events, and environmental and background factors (Winston and Miller, 1994), both the needs and outcomes assessment phases of programming should use multiple measures.

Before collecting any new data, the co-curricular planning team should examine information already available. When generating new data, informal focus groups and interviews can be used, along with minutes of student organization meetings, attendance figures from similar past programs, institutionally-developed surveys, and nationally-normed instruments such as the ACT student profile and the CIRP survey of incoming freshmen developed by the Higher Education Research Institute. Planners should carefully consider the reliability and validity of an instrument before using it. They should also look for indications that a particular instrument may be culturally biased–a growing concern as our student bodies become more diverse. A number of available books and research articles explain how to plan programs for specific student populations. These are listed in the bibliography at the end of the chapter.

Phase two, **determination of program goals and objectives**, is based upon the results of the student needs assessment. Since not all student needs can be met through a single program, the planning team must establish goal priorities. In order to do so, team members can interpret the collected data and determine what student outcomes (behavioral and/or cognitive) should result from the proposed program. It is vital that goal setting be selective and collaborative, actively involving all members of the team. This phase must also be realistic, taking into account available resources as well as potential barriers and limitations. Barriers might include existing policies, political controversies, and staffing limitations. Strategies for overcoming them should be identified, but if they appear insurmountable, it is realistic for the team to consider scaling back or scuttling the program. Finally, goals must be measurable to provide a basis for later evaluation of the program. The team should decide what quantifiable outcomes (objectives) would be necessary in order for the program to be considered a success. At this point, a method of measuring the outcomes may need to be identified and pre-tested.

The third phase involves team **brainstorming of potential programs** that might fit the student needs and program goals and objectives defined in the earlier two phases. This is a creative, collaborative process. Existing programs are fair game for discussion, particularly if they can be expanded or changed in some way to accommodate the activity or event under consideration. At the end of this stage, the team should narrow its options to one preferred program or event or a series of related programs.

During phase four, the planning team **develops the co-curricular program**. This stage requires a brutally realistic appraisal of costs and any other limits to program effectiveness. Stage and Manning (1992) have designed a matrix that can be used for making decisions about programming costs. Program objectives can be placed on the left-hand side of the matrix, while various cost levels (low, medium, and high) are placed along the top. When the budget is tight, an increasingly common condition, tradeoffs have to be made to achieve program objectives.

The fifth phase of the process is **program implementation**. Depending upon the kind of program, the team may decide to conduct a pilot or trial program with a small group of students. Particularly when the full-scale event will be expensive to produce, a pilot program that is evaluated thoroughly following implementation can be highly cost-effective. Whether or not the program is a pilot or the "real thing," students and staff who are not on the planning team will probably be involved in its implementation, and care must be taken to ensure that these individuals understand why and how the program was developed. In addition, members of the planning team should attend the event itself so that they have direct experience so important in the final evaluation stage.

The final phase, which should be ongoing if the program will be implemented on a regular basis, is **evaluation or outcomes assessment**. As Stage and Manning (1993) point out, this stage is very much like the needs assessment phase in that several kinds of evaluation should be conducted in order to get the broadest possible range of responses. In addition to the evaluation methods described for use during needs assessment, typical outcome measures include:

- Portfolio analysis (in which examples of a student's work or experiences in planning or implementing an activity are gathered together);
- Student satisfaction instruments;
- Persistence and graduation rate data;
- Developmental transcript analysis (Winston, Miller, and Prince, 1979);

- Pre- and post-testing for learning, behavioral, or attitudinal change;
- Findings from student focus groups; and
- Institutional climate/environment surveys.

For greatest effectiveness, these measures should be used in conjunction with needs assessment data generated during phase one of the planning process. Outcomes assessment should combine quantitative and qualitative measures as well as cross-sectional and longitudinal designs. A systematic assessment effort can use several different approaches, including functional, environmental interaction, developmental, or cross-functional for effective analysis and display of co-curricular data. (See Chapter 10 for a full discussion of these different approaches.) This final outcomes assessment phase must lead, in circular fashion, back through the other five stages as part of a continuous process in order for the planning cycle to be effective and dynamic.

The planning team should develop, in advance, strategies that can be used to deal with low student response rates and low program interest and participation. This is particularly true of co-curricular planning for nonresidential students. Strategies may include:

- Obtaining survey responses from audience members or participants immediately following an event/performance;
- Conducting assessments in classrooms where students are a "captive audience";
- Designing a personal follow-up process when participants or groups can be identified;
- Providing incentives (food, prizes, money) to respondents;
- Including self-addressed return envelopes or postcards with mailed surveys; and
- Using telemarketers to survey program participants.

On campuses with touchtone registration systems, the researcher can program the system to ask a series of questions and automatically dial a random sample of students. The campus management information system

The planning team should develop, in advance, strategies that can be used to deal with low student response rates and low program interest and participation.

should also be used as it can collect and assimilate a tremendous amount of specific data for analysis. Although this kind of information is readily available on most campuses, it is seldom used for program planning.

The "Let Us Light Candles" program illustrates this six-step process. Initially, a member of the student affairs staff conducted a qualitative needs assessment by interviewing a cross-section of students, staff, and faculty at the university. Results of the assessment indicated a high level of interest in the proposed program and confirmed that it would fill an important educational need. To form a planning team, the student affairs staff member approached faculty in the English and music departments as well as a student member of the campus activities board. Together, these team members developed a set of goals and objectives to meet the needs articulated in the assessment phase. The primary outcome defined for this program was to educate the campus and community about diverse holiday traditions.

The team spent the next several weeks brainstorming ideas as to how the goals and objectives could be accomplished and what artistic and program components would need to be included. Once the brainstorming had concluded, and the ideas had been translated into useable concepts, the team proceeded to develop the program. This included writing the narrative, selecting the music, designing a set, developing a promotional plan, and delineating a budget. During the fifth phase of the effort, the team invited students and instructors to two matinee performances. Following each program, an informal survey was conducted to gauge general reactions to the program and to discover what members of the audience had learned. In retrospect, team members felt they should have developed a formal evaluation tool to determine more accurately the impact and usefulness of the program and to discover whether the program met the originally stated goals and objectives. Using the survey instrument, each year's performance would then reflect the evaluation results of the previous year's program. This information could have been critical in making needed

> *The campus management information system should also be used as it can collect and assimilate a tremendous amount of specific data for analysis.*

changes and in determining whether or not the program should have been offered the following year.

The program was developed within a relatively short time frame (and without the benefit of Russell's planning model!). Nevertheless, the planning process for this program can be used to illustrate some of the steps that can be taken to plan a successful new co-curricular event.

"Let Us Light Candles" can also be used to illustrate how to measure co-curricular outcomes, utilizing several different but appropriate tools. A survey could be distributed at each performance, asking audience members whether they learned something new about the holiday traditions presented and whether their expectations concerning program content and quality were met. A pre-test could be administered to students to determine their level of awareness and understanding of various religious traditions before attending the performance. A post-performance assessment could be administered to measure changes in knowledge (concerning various religious observances presented) or behavior (whether respondents exhibited increased tolerance for the ways in which other cultures and religions celebrate the holidays). Focus groups conducted before the event and immediately afterward could also indicate whether a desired learning outcome occurred. Finally, co-curricular planners would want to see some quantitative data in order to know whether or not attendance figures met expectations and whether revenue projections for the event were reached.

MANIPULATION, DELIVERY, AND ACTIONABILITY ISSUES

Why is the data collected on co-curricular programs often not useful to academic planners? It is difficult to find information useful or meaningful when one cannot gauge the effect of a program on the institution's "bottom line." In order to demonstrate that co-curricular programs have an important impact on students that in turn affect the institution in favorable and significant ways, program planners must demonstrate that students who attend/participate in these programs learn or develop in ways that differentiate them from their peers who do not attend/participate. While on the surface the impact of most co-curricular programs is highly subjective, a direct relationship does exist between the retention of satisfied students and the budgetary implications of such satisfaction. If we know that satisfaction results from student expectations being met by the university, and the university promotes its co-curricular programs as part of the student recruitment process, then it follows that these programs influence recruitment, retention, satisfaction, loyalty, and graduation rates.

One way in which planners can discover whether co-curricular programs are important to student satisfaction is to use the university database to survey prospective students who visit the campus. This information can help determine whether the availability of specific programs is instrumental in a student's decision to attend the institution. The university's institutional research office can correlate the data with students' academic performance and with retention and graduation rates to determine the impact of various programs on the university's bottom line.

Another way to measure co-curricular impact is to analyze the experiential portion of a program. For example, students who are involved in the promotional aspects of "Let Us Light Candles" can have their hands-on experience analyzed as it applies to learning in a marketing class. Other courses for which this experience could be relevant include theater set design, musical performance, box office management/audience development, public relations, and promotional writing. This concept could be further expanded through the development of credit-bearing internships and practica in a variety of academic disciplines. Related measures include instructor and student evaluations of the experience, data on how many students have taken advantage of experiential learning, and whether this number has increased each year, and alumni surveys indicating how helpful the experience was to students' career growth after graduation.

How can co-curricular data be interpreted, displayed, and distributed so that it is used effectively by other planners on campus? Planners tend to use data most when it is summarized in a brief, concise format. This is problematic in the area of co-curricular programming. Because of the overlapping planning functions in this area, information is often collected by several different offices

and is not widely distributed or shared in a systematic way. It is essential that data on co-curricular programs and outcomes be made available to both student services and academic affairs planners so the institution can make good decisions regarding limited resources and so the importance of such programs is understood.

There are a variety of technological tools available to assist in data display and dissemination. Planners should be able to access data via electronic mail and through online databases. Other formats may include executive summaries, presentations on videotape, newsletters, and news releases in the campus and community newspapers. Specialized reports focusing on the mission and goals of various offices and divisions within the university can also "get the message across" effectively. Winston and Miller (1994) suggest that student quotations gleaned through interviews and focus groups can "humanize" data and make it more meaningful than graphs and statistical tables.

It is essential that data on co-curricular programs and outcomes be made available to both student services and academic affairs planners so the institution can make good decisions regarding limited resources and so the importance of such programs is understood.

RECOMMENDATIONS

First, it is vital that co-curricular planning be accomplished within the context of the institution's mission statement and that it be influenced by the vision of the chief executive. When the mission statement is inaccurate or weak and when the chief executive has failed to articulate a vision for the institution, the planning process becomes extremely difficult.

Second, the planning process should not become too prolonged. Co-curricular planning must reflect the institutional environment, which is in a constant state of flux. Programs must often be developed and implemented quickly in order to take full advantage of current events on campus and in the larger community.

Third, collaborative linkages between student and academic affairs must be built into the planning process. These two areas should work as functional teams (Garland and Grace, 1993) and take joint ownership of co-curricular planning and outcomes assessment. The

PRINT REFERENCES

Cheatham, H. E., ed. 1991. *Cultural Pluralism on Campus*. Alexandria: American College Personnel Association Media.

Garland, P. H. and Grace, T. W. 1993. *New Perspectives for Student Affairs Professionals: Evolving Realities, Responsibilities and Roles. ASHE-ERIC Higher Education Report* No. 7. Washington, DC: George Washington University, School of Education and Human Development.

MacKinnon-Slaney, F. Spring, 1993. "Theory to Practice in Co-Curricular Activities: A New Model for Student Involvement." *College Student Affairs Journal* 12(2): 35–40.

Norris, D. M. and Poulton, N. L. 1991. *A Guide for New Planners*. Ann Arbor: Society for College and University Planning.

Pascarella, E. T. and Terenzini, P. T. 1991. *How College Affects Students: Findings and Insights from Twenty Years of Research*. San Francisco: Jossey-Bass Publishers.

Russell, R. 1982. *Planning Programs in Recreation*. St. Louis: Times-Mirror/Mosby.

Seldin, P., and Associates. 1990. *How Administrators Can Improve Teaching*. San Francisco, CA: Jossey-Bass Publishers.

Stage, F. K. and Manning, K. 1992. *Enhancing the Multicultural Campus Environment: A Cultural Brokering Approach. New Directions for Student Services* No. 60. San Francisco: Jossey-Bass Publishers.

Stage, F. K., ed. 1992. *Diverse Methods for Research and Assessment of College Students*. Alexandria: American College Personnel Association Media.

Tinto, V. 1993. *Leaving College: Rethinking the Causes and Cures of Student Attrition* (2nd ed.) Chicago: The University of Chicago Press.

Winston, R. B. and Miller, T. K. 1994. "A Model for Assessing Developmental Outcomes Related to Student Affairs Programs and Services." *NASPA Journal* 32(1): 2–19.

Winston, R. B.; Miller, S. C.; and Prince, J. S. 1979. *Student Developmental Task Inventory* (2nd ed.) Athens: Student Development Associates, Inc.

Wright, D. J., ed. 1987. *Responding to the Needs of Today's Minority Students. New Directions for Student Services* No. 38. San Francisco: Jossey-Bass Publishers.

ELECTRONIC SAMPLER

http://sshe7.sshechan.edu/mayplan.html
   Imperatives for the future: A plan for Pennsylvania's state system of higher education.
   An excellent document to peruse on how co-curricular facets of higher education are woven through an entire strategic plan.

http://w3.wo.sbc.edu/Co-curricular/home.html
   The Sweet Life@SBC. Office of Co-Curricular Programs, Sweet Briar College.

http://www.siu.edu/plan.html
   Priority Issues for SIU. Southern Illinois University.
   This is the pertinent portion of the Southern Illinois University strategic plan.

http://www.uwp.edu/
   Home page. University of Wisconsin-Parkside.

co-curriculum is by definition "experiential learning augmenting the cognitive and theoretical perspectives of the classroom" (MacKinnon-Slaney, 1993, p.35), and these two components must be planned and assessed in an integrated way if the resulting programs and evaluative data are to be understood and supported by both the student and academic affairs communities. Through reengineering analyses, some institutions have made bold organizational changes to foster collaborative linkages. Combining the position of the academic vice president with that of the student development officer has met with success in community colleges and four-year institutions of moderate size.

Fourth, new information technology should be used whenever possible to improve the analysis, presentation, and dissemination of data. Email, online databases, and computer analysis and formatting are examples. Although usually limited to processing transactions, administrative software systems should be examined as well for their potential to capture and report student development information usable to a variety stakeholders including students, managers, advisors, and faculty.

Fifth, co-curricular planning is not a static process. Evaluation, as the last step in Russell's (1982) planning model, has to be revisited continuously . Often, evaluation needs to be done at times other than the conclusion of a program because new information that could alter program delivery is constantly being collected.

Sixth, it is vital for co-curricular planners to demonstrate how programs in this area benefit the curricular and institutional "bottom lines." Illustrating the budgetary implications of retaining and graduating satisfied, successful students is one approach. The co-curriculum affects the academic bottom line directly when departments establish internships, practica, and volunteer experiences that tie in with different programs to give students "hands-on" experience and complement the academic component.

Finally, because campuses comprise numerous subcultures and diverse racial and ethnic groups, it is difficult to define the exact students we are targeting for co-curricular programming efforts. Co-curricular planners need to incorporate multiple perspectives into the planning process in order to serve various student constituencies. Diverse perspectives must be sought from faculty, staff, and students by incorporating a variety of ethnic and age groups into all phases of the planning process. ◆

Academic Planning within the Larger Context

Integrating Academic and Facilities Planning

Dilip M. Anketell

Connecting Academic Plans to Budgeting: Key Conditions for Success

Thomas K. Anderes

The link between academic planning and facilities planning is often strong in theory but weak in practice. Facilities planning can be successful only when it is integral to the overall mission and goals of an institution, and when all facets of the academic community are represented at every step along the way of the planning process.

Integrating Academic and Facilities Planning

Dilip M. Anketell

INTRODUCTION

The integration of academic and facilities planning usually occurs either through a broad range of activities that incorporate academic needs into the design, construction, and use of a new building, or when institutions coordinate key elements of their strategic plan into a concise planning tool.

A fundamental tenet of the planning process dictates that the "academic plan" guides and directs the physical and facilities planning on any campus. However, defining and crystallizing academic objectives into an orderly set of priorities and principles is difficult for institutions governed by faculty accustomed to independence and autonomy. Increasingly, the complexity of higher education institutions and the regulations that are imposed on them make specialization, compartmentalization, and even competition more common on campus than collaboration. Increased specialization often leads to a lack of communication and knowledge about the overall mission of the organization. Thus, physical and facilities planners often become frustrated when they attempt to convince their academic colleagues and executive management to develop an academic plan.

Although this chapter focuses primarily on the processes that integrate academic and facilities planning, some fundamental questions must first be explored.

- Why plan?

- How do planners get key decision makers to plan?
- Should planners be a part of the decision-making process?
- How can planners establish and maintain an institutional commitment to continuous planning?

Effective planning leads to a rational process of defining and clarifying purpose or mission. An institution's academic plan, an identification of program strengths, areas of expertise, and selected priorities where the institution wants to focus its attention and resources, should serve as the foundation for an integrative planning process. The lack of a clear, well defined academic plan, however, inhibits the planning process, much like trying to start a car without an ignition key.

CORE PLANNING QUESTIONS

Planning is a fragile profession, inherent in its grounding in the soft sciences, heavily dependent on the political climate, and the acumen of the planner-proponent for its success. Universally embraced as essential to sound policy practice, planning is rarely mandated or required by statute. Further, as middle managers, planners often fail to exert significant influence on decision makers or the decision making process. Yet, effective planning

Dilip M. Anketell

is an Educational Planning and Management Consultant with dilip m. anketell & associates, Riverside, California. Anketell is the Associate Convener of SCUP's Facilities Planning Academy and a frequent presenter at SCUP's annual international conference.

requires clear support from the president or chancellor and their executive officers.

Why plan? Higher education is redefining and transforming itself from inside and outside the academy. Changing environments, external competition, new clientele, uncertainty of resources, a growing diversity of stakeholders and mission complexity together demand the use of managerial tools to prevent organizational fragmentation. To successfully manage the transformation of higher education and guide its future, institutions must view comprehensive and integrative planning as an essential tool.

How do you get decision makers to plan? Often, the arrival of a new chief executive officer provides an opportunity to begin a planning process because administrative change affects reassessment and evaluation of existing policies and procedures. External challenges also encourage planning efforts because society today demands accountability from higher education as well as other institutions. To provide educational services efficiently, institutions must determine priorities and judiciously allocate scarce resources. (The University of California, for example, was forced to embark on long range development planning to justify funding support for enrollment growth and the creation of new campuses.)

Should staff planners be a part of the process? Involvement of a staff planner can improve communication. The planner can provide feedback on questions about program-to-facility compatibility, costs, adjacency requirements and other issues, including feasibility. Collaboration between academic and physical planners through team-based project management fosters ongoing commitment to planning by senior management.

What type of plan? Historically, campus plans followed the "city beautiful" style of planning, commonly referred to as "master plans." The deliverable product usually resulted in an elaborate multicolored drawing, depicting existing and future buildings with adjacent malls and walkways. The illustrative drawings, often limited in text, provided the viewer/ reader a clear vision of the campus at the time

During the past decade, an approach similar to a general city plan that includes many constituencies has evolved as an effective way to depict campus growth.

of construction completion, but described little about the extensive, necessary decision process followed to reach that point.

During the past decade, an approach similar to a general city plan that includes many constituencies has evolved as an effective way to depict campus growth. An outgrowth of concerns over environmental problems, the participative approach to a Long Range Development Plan (LRDP) replaced "master plans" in the planning vocabulary. LRDPs establish broad land use policy and direction for campus growth, and include text that outlines and prescribes enrollment trends, planning assumptions and land use requirements.

BASIC CONCEPTS

Comprehensive planning requires a participative team approach to achieve a broad perspective of the institution's vision. Comprehensive planning also requires a continuous process, segmented at specific, regular intervals only to create milestones or benchmarks to manage data.

Figure 1 (Campus Planning and Implementation Wheel) illustrates the comprehensive planning approach. The initial step, the development of the academic plan, defines the vision and mission statement to establish institutional direction and provides a framework for the deliberations that will follow. These plans often contain broad statements of direction for each division college or school. However, the plan must also include sufficient details of future growth (or retrenchment) for campus planners. The academic planning document should contain:

- The planning horizon (time frame);
- A list of existing programs, enrollment history and future projections;
- A list of new program initiatives, including
  - start dates by program level (AA, BS/ BA, MS/MA, PhD)
  - enrollment trends by level to build-out
  - program growth rate estimations;
- Existing program space and needs projections;
- New program initiatives and projected space needs;
- New program adjacency requirements;
- Annual operating budget development; and
- Annual capital program budget development.

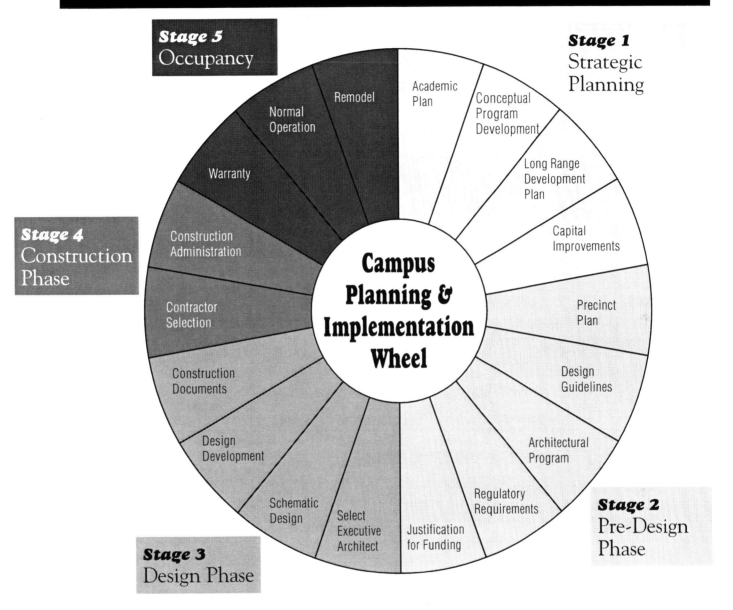

FIGURE 1
Campus Planning and Implementation Wheel

Stage 5 Occupancy

Stage 1 Strategic Planning

Stage 4 Construction Phase

Stage 2 Pre-Design Phase

Stage 3 Design Phase

Campus Planning & Implementation Wheel

Remodel · Normal Operation · Warranty · Construction Administration · Contractor Selection · Construction Documents · Design Development · Schematic Design · Select Executive Architect · Justification for Funding · Regulatory Requirements · Architectural Program · Design Guidelines · Precinct Plan · Capital Improvements · Long Range Development Plan · Conceptual Program Development · Academic Plan

Conceptual program development. This next stage defines the general campus appearance and configuration. The planning team should include consultants (architectural and planning), campus and system representative space planners, and the long range (physical) planning committee. Specialty consultants (e.g., engineers, landscape architects, technology specialists) should be included in the consultant team as required.

The first step in this process is a program needs assessment that includes interviews with all vice presidents/vice chancellors, deans, and unit heads. In addition, environmental scan-ning assesses space and facilities at comparable or competitive institutions.

Following the data collection phase, the team should develop conceptual programs for each identified unit/division or college/school. The team should review draft forms of program models with various client groups and when necessary, develop a phased implementation plan. The quantitative description of each program should include faculty counts (full time equivalent), full-time employees and FTE students served. The facilities inventory should include net square footage requirements, net-to-gross efficiency factors appropriate for each component type, and the resulting gross square footage required by each component and phase. These data can then form a base to generate prototype building footprints for broad categories of campus building types.

The process should also produce a report narrative on the various programs, a phasing implementation schedule, a transportation and parking report, a residential and non-residential housing report, and an inventory of land uses and acreage requirements.

The **Long Range Development Plan (LRDP)**, the third segment in Stage 1 of the strategic planning process, can be organized into four major categories: organization, process, content and deliverables.

To establish the foundation for a successful LRDP, there must be visible and absolute community, campus and central administrative support for the endeavor. In addition, this consensus of broad support should help articulate the goals of the plan and should clearly define the terms of process and the anticipated results. Next, the project must receive adequate funding and appropriate staffing, or the project will fail. The fewer administrative staff involved in the process, the greater the number of consultants who must be contracted, resulting in a lower commitment to the study than desired. Two final ingredients, a clearly articulated and adopted academic mission, and a detailed, cogent conceptual program form the basis for a successful LRDP.

Organization. Review committees are an important element in the process, and the planning team must develop policy that identifies the membership of each committee and defines their respective roles. For example, if a blue ribbon advisory committee is established, the composition of membership and its role and ranking compared to other standing committees, such as an academic senate committee, must be clearly defined and channels of communication between the groups established.

Tasks usually performed by the institution's administrative staff include the hiring of new personnel as required, preparation of the Request for Proposal (RFP) to hire a consultant (or consultants), and provisions for logistical support to the various committees established. One of the first staff tasks is to circulate and obtain approval of the RFP from the various committees or administrators. Selection of the consultant should be a decision made by representative committee members, as a first step toward consensus building and to ensure support of the process.

Once the consultant is selected and contractually secured, the administrative staff should define the philosophical position[1] of the planning office and prescribe the ground rules for the consultants. Further, some institutions select consultants based on stylistic compatibility, expertise, and experience not possessed by staff. These philosophical ground rules may vary among campuses, according to the degree of reliance on consultants during the process.

Operationally, at least one member of the in-house team should accompany the consultant to all meetings. Further, all communication flows through the in-house project team leader to the consultants.

The agenda for the kick-off meeting between the in-house team and consultants should include the generation and discussion of ideas, a confirmation of issues that require attention, and the development of a schedule for the plan. The first meeting should also provide the consultants' team members an understanding of the campus culture, its organizational components and communication channels, and all pertinent operating policies and procedures.

The initial meeting should also identify specific tasks and logistics to manage and assign individuals responsible for them. Included in these discussions should be the establishment and content of a mail and email distribution list that will maintain open communications among all members of the committee. The list should be as broad and inclusive as possible. Attempts to scale down the list often lead to problems later which could result in significant expense and delay. An open, inclusive process will strengthen the constituent group's sense of ownership and will result in a successful process and plan.

The fewer administrative staff involved in the process, the greater the number of consultants who must be contracted, resulting in a lower commitment to the study than desired.

---

[1]As an example of what is meant by "philosophical position," the University of California , Riverside (UCR) identifies all contracted consultants as extensions of the university planning office.

Process. The process to develop an LRDP begins with the identification of priorities in the academic plan and refinement of the mission statement. These requirements must then transfer directly into a physical plan that will evolve from active participation of planning committee members representing all facets of the institution. The typical review process begins with the concept definition, follows with client committee review and revision, and concludes with public review and comment.

The concept definition phase begins with data classification and categorization into various schematic types:

- Physical;
- Biological;
- Transportation;
- Infrastructure;
- Housing;
- Local plans and ordinances;
- Land use (on-campus and surrounding area);
- Zoning; and
- Building conditions, use and adaptive reuses.

Content. Data collected in the "physical" category include climate (temperature, rainfall, wind) as well as topographic and soils information. Biological data should include natural fauna and flora, recognized riverland stream right-of-way areas, and endangered species. Transportation includes campus parking patterns (e.g., data on origins and destinations), methods of travel (bus, train, carpool, bicycle, walking), street and intersection volumes and capacities, and freeway and highway accessibility routes. Housing data should consider availability, type, location and cost of (on- and off-campus) housing for students, faculty and staff, and should project any new housing projects that will be available later in the area. Infrastructure data should describe all utilities (power, water, sewer, storm drains, telephone, media, heating and cooling), and should include projections of future expansion.

Land use and zoning data are particularly important to private institutions governed by local ordinances. Public institutions can avoid land use conflicts and enhance their standing with local jurisdictions by involving them in the process, particularly if growth into adjacent

neighborhoods is anticipated. Including local planning and redevelopment officials, public utilities, and public works staff creates cooperation and trust that will improve information dissemination and expand and enhance the support base for the planning effort. Local officials and institutional "planners" recognize the campus as an integral part of the local, regional, and in some cases, national landscape.

Data collection and reports on building condition and use, as well as adaptive reuse surveys, should cover all campus (i.e., academic and non-academic) facilities. The utility of these data will become evident as alternative land use plans are developed, and ultimately, when the capital program and associated budgets are developed.

While the first Long Range Development Planning Committee meeting outlined the study, defined the concept, and identified and assigned specific tasks and responsibilities, the second committee meeting should present key notions of the members' vision of the institution. Discussion should include topics such as assets, liabilities, opportunities, barriers and a preferred future. Assets should encompass both the natural (e.g., unspoiled hills surrounding the campus) and the human-made (e.g., historic buildings). Liabilities may include a freeway adjacent to the campus with its associated noise and air pollution. Challenges associated with those items which, with remedial action, could become an asset to the campus can include both natural and constructed features, such as a series of poorly situated temporary structures blocking an otherwise attractive view to a lake or building. Such issues should be identified with text, maps, and photographs. This technique will produce an inventory of existing data and will reveal missing information that can assist planners to frame options that are politically feasible and technically accurate.

Next, the committee should thoroughly review the data collected and formulate its environmental assessment, developmental opportunities and constraints, site analysis/visual assessment, transportation, roads and intersec-

Public institutions can avoid land use conflicts and enhance their standing with local jurisdictions by involving them in the process, particularly if growth into adjacent neighborhoods is anticipated.

tions, parking and utilities capacities, growth limitations that may affect adjacent city plans, and an inventory of campus/community issues and conflicts. Here again, the use of text and illustrations is particularly useful.

Alternative physical planning scenarios first prove useful during development of alternate land use plans. An open, honest and responsive process results in the greatest level of consensus and support. Color maps, charts, and photographs are useful tools in this process. At this early stage participants should be encouraged to become actively involved and add their own interpretations to the drawings. A facilitator should record these interpretations on wall charts to demonstrate to the participants the importance of their opinions. At the next committee meeting, these interpretations should be distributed as part of the previous meeting's minutes so that participants realize their comments are part of an official record and are earnestly considered.

Deliverables. Constantinos Doxiadis compared the lifespan of physical plans to biological organisms (Doxiadis, 1969), where various organs represent land uses and arteries and veins represent transportation infrastructures. If transportation is a function of land use, then several alternative land use plans may result

If transportation is a function of land use, then several alternative land use plans may result along with a corresponding number of transportation alternatives.

along with a corresponding number of transportation alternatives. Each alternative should be given due consideration, not only by the committee, but through campus and community workshops and task forces that involve students, faculty, and staff and community members. Alternatives should also be publicized in project newsletters.

The development of alternative plans should identify an ideal plan superimposed over existing conditions. When tested through a formula-weighting system for compliance with vision, mission, goals, phasing and costs, etc., the ideal plan should earn the highest value and the lowest cost. It becomes the benchmark against which other alternatives are tested and compared.

Alternatives should also include differing, and in many instances, competing visions. An example might be the city's vision

to see the campus expand across its recognized boundaries and become a more visible player in the community, versus the institution's vision of a cohesive single unit with minimal involvement or intrusion into the surrounding community. Many campuses today face conflicting issues to provide broad access to facilities, but also maintain a safe, secure environment.

Assuming consensus can be reached on the evaluation criteria, choosing and ranking alternative plans can be done collectively. Often, elements from various plans may appeal to different groups. Then, an opportunity may exist to build consensus by adopting specific elements and creating a new alternative. Since land use planning decisions are not based on absolutes, this outcome presents one of the easiest opportunities to participate in the decision making process and, when managed correctly, can generate support and ownership at a critical point in the process. Any stakeholder's lingering perception of needs left unaddressed at this point can seriously damage the final outcome of the plan, particularly if the perception causes either active or passive disassociation with the plan.

Once adopted, the committee must quickly transmit the plan to appropriate decision making bodies on campus for consultation. The LRDP document should include:

- An executive summary;
- An introductory statement of purpose and need;
- Plan context;
- Planning determinants;
- A description of the plan;
- The process for plan implementation; and
- Appendices.

The **Capital Improvements Plan** comprises the final segment in Stage 1—Strategic Planning portion of the diagram. The organizational structure necessary to review and approve a capital program on campus depends on a variety of circumstances that may include campus culture and organization, precedents and history. Composition of the committee should represent all academic units, administrative decision makers, students, staff, and academic senate or appropriate faculty governance assemblies. To provide continuity in the process, membership should include key members of the Academic Planning and Long Range Development Planning Committees.

The first step in the development of a capital program should be a two-page project summary that includes a paragraph or two covering problem identification, alternative solutions, project description, quantitative justification, and status of project.

Priority ranking and scheduling of projects is the next step in the development of the capital improvement plan. Priority ranking for scheduling projects should correspond as nearly as possible to the delivery schedule of programs in the academic plan. Variations from the academic plan schedule should occur only when new information, unavailable during development of the academic plan, results in a rearrangement of academic priorities. Finally, the time frame (planning horizon) for the multi-year capital improvement program should match the time frame used for the academic and physical plans.

Private institutions may choose to combine academic and non-academic projects on a single master capital improvements schedule. A consolidated list also often benefits public institutions who must coordinate and manage staff workloads. Many public institutions also require a separate program schedule for non-state funded projects.

Once Stage 1 is complete, Stage 2, the **Pre-Design Stage** follows, measuring the results derived from Stage 1 against any recognized benchmark or regulatory guidelines and standards to determine whether the plan is accurate, pragmatic, affordable, realistic, and complies with recognized local, state, and federal construction codes.

When the Pre-Design Stage confirms or adjusts the results of the strategic plan derived in Stage 1, then the project moves to Stage 3, the **Design Phase**, where actual construction drawings develop after selection of an executive architect to oversee the project. Building projects move steadily from schematics through design/development and finally to construction documents.

Stage 4, the **Construction Phase**, begins the actual construction process, from hiring contractors to administering specific construction projects, and continues to the point of Stage 5, **Occupancy** of the building(s). Stage 5 includes the period when the building and its equipment is new and under warranty, through

normal operation until time for renovations to occur in the building because of age, deterioration, or change in program accommodations.

The Planning Wheel outlines the process for new construction, but additional planning must occur to fully utilize existing facilities once space is vacant.

COMPREHENSIVE PLANNING APPROACHES AND PRACTICES

Comprehensive, consistent planning practices require a pragmatic approach, meeting with all deans and unit/division heads to ascertain the visions, goals, and program objectives for their specific areas of responsibility. Prior to these meetings, enrollment and other growth trends or retrenchment analyses must document justifications for further facilities planning.

The strategic planning process described in Stage 1 of the Planning Wheel can apply directly to space assignments and renovation of existing facilities. Once the academic priorities are established and decisions are made about who will move into new facilities, a second planning cycle can begin to "backfill" vacant space.

A series of important decisions must follow:

- **Will the existing structure remain?** Does the master plan call for demolition of the structure and an adaptive reuse of the site? Is it cost-beneficial to renovate the structure? Does the structure have historical or architectural (or both) value? Is the structure tied to any legal commitments of the property?

- **What is the current condition of the structure?** Will it require more renovation funds than are available or can it be justified? Can new occupants move in with a basic maintenance upgrade of paint, carpeting and lighting?

- **Are renovation funds available?** Funding for immediate or near future (within eighteen months) renovations requires careful and timely planning. In some cases, the availability amount of renovation funds can determine the extent of renovation scope and may determine who can actually move into the space.

Comprehensive, consistent planning practices require a pragmatic approach, meeting with all deans and unit/division heads to ascertain the visions, goals, and program objectives for their specific areas of responsibility.

- **What academic priorities might fit into the vacant space?** When possible, space allocation decisions must be made according to strategic academic and administrative priority needs. Occasionally, limited renovation funds may dictate assignment of space on the basis of function. Thus, vacant space may be assigned to functions that rank lower in priority, but fit the type of space available better than other higher priority units.

Once program need for facilities is warranted, academic leadership should be advised of the study being undertaken and, when possible, should participate fully.

Consensus must develop on the feasibility of the schedule and the necessary action steps (process). Once program need for facilities is warranted, academic leadership should be advised of the study being undertaken and, when possible, should participate fully. The template for the document, identified earlier in this chapter, should be approved prior to undertaking this in-house academic planning exercise and should form the basis of this approach. Finally, all parties should have the opportunity to review and comment on the entire draft document.

Several inherent challenges exist with this approach. First, such a comprehensive project must garner top priority for operational and executive level support among other mandatory, regular, daily activities. Lack of top priority can cause delays and short-cuts of important steps in the process, input, review, and feedback responses that can lead to inaccuracies, frustration, and failure. Ultimately, the loss of credibility in the process can occur.

Other inherent weaknesses and unresolved issues also must be considered, such as:

- The credibility and competence of in-house staff;
- In-house biases, preconceptions, and motives;
- The lack of an impartial third party (provided by a consultant); and
- Variations in the management styles of deans on the issue of inclusiveness and decision making.

Some executives may include all department heads; others may choose a more limited approach. The range of approaches will vary according to the size of the constituency, the level of buy-in and sense of ownership.

The length of time required to undertake such studies and the reliability of the data collected create two common, difficult obstacles in this approach. Another challenge may be securing active participation in an academic community, where process is often more important than outcome.

In-house physical planning activities begin with a thorough, objective analysis of staffing levels, expertise and workload. The enormous amount of data that must be collected, analyzed and synthesized makes it unlikely that any campus has the breadth of in-house expertise to undertake such efforts without contract assistance. Specialty consultants can fill the identified voids where in-house staff expertise is missing. For example, specialty consultants should be considered for architectural and infrastructure engineering. A land use planner also should be considered, unless campus staff has a proven track record in this activity. Fresh perspectives of outside consultants can be useful, creative, and energizing to the process.

Coordinating the work of multiple consultants can be difficult, particularly if in-house staff cannot perform the task or lack the necessary experience. As one strategy, hire one consultant (e.g., the land use consultant) as contract manager, and require the contract manager to hire additional specialty consultants as necessary.

Ideally, physical planning should parallel academic planning, eliminating dual meetings and providing program-to-building fit. Comprehensive analysis and feedback are simultaneous, and adequate facilities data are available from the start. If concurrent start-up is not feasible, the physical planning process should begin after the first round of interviews with deans.

The range of data to collect is similar to what was proposed earlier in the Conceptual Program and Long Range Development Plan. The thoroughness and accuracy of data create confidence in the staff and build support and involvement in both process and outcome. Participants should be encouraged to suggest and provide additional data for the study, and once received, data should be used to validate and verify opinions.

Environmental scanning is a good starting point for data collection. The available data bases that have been established during the last decade form a sound foundation for data management. Several national organizations with local chapters (United Way, for example) are an invaluable resource. City, county, regional and state planning agencies should be contacted, as well as federal agencies–National Weather Service, Department of Agriculture, Housing and Urban Development, Education, Interior, Transportation and Defense. The long list of data sources should be tailored to setting and time constraints, but time limitations must not compromise data collection.

The time frame for each planning effort should be kept to a minimum, to sustain interest and participation. Regardless of approach, the LRDP should be accomplished in a single academic year. Ideally, a schedule that begins during the fall quarter/semester so that final documents can be submitted, reviewed and approved by the end of the academic year or the middle of the next fall term is most effective. Even when academic and physical planning efforts cannot occur simultaneously, the entire planning process should be completed in a year and a half. Protracted delays can seriously threaten the validity of the data.

MANIPULATION & DELIVERY

The Academic Planning Statement should include segments on the following:

- Distinctive academic features of the campus;

- Enrollment history and projection;
- Campus goals and objectives
  - teaching
  - research
  - service
  - and, diversity; and
- Current academic strengths (by academic unit).

The following sections should be completed after review, approval and adoption of new programs:

- Implementation procedures
  - funding and faculty allocations
  - space planning and allocation; and
- Development of new programs (by academic unit).

The text for each new program initiative should contain:

- History and background;
- Academic & economic trends (environmental scanning);
- Justification (mission-related goals and objectives);
- Program characteristics and levels (AA, BS, MS, PhD);
- Program content (courses) and mode(s) of delivery;
- Faculty compensation and size;

TABLE 1
Long Range Academic Plan 1995–2004
Program Schedule and Cost ($'000)

YEAR Academic Program	1995	1996	1997	1998	1999	2000	2001	2002	2003	2004
DANCE										
MFA	MFA									
PhD		PhD								
Number of faculty	3	2								
Start-up funding	150	80								
Salaries	210	100								
Supplies/Equipment	15	10								

- Enrollment growth to build out;
- Space requirements and type;
- Funding level and source(s);
- Projected schedule (start-up dates); and
- Performance assessment procedures.

Using a member of the academic planning committee to head a subcommittee in this effort will maximize participation by the faculty.

The final item in the document should be a multi-year academic program delivery schedule. Table 1 provides a suggested format for such a table.

Open forums should present a draft of the academic plan and solicit feedback. The forums should begin with focus group sessions within each academic area, and should follow with general campus sessions that include students and staff. It is important that non-academic audiences understand forum presentations as primarily information sessions, although comments may be entertained. It is helpful to conduct debriefing sessions after each forum to better understand the depth of community sentiment. The final step in the process is review, comment, and adoption by the appropriate governance body (e.g., the academic senate).

*I*t is important that non-academic audiences understand forum presentations as primarily information sessions, although comments may be entertained.

In the physical planning phase, alternative land use plans are not only useful, but essential. This is also the first of many interactive steps in the development of the final selected plan. An open, honest, proactive and responsive process is essential to ensure buy-in and support. The use of color maps, charts, and photographs are all standard tools of the trade. At this early stage participants should be encouraged to be actively involved, including being invited to add their own solutions on the drawings. Using a facilitator/recorder to present comments on a wall is also helpful in reassuring the audience that their feedback is not being filtered out. These recorded notes should then be distributed to the follow-up meetings as minutes.

Drawings should be large enough to display for discussion during the forum and should be easy to reduce for photocopying and incorporating into text. Key plans should include:

- History of campus growth;
- Regional setting;
- Local setting;
- Existing conditions;
- Existing land use;
- Vehicular circulation and parking;
- Pedestrian and bicycle circulation; and
- Infrastructure utilities (sanitary sewer, storm drain, water, gas, electricity, steam, chilled water, and telecommunication—voice, data and video).

Multiple drafts are common during this process. The first is an administrative draft developed for in-house staff review. The second draft is for the committee and campus at large, and the third draft (including a tightly written executive summary) is reviewed by the trustees/regents. Then a camera-ready report should be prepared, reviewed, and published.

ACTIONABILITY ISSUES

Both the Academic Plan and Long Range Development Plan should express commitment to:

- Establish appropriate administrative procedures that comply with the goals and objectives of each plan; and
- Review and revise the plans as appropriate.

Institutions should review their academic plan every two to three years, and their physical plan every three to five years. Ideally, the development, maintenance and updating of academic and long range development plans should be incorporated into the bylaws of the trustees or regents and should be implemented through that body's standing orders. On a campus, planning should be mandated through administrative policies and procedures, academic senate bylaws, and standing orders. Bylaws and orders should include the establishment of administrative and academic committees to oversee the plans and their implementation, including any deviations from the approved documents. Parallel academic and administrative systems should ensure necessary checks and balances and adherence to time frames.

CONCLUSIONS AND RECOMMENDATIONS

Planning must be viewed as essential and adequately supported for an institution to maximize benefits. Planning and its processes must be supported at the highest levels if it is to succeed; anything less dooms the process to failure. Competition from alternative education providers makes planning essential to sound academic and fiscal management. If the chief executive officer does not support planning as central to the life of the institution, planning exercises become empty rituals.

External pressures and threats do not energize faculties; in fact, the opposite may be true. Garnering faculty support requires inducements. The planning process should present an opportunity to understand academic directions and needs and to find ways to fund them. Planning can prioritize need and allocate finite resources. To suggest more may garner short-term support, but long-term support and trust will lessen if funding is not quickly forthcoming. Successful planning requires support from all facets of the campus community.

The planning process must be open, inclusive and responsive to input. Sustained support for planning, regardless of process, depends on openness, inclusiveness and responsiveness. If ground rules and limitations are set, they should be defined and enunciated clearly at the outset. Attempts to impose limits during the process will result in mistrust and disinterest. The more open and inclusive the process, the larger the number of stakeholders.

Feedback and responsiveness are important, as is meeting deadlines when surveys are completed. Drafts should be delivered to deans and department chairs according to schedule. Similarly issues should garner prompt responses and, depending on their relevance to the entire process, should be widely distributed. Participants should be notified when delays occur as quickly as possible, with an explanation and notification of a new time frame.

Participation should be encouraged at every academic and administrative level to foster an open, inclusive and responsive process. Chairpersons, for example, should rank the new program initiatives and then participate in ranking programs at the next level.

Schedules should be carefully managed to ensure adequate time for input and feedback. Delays are, in most instances, unavoidable; but minimizing them will enhance the process. A serious staff commitment can make the difference. At least one (and preferably two) staff members should be assigned exclusively to planning tasks. No extraneous duties and responsibilities should add to their workload.

PRINT REFERENCES

Brubaker, W. C. 1983. *Campus Planning: Redesign—Redevelopment—Rethinking: Proceedings of A Professional Development Symposium.* Waco: Myrick, Norman, Dahlberg & Partners, Inc.

Creighton, J. L. 1981. *The Public Involvement Manual.* Cambridge: Abt Books.

Dandekar, H. C., ed. 1988. *The Planner's Use of Information.* Washington, DC: Planners Press.

Dolence, M. G. and Norris, D. M. 1995. *Transforming Higher Education—A Vision for Learning in the 21st Century.* Ann Arbor: Society for College and University Planning.

Doxiadis, C. A. 1968. *Ekistics: An Introduction to the Science of Human Settlements.* London: Hutchison & Co. Ltd.

Fink, I. and Fardet, N., eds. 1992. *Campus Planning and Facility Development: A Selected Bibliography.* Berkeley: Ira Fink and Associates, Inc.

McClendon, B. W. and Quay, R. 1988. *Mastering Change: Winning Strategies for Effective City Planning.* Washington, DC: Planners Press.

Morrison, J. L.; Renfro, W. L.; and Boucher, W. I. 1984. *Futures Research and The Strategic Planning Process: Implications for Higher Education.* Washington, DC: Association for the Study of Higher Education.

Norris, D. M. and Poulton, N. N. 1991. *A Guide for New Planners 1991.* Ann Arbor: Society for College and University Planning.

Solnit, A. et. al. 1988. *The Job of the Practicing Planner.* Washington, DC: Planners Press.

Smith, F. J. and Hester Jr., R. T. 1982. *Community Goal Setting.* Stroudsburg: Hutchison Press Publishing Co.

ELECTRONIC SAMPLER

http://www.appa.org
  APPA (The Association of Higher Education Facilities Officers).

http://www.cefpi.com/cefpi/
  Council of Educational Facility Planners, International.
  Includes options for searching the abstracts of their journal.

http://www.clark.net/pub/peter/1electr.htm
  WorkSpace Resources: Design information, FAQs, Links and Product Resources for Ergonomic Computer Furniture, Casegoods, Seating and Accessories designed for the Modern Office and the Electronic Classroom.

http://www.conway.com/index.htm

http://www.conway.com/webtools.htm:
  SiteNet. Site Selection Magazine.
  A variety of online resources for facilities planners though not necessarily in higher education.

http://www.fmdata.com/cgi-shl/dbml.exe?template=/services/home.dbm
  FM Datacom, The Internet Home of Facilities Planning and Management Data.

http://www.itp.berkeley.edu/PlanningForTechInEdu.html
  Repertoire of Strategies for Instructional Technology in Higher Education. Instructional Technology Program, University of California, Berkeley. Marcia C. Linn.

http://www.nchems.com/
  NCHEMS: (National Center for Higher Education Management Systems).

http://www.westgov.org/smart/
  Smart States Initiative. Western Governors Association.
  Includes information on their Virtual University.

Adequate flexibility must be built into the schedule, particularly at the initial interview/data gathering phase. Time frames should include opportunities for rescheduling and/or substituting interviewees. Schedule periodic meetings (bi-weekly or monthly) with the director and key decision makers to evaluate progress. Anticipated delays must be communicated to all parties. Keeping participants informed is vital to the process and ensures their continued interest. A newsletter is useful to disseminate information, either as printed text or through an electronic medium.

Adequate, appropriate policies, procedures and committee structures must be established to ensure compliance with the plan and subsequent review and revision as a "living" document. To ensure that the plans are "living" documents, campus policies, procedures, and committees are essential. Most institutions follow such procedures (for the approval of new academic programs and buildings) and, in most cases, a modest revision of existing bylaws and standing orders will accommodate the review and approval of programs to ensure compliance with the plans.

Modifying the bylaws of the trustees/regents will ensure that plans are followed, and can survive administrative personnel changes. Within these amendments, statements should require that both plans receive periodic review. Thus, the two plans are "living" documents.

Progress toward implementation of the plan should be tracked through continuous, regular updates of the documents. Once studies are completed and plans adopted, there is a tendency to reduce planning resources or redirect them to other projects or needs. To ensure that plans are maintained, updated and tracked for progress, a commitment to continued financial support is imperative. Otherwise, the relevance and validity of planning documents will be questioned.

A staff person should be assigned as "keeper" of the studies, responsible for tracking progress, amendments or revisions, and providing staff support to committees and central administration as required. Additional funding should be available to introduce technological improvements and to monitor, gather and evaluate data as they are collected. On-going commitment will ensure the usefulness of planning documents and their relevance to annual and long term planning and budgeting processes on campus. ◆

𝒯his chapter defines why and how academic plans and processes should be connected with budget development and funding allocation. Examples are offered of successful practices that benefit planners at any level of the organization.

Connecting Academic Plans To Budgeting: Key Conditions For Success

Thomas K. Anderes

CORE PLANNING QUESTIONS

In an era of increased demands for accountability and "return on investment," planners and academic leaders are faced with three core issues:

- What does it mean to connect plans with budgets?
- Why is it important to connect planning and budgeting?
- Under what conditions can planning and budgeting be connected in such a way to improve both processes?

Budget terminology that commonly substitutes for "connecting" includes integrating or linking. It refers to a formalization of the relationship between planning and budgeting processes that establishes visions, goals, objectives, priorities, and indicators as the foundation upon which budgets are constructed and implemented. Budgets are extensions of planned priorities, implemented within the general boundaries and intent of the plan(s). The degree to which planned priorities and objectives are achieved is an important consideration in determining the effectiveness of resource deployment.

Higher education leaders, while embracing the basic concept of connecting planning and budget, frequently do not adequately structure the relationship between the two in such a way that priorities and processes are shared and coordinated. The outcome, often enough,

is that decisions are administratively expedient under the pressure of budget requirements, but not necessarily cognizant of priorities established by institutional planning.

There are a number of very good reasons why viable linkages between planning and budgeting should be developed and maintained.

Legitimize planning. The measure of a successful plan is frequently tied to whether or not its objectives and priorities were included in the budget development process, and whether or not it received funding. For example, increasing concern for a learner-centered environment demands attention throughout the various phases of planning. The degree to which learner-centered initiatives are adopted and, ultimately, planning processes are successful, depends on their acceptance as budget priorities.

Legitimize budgeting. The long term reliability of a budget should be determined by its continuity in seeking funding support for priorities (old or new) not yet fully realized. Further, the credibility of a budget request should be judged on how well it represents institutional planning priorities.

Follow through on expectations raised in planning. Internal and external constituents must feel that their ideas and participation

Thomas K. Anderes

is Vice Chancellor for Finance and Administration for the University and Community College System of Nevada, Reno, Nevada. Anderes is the Associate Convenor of SCUP's Institutional Decision Making and Resource Planning Academy.

have value. Identification of planning priorities in the budget, and evidence of progress toward achieving them, will help satisfy individual and group expectations.

Secure institutional support. There will be greater confidence in institutional direction when a coherent plan underpins the budget. The acceptance and support of a plan requires active coordination of outcomes with representatives of faculty, staff, and students.

Provide continuity over time in the achievement of goals. It is essential to understand what has been accomplished if there is to be an assessment of future goals and the likelihood of achieving them. When priorities are not funded, future planning processes must reassess their relative value and determine their potential for success in future budget exercises.

Track performance. Specific objectives should be developed and tracked throughout the process—from planning to budget development, and from budget development through funding allocation. The ultimate test of performance lies in measuring expectations against outcomes. It also helps when budget success criteria move from tracking of inputs to demonstration of actual goal achievement.

Reduce decisions made outside of program priorities. Although priorities that were not considered in the planning phase will arise later, they should be minimized. The success of planning is related, in part, to how well priorities are anticipated. Frequent revisions of planning priorities in the budget process signal insufficient depth of information for adequately predicting change, or limited interest in the planning outcomes.

Constructing connections between processes entails a number of commitments which should be understood at the earliest stages of planning. The connection of planning to budgeting can generally be accomplished in a number of ways. One alternative is to construct a comprehensive process that weaves the two together, linking schedules to

> *The connection of planning to budgeting can generally be accomplished in a number of ways. One alternative is to construct a comprehensive process that weaves the two together, linking schedules to key actions, and, ideally, including an overlap of participants. The preferred approach, it is also the most difficult to build and maintain.*

key actions, and, ideally, including an overlap of participants. The preferred approach, it is also the most difficult to build and maintain.

A second, less integrated approach is to maintain separate planning and budget development processes and then translate the major planning priorities into the budget. This method limits interaction between the planning and budget phases, and can create timing problems. Budgets always have a fixed time cycle, imposed by external funding agencies, whereas planning schedules tend to be more flexible and open-ended.

A third approach entails a more random selection of objectives and priorities from plans generated through separate division or college planning processes. This approach is often seen where the chief executive permits planning at the unit level to continue, but seldom feels constrained to operate within the larger planning context. Under these conditions planning is more symbolic and ritualistic than purposeful and connected to effective resource allocation for the long-run good of the institution. It is the least desirable alternative when more time and resources make a better choice possible.

Specific conditions for effective implementation of a planning-budgeting process are listed below. They will be explored further in two "real life" examples. Key conditions for effective implementation include:

- Active leadership from top institutional and/or system representatives;

- Broad participation by key internal and, where appropriate, external constituencies and stakeholders;

- A clear intention to integrate planning outcomes into budget development and funding allocations;

- Forums to provide sufficient background information to interested participants;

- Feedback to constituencies when decisions are made, particularly when decisions create commitments; and

- A mechanism to assess progress on planned objectives and feed findings back into ensuing planning budget processes.

The examples of how planning and budgeting have been connected, one at the institutional level and one at the system level, are representative of the comprehensive alternative. A comparative review of key factors or conditions highlights the reason for success.

PLANNING AND BUDGETING — AN INSTITUTIONAL PERSPECTIVE

The University of Wyoming, a state land grant university, decided to develop a comprehensive planning and budget review process to coincide with a change in institutional leadership. The institution had no long term plans or planning process in place; consequently, it did not link planning with budget development. There was also a significant lack of information regarding how funding allocation/decisions were made, and how different fund sources could be used.

At the direction of the new president, the academic and finance divisions built a shared process and created key conditions which purposely incorporated the following key elements:

- A *presidential vision* established the foundation for the processes.

- *Educational work sessions* provided current status reports on programs, budgets, projected future funding and other background information.

- Distinct *planning and priority setting* sessions were *linked into budget* development.

- *Follow-up sessions* during the planning and budget phases provided status updates to the university community and sought input from them. They also provided *feedback* regarding decisions included in the budget.

- The process was *broadly representative* of key institutional constituencies and was focused through a *core decision making committee*; the committee linked discussions on academic and administrative programs with funding decisions.

The overall success of the eight-month process was tied to the attention placed on implementing the key conditions, and to the cooperative efforts of finance and academic divisions in creating and committing themselves to a comprehensive assessment of institutional goals and funding outcomes. Specific strengths (as reflected through key conditions) led to the general success of the process.

Strengths. The process was broadly participative, including over 50 individuals representing all major campus constituencies on an institution-wide oversight committee. Individuals were engaged in all aspects of planning and budget development.

The president provided a vision statement that helped the oversight committee and other campus groups understand his basic directions for the future. His expressed goals acted as a point of reference and assessment in both planning and budgeting phases.

The educational/informational sessions helped to connect people with process in a manner that had not occurred in many years. Substantial background and definition raised individual levels of awareness on funding, programs, priorities, external requirements and other issues that had previously been avoided. Wide-ranging discussion asked why various processes were in place and how change could be effected. These sessions were ultimately most instrumental in opening communication among all constituencies and establishing a foundation for cooperation.

The link between plans and budget was achieved because of the continuity of people involved and the continuity of moving directly from a planning mode to budget development. Everyone had a vested interest in ensuring that planning priorities would be incorporated into the budget development phase.

Follow-up meetings, to communicate decisions and seek further input, were sporadically useful. Though not always well attended, they achieved the objective of maintaining open avenues for dialogue.

The oversight committee acted as the core reviewing body on both program planning and budget allocation. There was specific focus on translating significant findings and outcomes generated through planning into the budget development phase. The planning-to-budget connection was achieved because of the continuing involvement of committee members—held accountable for inclusion or exclusion of planning outcomes throughout the budget development process.

Finally, there were follow-up sessions, open to faculty and staff, to discuss planning progress and seek further advice. A final summary review of decisions carried forward in the budget was discussed with the university community.

Weaknesses. The process also had weaknesses that compomised the outcomes. The length and intensity of the process (eight months) put a sig-

The link between plans and budget was achieved because of the continuity of people involved and the continuity of moving directly from a planning mode to budget development.

nificant strain on participants who were engaged in regular job tasks during the planning process. The need for regular input from most committee members, in both the planning and budget phases, was demanding.

The core committee membership exceeded 50 representatives of faculty and staff, deans and directors. Although the participation rate was quite good in key decision-making meetings, the administrative effort required was immense (coordinate drafts, schedule meetings, disseminate materials, build agendas, and so on).

Forums established to hear university reactions and feedback on evolving plans and priorities were poorly attended by the wider university community. Historical precedent had suggested that the administration would not seek broader sources of input.

Nevertheless, strengths greatly outweighed weaknesses, and the university was pleased with the process and outcomes.

To provide both consistent and flexible support to all institutions, the system must establish directions and priorities that address the most pressing issues of the state. The thrust of system planning and budgeting is to create a useful and extended vehicle that will highlight solutions to state-wide problems.

PLANNING AND BUDGETING— A SYSTEM PERSPECTIVE

Planning and budgeting for a state system represents a challenge different from that posed at the institutional level. To provide both consistent and flexible support to all institutions, the system must establish directions and priorities that address the most pressing issues of the state. The thrust of system planning and budgeting is to create a useful and extended vehicle that will highlight solutions to state-wide problems. However, the key conditions for a successful connection between planning and budgeting are much the same as at the institutional level.

A recent example of system planning and budgeting strategy at the University of Wisconsin encompasses a number of conditions that are applicable to all planning situations. Over an eight-year period, the Wisconsin system guided its two- and four-year institutions through a series of budget development and allocation approaches, built on planned policy initiatives and focused on improving the quality of instruction. A num-

ber of variables influenced the success of each phase of planning (Sell, 1993).

System "vision" and leadership. The most urgent system concern and catalyst for change was the demand to improve support for undergraduate education. Following an analysis of academic programs, and in response to declining state funding, the system decided it would be unrealistic, if not unfair to students, to continue policies that assumed simultaneous achievement of quality and access. They opted for quality. That strategic decision drove a number of plans and policies, ultimately incorporated into the budget(s)–in particular, an enrollment management policy linked to tuition revenues.

Participation by key constituencies. A variety of public forums on policy alternatives included gubernatorial and legislative task forces, public hearings, and cross-institutional working groups, thereby insuring group participation and input from interested constituencies. Planning continued at the institutional level in response to system enrollment and curriculum strategies.

Planning to budget connections. A pervasive goal of the system was to use academic planning and policies as the basis for budget development and funding allocations. The budget was the vehicle for offering incentives to institutions in achieving system goals and, in turn, to institutions in achieving institutional goals. The stated strategic initiative–to improve undergraduate education–would succeed only if the state appropriated additional funds, and only if institutions and the system identified base funding to supplement state sources. The integration of policy and budget was continuous through management of system-wide enrollment policies and maintenance of a central reserve to balance sector growth and decline.

The system implemented a number of additional policies to help achieve the ultimate goal of improving undergraduate education, thus creating an extended and meaningful interaction between plans and funding. The eight-year period implied a substantial commitment by a number of constituencies to support system policies. When the goals had to change because of fiscal constraints and shifts in enrollment, the plan adapted and survived.

COMPARISON OF INSTITUTIONAL AND SYSTEM PLANNING

The general success of the Wisconsin and Wyoming experiences can be tied to a number of conditions. Though not mentioned explicitly in either case, it is obvious that leadership must be truly persistent and flexible (and, at key junctures, firm) if the processes are to succeed.

Contemporary management theory makes it clear that leadership, whether institutional president or board, must offer and actively support a "vision" (Norris and Poulton, 1991). The successes of Wisconsin and Wyoming can be traced, in part, to initial efforts of leadership to validate the importance of building a plan that addressed an identified agenda.

Both examples recognized the need to build plans around the input of interested and affected constituencies. Broad participation offered avenues for input and afforded opportunities to show all constituencies the strengths and weaknesses of various alternatives. Participation also increased a sense of individual ownership and greater understanding of process, plans, funding, and timing. As the Wisconsin plan suggests, "buy-in" by external parties was significant for long term support.

The objective of both the system and the institution–to integrate planning and budgeting–was a critical and necessary condition for success. Early recognition of the integration of the two processes was important to Wyoming because it emphasized to institutional representatives their active engagement in decisions affecting their budgets. The Wisconsin experience may have been even more significant because the potential for failure was greater, given the changes at both institutional and state levels. Wisconsin's ability to construct a process that acknowledged the needs of the governor and legislative offices, while making higher education programs a priority, resulted in a formidable accomplishment.

RECOMMENDATIONS
Wisconsin and Wyoming offer two instances of a meaningful connection between planning and budgeting. Such integration demands substantial commitment from the earliest stages through budget allocation. Adherence to key conditions greatly enhances opportunities for positive processes and useful outcomes. In any planning and budgeting process, the following key conditions should be recognized:

Active leadership. Whether a process is implemented at the department, institution, or system level, active and informed leadership is a must (Drummond, Vinzant, and Praeder, 1991). If participants feel that leadership is not interested in their input, their efforts will not match leadership's enthusiasm and expectations. Outputs will be of relatively limited value and have little impact on budget decisions.

Broad participation. There is significant benefit in including a representative cross section of all groups affected by planning and budgeting outcomes. Realistic objectives, capable of being implemented successfully, are more likely to be selected. Buy-in is also increased. Conversely, there is significant risk in excluding groups that may hinder a process which seems not to recognize them. It is important to construct a means of participation that balances maximization of input with efficiency, timing, and cost.

Intention to connect planning and budgeting. The simplicity of connecting planning priorities with the budget at the onset of a process should not be overlooked. An intention to do so must be declared at all stages and to all participants. Interest on the part of some participants will lessen if the link between planning priorities and budget priorities does not match their expectations.

Informational forums. Most participants in comprehensive planning and budgeting exercises are not familiar with the process, nor do they have experience with issues, funding structure, or external exigencies that cut across an institution or a system. They participate as experts in a particular discipline or administrative field. Thus, informational forums that bring participants to a common understanding of the more important factors they will use in drawing conclusions are extremely useful.

Feedback on decisions. Participants in the planning processes should be apprised of decisions reached at key junctures. The need to communicate progress is highlighted when earlier outcomes have not been shared and individuals feel their roles were not valued. To truly involve people can greatly increase acceptance of planning outcomes and budgets built on those outcomes.

The ultimate test in determining whether planning and budgeting are connected is the degree to which planning outcomes are funded. Planning is a strong component of institutional decision making when priorities evolve through

Contemporary management theory makes it clear that leadership, whether institutional president or board, must offer and actively support a "vision"

budget development and are legitimized by allocation of resources. The continuing viability of priorities must be based on their ability to achieve the success projected for them in the planning process.

FINAL THOUGHTS

If an institution or system structures a planning and budgeting process that:

- Has active leadership;
- Is broadly participative;

PRINT REFERENCES

Drummond, M.; Vinzant, D.; and Praeder, W. 1991. "Paying for your Vision—Integrating the Planning and Budgeting Process." *CAUSE/EFFECT* 14(3): 21–27.

Nedwek, B. 1996. *Memorandum on linking strategic planning and budgeting.* Saint Louis University.

Norris, D. M. and Poulton, N. L. 1991. *A Guide for New Planners.* Ann Arbor: Society for College and University Planning.

Sell, K. R. 1993. "Coordinating Budgeting and Academic Planning to Affect Institutional Commitment to Teaching and Learning." A paper presented at the State Higher Education Finance Officers Conference, Denver, 1993.

ELECTRONIC SAMPLER

http://daps.arizona.edu/
Decision and Planning Support. University of Arizona.

On this site you will find the University of Arizona's Factbook, Standard Survey Response, and Public Records pages, as well as links to key planning and budgeting documents.

http://tikkun.ed.asu.edu/aera/home.html
AERA (American Educational Research Association).

AERA is concerned with improving the educational process by encouraging scholarly inquiry related to education and by promoting the dissemination and practical application of research results. The site has a list of searchable resources, including papers from conferences and articles in AERA publications, at http://tikkun.ed.asu.edu/aera/resour.html.

http://www.cause.org/information-resources/ir-library/html/cem9622.html
Current Issues for Higher Education: Information Resources Management.

http://www.library.utoronto.ca/www/budget.htm
Concerning the University Budget. University of Toronto.

Canada has been experiencing severe higher education financial stress. This site has a message about this issue from the President of the University of Toronto.

http://www.nacubo.org/
NACUBO (National Association for College and University Business Officers).

Includes the online version of their publication *Business Officer* with articles such as: "Little to Gain, Much to Lose: The Potential Impact of Income Tax Restructuring Proposals" which can be reached directly at http://www.nacubo.org/website/bomag/ltg1096.html.

- Translates planning priorities into budget development;
- Provides informational support to participants;
- Provides feedback on decisions to the community served; and
- Measures performance,

then the potential for successful integration of planning and budgeting will be high.

In this era of heightened concern for accountability and quality, the process of translating priorities into budget development should be carefully reviewed to guard against it serving to reinforce incremental decision making and a narrow vision for the future of the institution. An effective plan linked to the budget (Nedwek, 1996) should:

- Be simple and readily understandable to multiple constituencies.

- Encourage entrepreneurial approaches and thoughtful risk-taking that are tied directly to the mission and objectives of the whole institution as well as those of individual planning units.

- Provide planning units, e.g., schools and departments, and senior management adequate flexibility to modify operating decisions within a fiscal year.

- Provide a means for establishing and measuring progress against stated planning unit objectives and strategies.

- Promote collaboration and partnership development among planning units to undertake new initiatives and to reengineer existing products and services.

- Seek an alternative to traditional line-item budget development that aligns costs in support of unspecified or loosely coupled sets of activities.

Incremental budgeting can undermine strategic thinking and priority-setting. Remodeling the budget building process to improve linkages with strategic planning requires a thoughtful, open dialogue among all stakeholders. The rationale in support of changes to the policies and procedures must be compelling to planning unit heads. The specific implementation processes must be reasonable and understandable. Every effort should be made to streamline budget development procedures and make use of online information technology tools. ◆

Linking Quality and Accountability

Linking Quality Assurance and Accountability: Using Process and Performance Indicators

Brian P. Nedwek

This chapter examines both the risks and the benefits of using performance indicators (PIs) to link quality assurance and accountability. As a control tool, PIs run the risk of creating disincentives for meaningful reform. On the positive side, when PI systems have an instrumental use in agenda building, monitoring, and in forecasting—they make educational delivery problems more analytically tractable.

Linking Quality Assurance and Accountability: Using Process and Performance Indicators

Brian P. Nedwek

CORE PLANNING QUESTIONS

A variety of forces are altering the way higher education will govern itself as it enters the next century. Burgeoning short-term enrollment blips are creating political tradeoffs; legislators scramble to redistribute general revenue from one underfunded program to another. Two- and four-year colleges and universities are challenged by inflationary spikes in the cost of goods and services necessary for their mission. Information technology is restructuring delivery strategies as place-bound learning loses its grip on facilities and planning. Faculties continue in their apparent indifference toward a systematic search for more effective and efficient pedagogy. The consuming public questions the cost of education, even as policy makers demand greater returns on their investment of meager public resources. Higher education has, in short, fallen from grace. No longer insulated by a presumption of inherent goodness and worth, the academy finds itself exposed to a cacophony of demands for quality and accountability.

The net result of change within and beyond the academy has been a variety of initiatives to link quality to accountability. Core issues have forced the academy to examine ways to account for performance directly. In the past, emphasis lay on factors of production in man-

aging institutions, and was preoccupied with academic input measures (number of books in the library, proportion of faculty with terminal degrees). Now academic leaders are under pressure to emphasize instead the factors and results of learning. Focus is no longer on accountability through access to the academy; rather, return on investment has redefined accountability. State legislatures and governing boards, impatient with slow progress on quality enhancement, are beginning to demand that the academy restructure its *modus operandi*. Performance Indicator (PI) systems are now fully implemented in at least 18 states, half of which are already experimenting with ways to make performance a criterion for resource allocation.

Management practices are beginning to change as well. In the past, facilities and academic planning, institutional research, policy analysis, and budgeting all performed independently. An unwillingness to integrate functions created a managerial environment marked by duplication of effort, absence of mutual understanding, even of core terms, and a preoccupation with turf. The result: symbolic rather than substantive

Brian P. Nedwek is Associate Provost for Saint Louis University, St. Louis, Missouri, SCUP's 1996–97 President. and faculty for SCUP's Workshop, "Making Transformation Work on your Campus." He has also served as the Convener of SCUP's Academic Planning Academy.

planning. However, some signs of change are appearing. Administrative activities are moving from independence to interdependence. Effective institutions are striving to become "learning organizations" capable of transforming knowledge about their processes, programs, and products into new insights (Garvin, 1993).

What is quality? Who should define it? How can accountability be balanced with quality assurance to renew mutual trust among ourselves and with our publics? Whose priorities are central? This chapter addresses these core planning questions, describing ways to manage for quality through the use of process and performance indicators. Simply, we show how linking accountability to quality enhancement represents a major shift in the academic leader's task of managing for quality.

*Q*uality viewed as fidelity to design is simply conformance to mission specification and goal achievement— within publicly accepted standards of accountability and integrity

BASIC CONCEPTS

Quality. Regardless of one's notion of quality–as a state of affairs or a philosophy of management–its essential component is fidelity to a program design through mission specification and goal achievement. The degree of "fit" between articulated goals and expected educational results is the key idea, as calibrated through management tools or traditional peer reviews. Quality viewed as fidelity to design is simply "conformance to mission specification and goal achievement—within publicly accepted standards of accountability and integrity" (Bogue and Saunders, 1992, p. 20). In this age of consumerism, quality means delivering to our key stakeholders what was promised by us and is valued by them.

Indicators. Performance indicators are data about conditions, processes, or results associated with core organizational functions at a particular level of aggregation. Once gathered and publicly disseminated, they become the normative link to the policy process and serve several substantive purposes: (1) to monitor environmental conditions or resource usage, (2) to measure performance against stated policy or program goals, (3) to forecast problems, (4) to build policy agendas, (5) to support resource allocation decision making, and (6) to create

bases for comparisons within and among institutions. PIs serve symbolic functions as well, especially when resources are unavailable to remedy a problem (Nedwek, 1996).

Although potential indicators are available to stakeholders in vast array, most can be grouped under a taxonomy reflecting a mechanistic view of organizations. Input, process, output, and outcome form a typical scheme, creating a robust list of indicators, but generating problems as well. First, such an approach fails to view measures in interrelated ways. Second, indicators are sometimes inversely related to each other, thus creating a *Catch-22* situation in which realization of one measure undermines realization of another. For example, an effort to increase ACT scores in a four-year period may run counter to a PI calling for greater socioeconomic diversity in the undergraduate population. Third, discerning the relationship between input characteristics and outcomes involves a leap of faith. The assessment movement has alerted academic leaders not to overlook process variables. Fortunately, there is an emerging literature that deals with process factors and their contribution to enhanced learning environments (Banta, *et al.*, 1996a; Ruppert, 1994).

In addition to types of indicators, PI levels are equally important and just as varied. Indicator construction is a relatively straightforward process of operationalizing goals and objectives at appropriate levels: nations, systems, institutions, programs, or individuals. Goals and objectives are usually deduced from mission statements, which may have only a tenuous connection to performance indicators. At the broadest geopolitical level, indicators for nations tend to be expressed as bold objectives or goals to be attained. Consider how the Congressional *Goals 2000: Educate America Act* calls for the adult knowledge and skills necessary for competing in a global economy.

Systems within states or provinces frequently apply a combination of input and outcome measures, the latter directed toward accomplishing various goals (minimized time to graduation, economic revitalization through targeted jobs training, social equity for protected classes of citizens). Several states are moving to assess specific domains (the outcomes of general education or those associated with majors, incidence of remediation). These measures can be unpacked into indicators to compare institutions within systems. Process measures used in state systems tend to be proxies (the percentage of lower division courses taught by tenured or tenure-track faculty, for example, or class size by student level).

At the institutional level, emphasis is on outcomes and outputs and, to a lesser extent, on input or resource characteristics. Common assessment domains include retention and graduation rates, licensure passage rates of graduates, extent of sponsored research, and number of baccalaureate degrees awarded by type of student. Process measures are frequently conceptualized as administrative efficiencies (for example, faculty workload indicators). It is useful to apply the level typology when building process indicators. At the individual level, for example, indicators could include "time-on-task" measures; program indicators could include some standard incidence or occurrences of principles of good practice in instruction; and system process indicators could include a variety of ratio conversions frequently found in bond rating measures.

Program level performance indicators can take the form of disaggregations of the same indicators used as institutional measures, or they can be tailored exclusively to specific degree programs. Nichols (1991) provides an excellent way to construct linkages between statements of institutional purpose and departmental or program outcomes, as well as relevant assessment criteria and procedures–an indicator level especially rich in systematic data for altering basic design, delivery strategies, or other program facets.

At the individual level, the focus is primarily on student outcomes, often expressed as competencies to be demonstrated or skills to be mastered. This level provides the most likely opportunity to connect performance data to academic process and thereby increase the formative utility of PI information. Applications at the individual level are often designed without systematic attention to several basic questions:

- What knowledge must be demonstrated that is deducible either from the program or the institutional mission statement?

- Which skills are conditions of graduation; which are merely desirable?

- Should PIs be limited to cognitive skills, or can affective and citizenship skills be included as well?

- At what levels of proficiency, and by what means, should essential skills be demonstrated?

- When should an outcome be present (which skills should be manifest after a core curricular experience): At graduation? One year out? Five years? When?

Table 1 displays an array of applications at each level.

APPROACHES AND PRACTICES

System applications. The State University of New York (SUNY) represents a hybrid approach to control through its use of five general areas forming the basic framework of institutionally developed goals and indicators. The core goal areas: (1) access to undergraduate education, (2) excellence in undergraduate programs and services, (3) nationwide competition in graduate study and research, (4) meeting state needs in economic development, environment conservation, health care, public education, and social services, and (5) management efficiency and effectiveness (State University of New York, 1993). The SUNY approach is especially instructive in its attempt to combine accountability with institutional autonomy using system and campus performance indicators. Each goal area includes traditional outcome and process measures (time-to-degree, graduation rates, and so forth), set against comparative time series or national norms.

The State of Texas illustrates a common approach using output and outcome measures. It includes rates on student retention, program and degree completers, licensure exam passage, sponsored research productivity, as well as output measures on number of degrees awarded by type of student. Like other states, Texas offers some proxy process measures, such as percentage of lower division courses taught by tenure or tenure-track faculty. The performance measures in Texas were assessed to determine whether a measure can be certified. A measure is certified "if reported performance is accurate within plus or minus five percent and if it appears that controls are in place over the collection and reporting of performance data to ensure accuracy" (Office of the State Auditor, 1995, p. 98).

Common assessment domains include retention and graduation rates, licensure passage rates of graduates, extent of sponsored research, and number of baccalaureate degrees awarded by type of student.

TABLE 1
Sample Performance Indicators Across Levels

	Nation	System	Institution	Program	Individual
Input	Every school in America will be linked to the World Wide Web	Percent of qualified resident students accepted and enrolled	Percent of fiscal resources spent on instruction	Number of merit scholars admitted to program	Percent of targeted courses providing individualized modules
	Proportion of eligible students receiving financial aid	Incidence of faculty awards by national foundations or academies	Proportion of library and media expenditures to total education and general expenditures	Percent of first-year MBA students with GMAT scores above 80th percentile	Availability of competency-based self-assessment services
Process	Consumer-based indicators within the Student Right-to-Know and Campus Security Act	Percent of lower division classes taught by tenure or tenure-track faculty	Proportion of courses with syllabi meeting the seven principles of good teaching practice	Number of required courses for major taught by tenure or tenure-track faculty	Time-on-task measures
		Ratio of unrestricted fund balance to unrestricted current funds	Faculty workload measures appropriate to institutional mission	First-year to second-year retention rates	Number of collaborative learning experiences
Outcome	Every adult American will be literate and possess skills necessary to compete in a global economy.	Percent of course completers; Percent of first time full time students earning degree within six years	Amount of classes incorporating group work into learning process	Percent of students passing CPA exam on first attempt	Individual skill demonstrations (e.g., student paper written in APA format)
		Number of graduates entering targeted careers	Sponsored research per FTE faculty or proportionate to total revenue	Citations per FTE faculty using citation index	Achievement of personal academic goals

Institutional applications. Two of the more elaborate institutional methods in four-year institutional settings were introduced by the University of Miami, using 114 key performance indicators, and Winona State University which links quality assurance and assessment planning through 18 goal areas. Following the critical success factors model, Miami officials developed PIs about important revenue generators and other significant characteristics of the university's position at a given point in time, and reported them as year-to-date snapshots along with comparisons against the previous year.

The University of Northern Colorado developed 20 prioritized key performance indicators of efficiency and effectiveness, simi-lar to the University of Miami model. Their approach proves especially useful to decision makers by numerically posting the current value, the five-year goal, and the ten-year goal of each measure. For an excellent discussion of the application of key performance indicators to strategic decision making, see Dolence and Norris (1994).

Winona State University's PIs are interesting, given the degree of detail in their development of a host of process performance indicators in curriculum, general education, instruction, the teaching/learning climate, student development, faculty development, administrative practices, and continuous process improvement activity. The process measures alone include more than 140 specific process indicators–for example, the proportion of departments that make provisions for new student orientation to the major department (Winona State University, 1994).

Two-year community colleges have a solid conceptual framework in the Core Indicators of Effectiveness initiative (American Association of Community Colleges, 1994). Their indicators are divided into three broad domains: internally directed, to enhance developmental education, general education, or transfer preparation; student process directed, to promote student goal attainment, persistence, and degree completion; and externally directed, to enhance career preparation, tailored services, and community development.

Community colleges, at either system or institutional levels, face the problem of trying to build indicators using four-year models rather than designing measures tied to the culture of their clientele. Measures involving degree attainment, for example, run counter to outcome measures better suited to community college students pursuing individualized educational plans. Thus, indicators of partnerships between sectors are typically expressed as transfer rates from community colleges to baccalaureate programs.

Program applications. The development of indicators at the program level should be a deductive process using the institution's mission or purpose statement. The Southern Association of Colleges and Schools (SACS) provides a useful approach to building measures consistent with statement of purpose. A program indicator is judged against such criteria as fit when it embraces institutional purpose, reasonableness, measurability, level of specificity, and congruity with program goals and objectives. This approach produces PIs as expected results.

Another approach is found among professional program applications. Across a wide range of health science programs (from the allied health professions and nursing to medicine), the specialized accrediting bodies make use of performance indicator methodologies. Similar applications can be found in schools of law and business. Whether one is relying on accreditation bodies or professional standards within fields of study, the work of Nichols (1991), provides an excellent source of examples linking institutional purposes with program intended outcomes and indicators. National professional associations provide a fertile source of student outcome measures that

can be expressed as performance indicators. See, for example, *Statement of Fundamental Lawyering Skills and Professional Values* (American Bar Association, 1992).

Individual applications. Performance indicators at the individual level can be developed with either the student or the classroom as the unit of observation. The student development literature contains a wide array of approaches toward designing developmental goals at the individual level. See Chapter 10 by Sharp and Grace on student development, and Warner Kearney and McLaughlin's (Chapter 11) on planning the co-curricular component. Performance indicators within classrooms can be constructed using complementary "principles of good practice," instructional standards, and measures of instructional effectiveness.

ANALYZING AND DISPLAYING PI INFORMATION

Data display. Leaders of public academic institutions interact with key stakeholders, especially legislators, in highly structured ways. Public hearings on appropriations and annual state reports form the most common arenas of interaction. Reports of performance data must be easily grasped and understood by busy legislators and bureaucrats. The *JCAR Technical Conventions Manual* sponsored by the American Association of State Colleges and Universities, the American Association of Community Colleges, and the National Association of State Universities and Land Grant Colleges (1995) is an excellent source of data display models. Across a variety of policy areas, the manual describes calculation protocols and communication recommendations.

Whether data display is tabular, graphic, or textual, it is essential that the producer of PI systems know: (1) what information is required, (2) by whom it is needed, (3) when various decision cycles occur, and (4) in what format the data is most accessible. The most frequently recommended characteristics of effective data display include:

Community colleges, at either system or institutional levels, face the problem of trying to build indicators using four-year models rather than designing measures tied to the culture of their clientele.

- Match the information to the sophistication of the receiver. Actively listen to information consumers and ascertain their needs before settling on a particular format.

- Keep in mind that reports written for one audience often find their way to other, unintended receivers. Information builders have more control over substance than dissemination.

- Keep the language clean, direct and simple.

- Integrate effective graphics with appropriate text.

- Use graphics selectively to convey central points to the intended audience.

- Use presentation software (such as Microsoft's *PowerPoint*™) to enhance an oral presentation.

The University of Miami's key success indicator (KSI) system relies on simple spreadsheets dividing the monitored measures in four time sequences (year-to-date, current month, prior year's YTD, and prior year's monthly data). To avoid an inundation of data, the KSI report is circulated with only significant deviations noted and highlighted. Substantial deviations or apparent patterns form the agenda of senior management's monthly meetings. As the system matures, senior managers change their style of involvement at staff meetings, becoming more committed and better prepared (Sapp, 1994).

Making comparisons public. The drive to compare institutions is increasingly common. At system levels, interinstitutional comparisons are central to resource allocation decisions. At the institutional or program levels, academic leaders need to articulate a defensible comparison group methodology. Typical comparative criteria include historical relationships, Carnegie classification, political jurisdictions, market competition, and aspirations.

Each comparative approach creates opportunities and risks for a chancellor, dean or other senior manager. Establishing comparison groups will drive data collection and interpretation as well as policy agenda in the state house. The selection of groups is a function of senior management's intended accomplishment. If the goal is internal improvement, comparative PIs will be fitted to institutions or programs with similar missions, resources,

> *Each comparative approach creates opportunities and risks for a chancellor, dean or other senior manager.*

and clientele. If the goal is to engage the policy process, especially funding, then comparative PIs will more likely be controlled by state or district agencies. Under the latter conditions, academic leaders should make every effort to be involved in the initial process of indicator construction. Once the rules are set, it is difficult to alter their basic architecture.

Growing interest in the recent introduction of media published "league tables" represents a special challenge for academic leaders. Despite their serious methodological shortcomings, popular press rankings appear to be influencing the legislative process, if not the choice process of parents and prospective students. Use of these rankings as comparative PIs is a double-edged sword. On one hand, rankings provide bragging rights. On the other, a surge of rising expectations in the legislature, board of trustees, faculty senate, or other stakeholders may result from their discovery that competitive institutions within the market area are ranked higher. An institution's inability to control numerous factors in the ranking process (reputation among peers, for example) may leave academic leaders in a highly vulnerable political position. For a solid discussion of the problems associated with college guidebooks and ranking systems, see Walleri and Moss (1995).

ACTIONABILITY ISSUES

Producing usable knowledge. The translation of PI information into actionable options that drive program improvements is an essential step in producing usable knowledge. To enhance the actionability of PI data, several impediments must be overcome. First, we need better understanding of higher education from a learner-centered perspective, a view that will enable us to develop richer and more usable process indicators. PI systems should incorporate process measures useful to faculty and academic managers, and thereby correct or eliminate whatever undermines quality. More work needs to be done on the "uncertain connection" between performance indicators and educational improvement (NCHEMS, 1993; Chickering, Gamson, and Barsi, 1989; Angelo, 1993).

Second, academic leaders must insist on capturing and reporting data that demonstrate how variations in academic processes explain differences in student results. The academy is sustained by a host of myths about what works best for whom. Many performance indicators are constructed on the basis of a "broadcast" method of pedagogy (a tenured, full-time faculty member holds forth for a given period of lecture time). Whether full-time faculty are truly more effective than adjunct faculty in enhancing the learning environment remains unanswered. Whether student learning is improved through collaborative experiences is unexplored. The folk wisdom provides a lens through which PI systems are often designed and implemented.

Third, PI systems are not a substitute for peer review methodologies. On the contrary, peer reviews provide a rich source of process assessment information that can help explain variability in student outcomes and can produce usable knowledge to improve existing practice.

Fourth, in private higher education as well as in the public sector, the policy process creates potential impediments to effective uses of PI data. When PI systems are serving accountability goals linked to performance funding, the danger will be the replacement of decision making by formula rather than informed debate. The policy agenda reflects the changing priorities of the politically elite, who themselves are highly mobile. Thus, the foci of agenda continue to shift as well. What is important today may be irrelevant to the next legislative assembly or board of governors. Thus, systems must be regularly monitored for content and construct validity and reliability.

Fifth, academic leaders are challenged by the need to move beyond simple cognitive outcome measures toward affective outcome indicators at the individual level (citizenship skills, value-clarification competency), or community development measures at the program or system level. Some promising work that applies across levels of systems within community colleges is beginning to emerge (American Association of Community Colleges, 1994).

Sixth, to engage in useful systematic comparisons we need to develop and use key performance indicators that have a direct bearing on the strategic success of the system, institution, or program (Taylor, *et al.*, 1991). The lack of connection between indicator and consequences can be magnified when budgeting is linked to PI systems. Performance budgeting systems focus primarily on reporting rather than producing data for internal improvement. (See Tennessee's THEC model for an exception. Banta, *et al.*, 1996b).

Performance funding models are finding their way into state systems at an increasing

PRINT REFERENCES

American Association of Community Colleges. 1994. *Community Colleges: Core Indicators of Effectiveness*. AACC Special Reports No. 4. Washington, DC.

American Association of State Colleges and Universities, American Association of Community Colleges, and the National Association of State Universities and Land-Grant Colleges. 1995. *JCAR Technical Conventions Manual*. Washington, DC.

American Bar Association. 1992. *Statement of Fundamental Lawyering Skills and Professional Values*. Task Force on Law Schools and the Profession: Narrowing the Gap. Chicago.

Angelo, T. 1993. "A Teacher's Dozen: Fourteen General, Research-Based Principles For Improving Higher Learning in our Classrooms." *AAHE Bulletin*, 45(8): 3–7.

Banta, T.; Lund, J.; Black, K.; and Oblander, F. 1996a. *Assessment in Practice: Putting Principles to Work on College Campuses*. San Francisco: Jossey-Bass Publishers.

Banta, T.; Rudolph, L.; Van Dyke, J.; and Fisher, H. 1996b. "Performance Funding Comes of Age in Tennessee." *Journal of Higher Education* 67(1): 23–45.

Bogue, E. and Saunders, R. 1992. *The Evidence for Quality*. San Francisco: Jossey-Bass Publishers.

Bottani, N. and Tuijnman, A. 1994. "The Design of Indicator Systems." In *Monitoring the Standards of Education*, edited by A.C. Tuijnman and T. N. Postlethwaite, pp. 47–78. New York: Elsevier Sciences, Inc.

Chickering, A. W.; Gamson, Z.; and Barsi, L. 1989. *Faculty Inventory: 7 Principles for Good Practice in Undergraduate Education*. Racine: The Johnson Foundation, Inc.

Darling-Hammond, L. 1992. "Educational Indicators and Enlightened Policy." *Educational Policy* 6(3): 235–265.

Dolence, M. and Norris, D. 1994. "Using Key Performance Indicators to Drive Strategic Decision Making." In *Using Performance Indicators to Guide Strategic Decision Making*, edited by V. Borden and T. Banta, pp. 63–80. *New Directions for Institutional Research* No. 82. San Francisco: Jossey-Bass Publishers.

Gaither, G.; Nedwek, B.; and Neal, J. 1994. *Measuring Up: The Promises and Pitfalls of Performance Indicators in Higher Education*. ASHE-ERIC Higher Education Reports, Report Five. Washington, DC: George Washington University.

Garvin, D. 1993. "Building a Learning Organization." *Harvard Business Review*. July-August, 1993: 78–91.

NCHEMS (National Center for Higher Education Management Systems). 1993. *A Preliminary Study of the Feasibility and Utility for National Policy of Instructional 'Good Practice' Indicators in Undergraduate Education*. Prepared for the National Center for Educational Statistics. Boulder.

Nedwek, B. 1996. "Public Policy and Public Trust: The Use and Misuse of Performance Indicators in Higher Education." In *Higher Education: Handbook of Theory and Research*, edited by John Smart, volume XI: 47–89. New York: Agathon Press.

Nichols, J. 1991. *A Practitioner's Handbook for Institutional Effectiveness and Student Outcomes Assessment Implementation*. New York: Agathon Press.

Office of the State Auditor. 1995. *An Audit Report on Performance Measures at 20 Universities, Health-Related Institutions, and State Agencies*. State of Texas. Report Number 95–141.

Ruppert, S., ed. 1994. *Charting Higher Education Accountability: A Sourcebook on State-Level Performance Indicators*. Denver: Education Commission of the States.

PRINT REFERENCES

Sapp, M. 1994. "Setting Up a Key Success Index Report: A How-to Manual." *AIR Professional File* No 51. Tallahassee: Association for Institutional Research.

State University of New York. 1993. "Quality Academics; Quality Productivity." Address at the Chancellor's Forum at the Sagamore Hotel in Bolton Landing, New York on April 6, 1992.

Taylor, B.; Meyerson, J.; Morrell, L.; and Park, D. 1991. *Strategic Analysis: Using Comparative Data to Understand Your Institution.* Washington, DC: Association of Governing Boards of Universities and Colleges.

Walleri, R. and Moss. M. 1995. *Evaluating and Responding to College Guidebooks and Rankings.* New Directions for Institutional Research No. 88. San Francisco: Jossey-Bass Publishers.

Winona State University. 1994. *Academic Quality Assurance and Assessment Plan.*

ELECTRONIC SAMPLER

gopher://vmsgopher.cua.edu/00gopher_root_eric_ae%3a%5b_edir%5dprogstan.txt

Educational Measurement Page. The Joint Committee on Standards for Educational Evaluation. James R. Sanders.

Contains JCSEE PR-1994 which was approved by the American National Standards Institute as an American National Standard.

http://128.250.89.9/andrewf/EdMeas.html

Internet Resources in the Field of Higher Education. Andrew Stephanou (Curator).

http://info.tei.uq.oz.au/TEI/announcement.html

Eighth International Conference on Assessing Quality in Higher Education, 1996, Queensland, Australia.

http://rrpubs.com/heproc/index.shtml

HEPROC: Higher Education Processes.

http://www.col.org/cretrans.htm

The Commonwealth of Learning Task Force Report on Credit Transfer, Accreditation and Quality Assurance.

http://www.cua.edu/www/eric_ae/

ERIC Clearinghouse on Assessment and Evaluation.

http://www.educom.edu/program/nlii/keydocs/massy.html

Using Information Technology to Enhance Academic Productivity. EDUCOM. William F. Massy and Robert Zemsky.

http://www.ed.gov/legislation/GOALS2000/TheAct/

H.R. 1804 Goals 2000:Educate America Act. 103rd Congress, 2nd Session. US Congress.

rate. Most reflect a degree of government involvement in academic affairs unknown just a few decades ago. Under the umbrella of social equity goals, systems are beginning to create bounties as incentives to state institutions. Missouri, for example, provides incentive funding to four-year state institutions that include $1,000 for each African-American awarded a baccalaureate degree, $500 for newly admitted teacher education students who score at or above the 66th percentile on enhanced ACT tests, and $1,000 for graduates in selected disciplines (foreign language, health, targeted sciences).

Making PI systems useful. The basic characteristics of useful PI systems depend of course on who are the users and what ends they intend to achieve. Nevertheless, it is reasonable to suggest several essential characteristics regardless of application. Academic leaders should expect PI systems to be:

- Easily understood by all stakeholders (faculty, students, managers, trustees, legislators), yet sufficiently complex to build an accurate picture of the situation (Darling-Hammond, 1992);

- Fueled by available data that are easy to capture and maintain;

- Designed with standards and comparisons appropriate to those units expected to achieve them;

- Sensitive to the diversity of missions within and among higher education systems, institutions, or programs;

- Complementary to other quality assurance methodologies (institutional peer review, self-study accreditation, bond rating studies);

- Valid and reliable direct linkages to strategic planning, decision-making, budgeting, and funding;

- Sensitive to political cultures within states and the political geography among states; and,

- Robust, to include resource, process, and outcome measures that foster an integrated approach to problem-solving and quality assurance enhancement.

SUMMARY

The instrumental use of performance indicators as administrative mechanisms of control runs the risk of creating unintended negative consequences. As a control tool, PIs run the risk of creating disincentives for meaningful reform. If reform does not capture the imagination and agenda of higher education, the likelihood of diminished public support for the academy will increase. On the positive side, when PI systems have an instrumental use in agenda building, monitoring, and forecasting, they make educational delivery problems more analytically tractable. ◆

Index